Nationhood and Political Theory

Nationhood and Political Theory

Margaret Canovan

Professor of Politics, University of Keele

Edward Elgar
Cheltenham, UK • Brookfield, US

Published by
Edward Elgar Publishing limited
8 Lansdown Place
Cheltenham
Glos GL50 2HU
UK

Edward Elgar Publishing Company
Old Post Road
Brookfield
Vermont 05036
US

British Library Cataloguing in Publication Data
Canovan, Margaret
  Nationhood and Political Theory
  I. Title
  320.1

Library of Congress Cataloguing in Publication Data
Canovan, Margaret.
    Nationhood and political theory / Margaret Canovan.
    Includes bibliographical references and index.
    1. Nationalism.   2. National state.   I. Title.
  JC311.C337   1996
  320.1'01—dc20   95–31939
                                                                         CIP

ISBN 1 85278 852 6

Typeset by Manton Typesetters, 5–7 Eastfield Road, Louth, Lincolnshire LN11 7AJ, UK
Printed and bound in Great Britain by Biddles Ltd, Guildford and King's Lynn

Contents

1. Introduction

During the present century national disputes of one sort or another have rarely been far from the top of the political agenda, and in recent years they seem to have become more common rather than less so. Hopes that global markets and satellite television would turn us all into citizens of the world (especially after the collapse of communism) have been dashed by the nationalist struggles in what used to be Yugoslavia and the Soviet Union. Nor can these upheavals be explained away as symptoms of backwardness, localized and temporary interruptions of a long-term trend toward cosmopolitanism. At the other extreme, even a country as prosperous and peaceful as Canada can be seriously troubled by questions of national identity.

There is no doubting the political significance of nationhood, and as one might expect, the academic literature on such matters is enormous. What is surprising, though, is that so little of the contents of those overflowing shelves could be described as political theory. Historians have chronicled the struggles of nationalist movements and sociologists have offered explanations for their success in attracting support, but for at least the past half century most anglophone political theorists have turned their backs on the whole business and gone on talking about their preferred topics – democracy (for example), social justice, freedom, rights, even community – as if nations were an irrelevance. It is true that recent events have prompted a few theorists to examine (and usually to refute) the arguments for a right to national self-determination, but most have made plain their belief that nations are too hard to define and national sentiments too dangerously irrational to form suitable topics for the clear-minded.

It must be admitted that theorists have had good reasons for dismissing or neglecting explicitly nationalist ideas, because those ideas do not stand up well to examination. In Chapter 2 I shall look at the theoretical case against nationalism, and confirm that it is indeed powerful. However, I hope to show that this is very far from being the end of the matter. The purpose of this book is to argue that questions of nationhood are not an optional extra for political theory, but should actually be at the heart of the discipline. The reason for this is that (as I hope to show in Chapters 3, 4 and 5) nationhood is actually a tacit premise in almost all contemporary political thinking. The current discourses of democracy, social justice and liberalism all in their different ways

1

presuppose the existence not just of a state, but of a political community. The question of how this body politic is constituted is regularly passed over by theorists, but I shall argue that all concerned, while writing in terms that seem to apply to all humanity, tacitly assume that nation-states can be taken as given. To make sense, democracy requires a 'people', and social justice a political community within which redistribution can take place, while the liberal discourse of rights and the rule of law demands a strong and impartial polity. The resounding silence of most of the thinkers concerned on the topics of boundaries, the generation of political solidarity and the sources of political power bears witness to their presuppositions.

If political thinkers really have been building nation-states into their theories without noticing that they were doing so, how has this been possible? The explanation lies, I believe, in the peculiar nature of nationhood itself, which will be considered in Chapters 6 and 7. Nations are extraordinarily complex political phenomena, highly resistant to theoretical analysis. The features that make them politically effective also render them intellectually opaque, repelling philosophers who come to them in search of clear and distinct ideas. But those same obscurities not only enable nationhood to generate powerful political communities; even more momentously, they make those communities seem natural, so that the task of generating collective power is made to look deceptively easy. Political philosophers who conclude that nationhood can be ignored because it cannot be satisfactorily defined often fail to realise that they themselves are relying on it to supply the power and solidarity taken for granted in their theories.

Two powerful objections may be raised against my claim that the nation-state is an unacknowledged presence in most current political theory. In the first place, it may be objected that while political theorists ought to pay more attention to their assumptions about political community, it does not follow that the political community concerned has to be a *nation*. Some theorists would argue that whereas national solidarity is too narrow to be compatible with the universalist commitments of liberal democratic political theory, a different kind of political solidarity is capable of sustaining those commitments: a kind that might be described as the local patriotism of citizens of the world. In Chapter 8 I shall consider this argument, but conclude that attempted distinctions between (good, humane) 'patriotic' political solidarity on the one hand and (bad, racist) nationhood are misleading, and that they do not solve the genuine problem of reconciling the universalist aspirations of liberal democratic theory with its particularistic underpinnings.

The following chapter is concerned with another objection to my thesis: if nationhood lies at the root of modern thinking about exalted ideals like democracy, social justice and universal rights, how are we to make sense of the fact that nationalist politics is so often undemocratic, unjust and illiberal?

I shall offer a number of answers to this objection. For one thing, nations and nationalisms vary a great deal, and the kind of nationhood presupposed in contemporary anglophone political theory does not correspond very closely to (say) Russian or German nationalist traditions. For another, while civil war and other ills are often blamed on the presence of nationalism, they might in many cases be more plausibly accounted for by the absence of nations. The most disturbing answer, however, is that even the mature, settled, comparatively civilized nationhood that sustains the collective power presupposed by liberal democratic political theory has itself almost invariably been generated by a history of popular mobilization and violence that will not bear looking into, and that cannot even be counted on to result in the creation of a political community. Machiavellian skeletons lurk behind the serene assumption that the collective power and solidarity to sustain democracy, justice and the rule of law can be taken for granted.

It is above all dilemmas of this last kind that are typically dodged in contemporary political theory. If political philosophy is expected to be more than a purely intellectual exercise; if it is supposed to have some purchase on the world and some relevance for political activity, then questions of power and its foundation have to be faced. From this point of view, the most significant feature of nationhood is its role in generating collective power, its capacity to create an 'us' that can be mobilized and represented, and for which a surprising number of people are prepared to make sacrifices. Despite all the economic, cultural and military trends pushing us in the direction of cosmopolitanism, this continues to be a stubborn fact. Nations are not of course the only collectivities that can be politically mobilized – religious communities and ideological parties are obvious alternatives – but from a political point of view they are peculiarly effective because they can attract so much support with so little by way of organization, doctrine and continuous mobilization. Where nations exist (and I shall argue that they are not very common) they function like batteries, capable of storing power for future use without needing to be active all the time. Political theorists who are used to political systems sustained by mature nationhood tend to take that political power for granted just as they take for granted electrical power at the flick of a switch. Across much of the world, however, neither assumption is safe.

If liberal democratic political theory presupposes the existence of a kind of political community that consorts uneasily with universal commitments, and that is in any case not universally available, what are the implications for political theory itself? In the final chapter I shall consider a number of strategies currently on offer for dealing with these tensions between universal principles and particular solidarities, but I shall argue that none is successful, and that although a greater awareness of the issues can help us, dilemmas in this area are inescapable. If my argument holds, the general conclusion must be not only that questions of nationhood deserve more attention, but that no contemporary political thinking can afford to neglect them. Let us begin, however, by considering why political theorists have found it so easy to ignore or dismiss such questions.

2.   The case against nationalism

National aspirations must be respected; peoples may now be dominated and governed only by their own consent. "Self-determination" is not a mere phrase. It is an imperative principle of action, which statesmen will henceforth ignore at their peril.[1]

These words, spoken by President Woodrow Wilson to the US Congress in 1918, express sentiments with which most citizens of Western states feel considerable sympathy. Political theorists, by contrast, have for the past half-century given short shrift to the principles espoused by Wilson and partially embodied in the ill-fated Versailles settlement that ended the First World War, and their suspicion has been well-founded. This chapter will consider why nationalist claims that appear to be so attractive have nevertheless been so easy to dismiss.

In all probability, when President Wilson spoke of the consent and self-determination of 'peoples' neither he nor his audience was sure whether they were considering the rights of collective 'peoples' or of individual people. In English the word 'people' is systematically ambiguous, referring either to a collective and continuing entity such as 'the Italian people', as in, 'the Italian people were divided and oppressed for centuries', or to an aggregate of individuals, as in, 'Italian people enjoy a higher quality of life than Londoners'. One reason for the vagueness of much nationalist discourse is that the two meanings are often confused or interchanged according to the convenience of the speaker. For the purposes of our analysis we will need to distinguish them, because nationalist claims have traditionally been theorized in two very different ways, one Romantic and collectivist, the other liberal and individualist.

On the Romantic-collectivist view, nations exist as wholes of which individuals are but parts, so that it is the collective nation that should form the basis of political organization. This implies (for example) that in the nineteenth century the Italian nation as a collective entity had a right to be unified and independent, whereas individual Italians had a duty to bring this about. Liberal-individualist versions of nationalism may reach what appears to be a similar polical conclusion, 'self-determination for the Italian people', but they begin from quite different premises. Since legitimate government is government by the consent of the individuals concerned, and since individuals identify themselves as members of nations, then there must be a right to national self-determination. So if in the days of Mazzini and Garibaldi an appropriate number of individuals thought of themselves as Italians and wished to be governed in a way that reflected that identity, then there was a *prima facie* case for their wish to be granted.

In spite of the frequent intermingling in nationalist claims of these two sorts of arguments, it is clear that from a theoretical point of view they are very different and probably incompatible. It will therefore be convenient to look at them separately. Romantic collectivism is by no means dead, particularly in the rhetoric of nationalist movements around the world, but it had its philosophical heyday in the nineteenth and early twentieth centuries and is framed in terms that seem markedly unpersuasive to modern political theorists. Let us therefore consider this kind of nationalist argument first.

ROMANTIC-COLLECTIVIST NATIONALISM

It seemed appropriate to begin with Italian examples when talking of nationalism because there has never been a more eloquent spokesman for the cause than the nineteenth-century Italian nationalist Giuseppe Mazzini. Nationalism as he understood it was a religion, a sacred calling far above material concerns. A fervent believer in God and in the progress of Humanity under the guidance of God's providence, Mazzini claimed that it is through service to one's own particular nation that each of us is called to serve the wider interests of humanity. Within the grand providential design, more primitive forms of polity once had their place: monarchy, in particular, had had the function of overcoming feudal divisions. In his own time, however, he believed that a new era was dawning in which dynastic states would be replaced by free republics, each corresponding to one of the nations into which God himself had divided mankind.

Looking at the map of Europe, Mazzini thought it obvious that national territories had been marked out by the divine hand. Italy in particular, 'the best-defined country in Europe'[2] was evidently intended to form a single country bounded by the Alps and the sea (though also, unaccountably, including Sicily, Sardinia, Corsica and other islands). When he was writing in the mid-nineteenth century borders did not yet conform to these natural frontiers, being instead a record of dynastic wars and marriages.

> But the divine design will infallibly be fulfilled. Natural divisions, the innate spontaneous tendencies of the peoples will replace the arbitrary divisions sanctioned by bad governments. The map of Europe will be remade. The Countries of the People will rise, defined by the voice of the free, upon the ruins of the

Countries of Kings and privileged castes. Between these Countries there will be harmony and brotherhood.[3]

Mazzini believed that within the general divine plan for humanity each of these natural nations had a particular mission, which was in the case of Italy to accomplish 'the moral unity of Europe'.[4] Looking back into history, he saw that the Rome of the Empire had imposed civilization and unity by force, and that the Rome of the Popes had followed this with a civilizing unity imposed by authority.

> ROME OF THE PEOPLE will give, when you Italians are nobler than you are now, a Unity of civilisation accepted by the free consent of the nations for Humanity.[5]

The high destiny of the nation in turn dictated the duties of individuals. Mazzini appealed to his readers to recognize their brotherhood with humanity, and especially with their fellow-nationals. Rejecting the false gospels of individualism and materialism, they should embrace the high calling to sacrifice themselves for the unity and liberty of their nation, living and dying in a way that befitted this vocation. 'Because you will be ready to die for Humanity, the life of your country will be immortal'.[6] The consummation of this struggle, the establishment of republican polities in which 'the Government will be the *mind* of a Nation',[7] would bring unity within the state and harmony without.

For the many English liberals who warmed to Mazzini's cause (regarding him and Garibaldi rather as more recent Western liberals regarded Desmond Tutu and Nelson Mandela)[8] the peculiar charm of his message lay in its combination of intense patriotic fervour with the broadest and most humane sympathies. For Mazzini, devotion to the nation was perfectly compatible both with the wider cause of humanity and with a respect for the rights and interests of the individual. A divinely pre-established harmony made the nation a rung on the ladder leading human beings to personal fulfilment in the service of humanity.[9] And because nations were part of the order of nature and had God-given destinies to fulfil, the call to self-sacrifice for the nation could not lead to oppression within it or conflict without.

I have presented Mazzini's thought at some length because it enables us to see clearly the assumptions upon which Romantic collectivist nationalism depends. The reason why a nation has the right to form a state and to call upon the allegiance of its members is that its existence and its historic destiny proceed from a natural order that is assumed to be the source of authoritative values. Other Romantic nationalists make similar assumptions without spelling them out to the same extent. On the naturalness of nations, for example, here is Herder assimilating a nation to an extended family:

> The family is a product of Nature. The most natural state is, therefore, a state composed of a single people with a single national character... For a people is a natural growth like a family, only spread more widely.[10]

For German nationalists in particular, the sign of a genuine nation was the existence of a distinct language. In the words of Fichte, 'Wherever a separate language is found, there a separate nation exists, which has the right to take independent charge of its own affairs and to govern itself'.[11] It would be a mistake to suppose, however, that Romantic nationalism could be refuted by pointing to the confusion of dialects spoken within a purportedly national territory. According to the doctrine, nations exist within time as well as space, and only gradually fulfil their predestined mission. The fact, for example, that at the time of Italian unification few inhabitants of the new state could speak Italian (as few as 2.5 per cent according to some estimates)[12] struck nationalists as an opportunity and a challenge rather than an objection.

There was in nineteenth-century Romantic nationalism a strong element of historicism, a tendency to look not so much at what the nation was at that particular time but at what it was destined to become. As Friedrich Meinecke (a fairly late and highly sophisticated examplar) put it, it is necessary to distinguish between 'an early period in which nations have a more plantlike, impersonal existence and growth and a later period in which the conscious will of the nation awakens.'[13] Given historicist assumptions, there is no more problem about discerning the gradually-emerging boundaries of historic nations than there is in identifying the boundaries of Marxist classes. During their embryonic stirrings, while they exist only *an sich*, their shapes may appear indistinct, but as they rise to conscious existence *für sich* and fulfil their historic destinies they become unmistakable.[14] Confidence in the march of history made it possible for Mazzini to envisage a fully nationalist Europe made up of only eleven genuine nations, and to dismiss the claims of the Irish (among others) to constitute a nation on the grounds that they possessed no national language and no special historic mission.[15]

Modern objections to Romantic-collectivist nationalism stem from bitter experience reinforced by doubts about historicism and collectivism. The most obvious weakness of the doctrine is that humanity does *not* in fact divide neatly into nations. In retrospect, the notion that it would be feasible to identify a limited number of natural nations that could fit together into a harmonious international order looks like a bad joke, or, worse, like an invitation to some states to realise their national mission by gobbling up others. Even the saintly Mazzini interpreted the 'natural' frontiers of Italy to suit himself, taking for granted that Sicily, Sardinia and Corsica were parts of the country in spite of being divided from it by the sea, and calling on his countrymen to reconquer Trentino, Istria and Nice in spite of the presence in these border regions of people with alternative national allegiances.[16] And if even Italy lacked indisputable natural frontiers, how were those of (say) Germany, Poland or Russia to be settled? Lacking Mazzini's faith, we no longer see reasons to believe that geography is destiny or that history has a direction that confers rights. At a time when even the Marxist version of faith in history has few remaining adherents, and when the prevailing intellectual mood is one of post-modern scepticism toward all 'grand narratives',[17] claims of a national 'mission' are not likely to be taken seriously in philosophical circles.

Similarly, for all the nobility of Mazzini's summons to fraternity and self-sacrifice, political theorists tend now to be more wary of the collectivism inherent in Romantic nationalism. Nationalists of this stamp see the nation rather than its members as the possessor of sacred rights, and stress that individuals are parts of something greater than themselves, with a duty to serve the whole. But experience of totalitarianism combined with the current stress on individual rights makes most Western political thinkers less sympathetic to claims of this sort.

It is true that this rejection of collectivism may be over-hasty: we shall have occasion later to consider whether it is indeed possible to manage without an unfashionably collectivist understanding of the body politic. However, when we now encounter claims about the political rights of the collective nation they have usually been shorn of Romantic historicism and recast in more subjectivist language, heavily influenced by the notion classically formulated by Renan that a nation exists if people will to belong to it.[18] In the process, the emphasis has shifted from the rights of the nation itself to the rights of the people who are its members, converging with arguments from the liberal notion of individual self-determination.

LIBERAL-INDIVIDUALIST NATIONALISM

Some analysts consider that the doctrine of self-determination is not really nationalist at all, and that only collectivist doctrines can be counted as such.[19] But this seems unnecessarily restrictive. It is true that the liberal doctrine of self-determination need not necessarily have any connection with nationalism, but in practice the demand for individual consent to government has regularly been translated into self-government for *peoples* and hence for nations. John Stuart Mill set the tone of the discussion when (arguing for national self-government 'where the sentiment of nationality exist in any force') he went on, 'This is merely saying that the question of government ought to be decided by the governed.'[20] Even Harry Beran, the most resolutely individualistic recent defender of the principle that consent is the only legitimate basis of political obligation, is prepared to deduce a nationalist conclusion from an individualist premise:

> Individuals have a right to personal self-determination. Therefore, groups have a right to group self-determination... Therefore, groups which are nations have a right to national self-determination.[21]

Recent champions of liberal nationalism, taking up communitarian themes, argue that since individuals are contextual beings whose identity is bound up with their membership of national groups, then respect for individual rights implies some form of national self-determination. Some of this nationalist thinking has moved away from the traditional claim for independent statehood towards more limited versions of self-rule within a supra-national organization on the lines of the European Union.[22] These modified versions of liberal nationalism come very close to liberal arguments for ethnic pluralism *within* states, and I shall postpone consideration of them to a later stage of the argument. However, the more traditional claim for full self-determination has recently been restated by Avishai Margalit and Joseph Raz.

Their position is particularly worthy of note because they make a point of eschewing utopian moral theory and assuming for the purposes of their inquiry that 'things are roughly as they are.'[23] Their argument proceeds from the importance for individuals' self-identity of membership in what they call 'encompassing groups' with 'pervasive cultures'.[24]

> The right to self-determination derives from the value of membership in encompassing groups... It rests on an appreciation of the great importance that membership in and identification with encompassing groups has in the life of individuals, and the importance of the prosperity and self-respect of such groups to the well-being of their members. That importance makes it reasonable to let the encompassing group that forms a substantial majority in a territory have the right to determine whether that territory shall form an independent state in order to protect the culture and self-respect of the group, provided that the new state is likely to respect the fundamental interests of its inhabitants, and provided that measures are adopted to prevent its creation from gravely damaging the just interests of other countries.[25]

This is a formulation that probably sums up the attitude of a great many liberal-minded people in the West. What could be more reasonable? On the face of it, liberal-individualist nationalism is a lot more plausible than the Romantic-collectivist kind, since it involves no appeals to 'mystical entities'[26] or to historic destiny. It is this version of nationalism that is most likely to gain the support of the casual observer, particularly if (as is usually the case) those claiming self-determination can point to ill-treatment by their current rulers. After all (we are inclined to ask), if Slovaks or Slovenes or

Scots want to follow the example of the Founding Fathers and 'frame a government for themselves', why shouldn't they?

Unfortunately things are not as simple as that, as the horrors of ex-Yugoslavia have reminded us. The case against liberal-individualist claims for self-determination, even when qualified in the manner of Margalit and Raz, is that they do *not* in fact take adequate account of 'things as they are'. The trouble is that things as they are include the role of force in politics, stabilized but never abolished by the existence of states. Liberal nationalist accounts of the 'right' to self-determination tend to take peace and order for granted, treating the world as if it were a legal order with enforceable laws. It is of the essence of nationalism, however, to be a revolutionary doctrine, calling for the destruction of existing states and the construction of new ones with different boundaries, and thereby upsetting existing legal frameworks. Revolutions of this sort can sometimes be carried out peacefully, but not often: characteristically they provoke civil war within which all the careful provisos and guarantees of liberal nationalism are overwhelmed by the logic of conflict. The vagueness of the liberal-individualist understanding of nationhood can only make this outcome more likely.

The point to note here is that our move from the Romantic notion of collectivist nations (each with its historic destiny) to individual people (each with his or her collective identification) was a jump from the frying pan into the fire. We may have escaped from the implausibilities of historicism, but we have also lost one crucial political advantage claimed for nationalism, namely that a limited number of historic nations, each with its destined territory, would fit together to form a just and stable political order. Once nations are defined not by historic destiny but by individual identification, there is no way of distinguishing 'true' nations that qualify for political independence from merely local or ethnic groups. Consequently, whereas the characteristic aim of the nineteenth-century nationalist was unification (of the South Slavs, for instance), the characteristic aim of the contemporary nationalist is secession (by Slovenes, Croats, Macedonians, Chechens...), encouraging competing definitions of the relevant 'people' and leading to the formation of smaller and smaller political units.[27] Meanwhile, in all cases, secession has costs that the rhetoric of self-determination ignores.

In an impressive recent book on the subject of secession, Allen Buchanan maintains that the 'pure self-determination or nationalist argument' is 'one of the least plausible justifications' for secession[28] because of the problems of demarcating the 'peoples' who are entitled to self-determination and the moral costs of trying to achieve a fit between peoples and states. As Buchanan sees, one of the most crucial problems concerns the implications of self-determination for control of territory. In principle, Romantic-collectivist nations came complete with the 'historic lands' that fitted their national mission.[29] Since the borders of these historic lands were usually disputed, this solution posed its own problems: but the right of self-determination for individuals does not obviously confer rights to territory at all. Is it simply the right to *leave* any particular territory – perhaps as a refugee? (James Mayall points out that since 1945 the principle of national self-determination has more often meant moving the people than the state borders.)[30] Or is it the right of the inhabitants of a particular area to decide the future of the area by majority vote? If so, how is the area of the plebiscite to be decided? Even more difficult, who is entitled to vote in the plebiscite? Those who happen to be there at the time the vote is held, perhaps after the area has undergone 'ethnic cleansing'? Or the 'historic inhabitants', however they can be decided? Even at the level of theory such questions cannot be addressed without reverting to some collective conception of the nation, with all its attendant difficulties.[31]

What is apparent, in other words, is that the notion of self-determination, which appears to offer a simple, liberal-democratic answer to nationalist disputes, merely creates further theoretical problems, and may in practice act as an incentive for one group to terrorize another into fleeing from disputed territory. Furthermore, since experience gives us few grounds for assuming that nationalist government will necessarily be *good* government,[32] those who embark upon the enterprise of redrawing state boundaries along national lines cannot reasonably argue that the benefits will outweigh the immediate costs. Looking at the current chaos in what used to be Yugoslavia, and at the breakdown of civilization that has followed attempts at self-determination, we may recall the accusation often levelled against nationalism, classically by Elie Kedourie,[33] that nationalists are naive, irresponsible ideologues who destroy political order for the sake of a theory, letting loose civil war, massacre, the creation of refugees and economic collapse.

Arguments of this sort seem to show that nationalist principles are deeply flawed, allowing political theorists to conclude, with Gordon Graham, that 'national government, as an ideal, is not generally something for which we have any reason to strive',[34] and to get back with a sigh of relief to the real issues of political theory. But this response is unduly complacent, because it takes for granted that there is in the modern world some easily available alternative to the nation-state as a basis for political order and civilized politics. While it is true that nationalist ideologues have made the mistake of taking political order for granted, exactly the same is true of mainstream political theorists, who have scorned attempts to create new states on nationalist principles while failing to consider what might be the foundations of the comparatively stable and legitimate states in which they themselves live.

One or two political theorists have recently begun to look again at nationalism, and to suggest that although (for the reasons we have discussed) states that coincide with national identities may not be feasible everywhere, there are good reasons to seek an accommodation between nationalism and the concerns of contemporary political theory. David Miller in particular has offered a sophisticated and highly-qualified defence of nationality which I shall discuss later.[35] In what follows I shall go beyond this to argue that nation-states may well be an indispensable condition for most of the projects of modern political theory, and are in fact tacitly assumed by its practitioners. I shall conclude, however, that hopes of an easy reconciliation between nationalism and liberal universalism are misplaced. The mistake that the more humane nationalists have made has not so much been to regard nation-states as desirable but to radically underestimate the difficulties and costs of achieving them in a world where nations are neither natural nor ubiquitous. Nations are political phenomena of great complexity, greater than is usually appreciated either by their opponents or their defenders, and they cannot be constructed, dismantled or adapted to order.

NATIONHOOD AS A TACIT ASSUMPTION IN POLITICAL THEORY

In the course of this book I hope to show that the existence of nations is a tacit presupposition of most current discourse in political theory, with serious implications for its content and relevance. The main argument has two aims, attempting firstly to establish that political theorists rely to a greater extent than is usually recognized on the presumed existence of political community, and secondly to show that the political community actually presupposed is in fact a nation-state.[36] The next three chapters will be concerned chiefly with the first of those stages. Leaving aside for the moment contentious questions about what a 'nation' is and whether alternative forms of political community are available in the modern world, I shall attempt to show that the current discourses of democracy, social justice and liberalism rest upon rarely examined assumptions that a particular kind of political community can be taken for granted.

Before we embark on this task it may be helpful to have some clarification of the kind of argument that is involved here, and particularly what it is not. In the first place, although there are hints here of a 'transcendental' approach in that I am endeavouring to show what must be the case for current debates in political theory to make sense, there is no aspiration to strict logical entailment: the present argument aims to be persuasive rather than deductive. As will become apparent later, the senses in which the various discourses of political theory presuppose a (national?) political community are partly logical and partly empirical, with a different balance between the two in different cases.

Secondly, what is attempted here is not a defence of nationalism or of national self-determination. For reasons that will become clear later, neither seems to me to be defensible in general terms. My purpose is rather to draw attention to the role of nationhood in concealing Hobbesian truths about the need for a stable body politic before any more ambitious political agenda can be pursued, and Machiavellian problems about the difficulties and costs of trying to generate power. Issues of this kind are frequently neglected in contemporary political theory, and I shall argue that this is at any rate partly due to the peculiar characteristics of nationhood, which have deceived many of its beneficiaries into supposing that powerful, stable political communities are easy to come by.

NOTES

1. D.P. Moynihan, *Pandaemonium: Ethnicity in International Politics* (Oxford, Oxford University Press, 1993) 78.
2. J. Mazzini, *The Duties of Man and Other Essays* (London, J.M. Dent, 1907) 53.
3. Mazzini, *Duties of Man* 52.
4. Mazzini, *Duties of Man* 58.
5. 'To the Italians', in *Essays by Joseph Mazzini* ed. B. King (London, J.M. Dent, 1894) 141.
6. Mazzini, *Duties of Man* 59.
7. Mazzini, 'To the Italians' 154.
8. C. Harvie, *The Lights of Liberalism: University Liberals and the Challenge of Democracy 1860–86* (London, Allen Lane, 1976) 97–104.
9. Mazzini, *Duties of Man* 41.
10. J.G. Herder, *Ideas towards a Philosophy of the History of Mankind* (1785), quoted in A. Zimmern (ed.), *Modern Political Doctrines* (London, Oxford University Press, 1939) 165.
11. 'Wherever a separate language is found, there a separate nation exists, which has the right to take independent charge of its affairs and to govern itself', J.G. Fichte, *Addresses to the German Nation* (Chicago and London, Open Court, 1922) 215.
12. G. Lepschy, 'How Popular is Italian?', in Z.G. Baranski and R. Lumley (eds), *Culture and Conflict in Postwar Italy* (Basingstoke, Macmillan, 1990) 66.
13. F. Meinecke, *Cosmopolitanism and the National State* trans. R.B. Kimber (Princeton, Princeton University Press, 1970) 12.
14. Marx and Engels sympathized with world-historical nations as well as classes, and had very little sympathy with groups who tried to resist what Engels called 'the right of historical evolution'. For example, Engels regarded Czech nationalism as 'ludicrous' and 'anti-historical', and also defended the German claim to Schleswig as 'the right of civilisation as against barbarism'. (R. Szporluk: *Communism and Nationalism: Karl Marx versus Friedrich List* (Oxford, Oxford University Press, 1988) 172–3).
15. P. Alter, *Nationalism* (London, Edward Arnold, 1985) 30.
16. Mazzini, 'To the Italians' 174.
17. J.F. Lyotard, *The Post-Modern Condition: A Report on Knowledge* (Manchester, Manchester University Press, 1984) xxiii.
18. E. Renan, 'What is a Nation?', in A. Zimmern (ed.), *Modern Political Doctrines* (London, Oxford University Press, 1939) 203.
19. A.H. Birch, *Nationalism and National Integration* (London, Unwin Hyman, 1989) 23; E. Kedourie, *Nationalism*, London, Hutchinson, 1960) 132.
20. 'Considerations on Representative Government' (1861), in J.S. Mill, *Utilitarianism, Liberty, Representative Government* (London, J.M. Dent, 1910) 360.

21. H. Beran, *The Consent Theory of Political Obligation* (London, Croom Helm, 1987) 138.

22. N. MacCormick, 'Is Nationalism Philosophically Credible?', in W. Twining (ed.), *Issues of Self-Determination* (Aberdeen, Aberdeen University Press, 1991); Y. Tamir, *Liberal Nationalism* (Princeton, Princeton University Press, 1993). Tamir's theory, an ambitious attempt to affirm national self-determination while overcoming its obvious shortcomings, will be discussed below.

23. A. Margalit and J. Raz, 'National Self-Determination', *The Journal of Philosophy* LXXXVII/9 (September 1990) 440.

24. Margalit and Raz, 'National Self-Determination' 448.

25. Margalit and Raz, 'National Self-Determination' 457.

26. MacCormick, 'Is Nationalism Philosophically Credible?' 8.

27. Cf. E.J. Hobsbawm, *Nations and Nationalism since 1780* (Cambridge, Cambridge University Press, 1990) 32–6.

28. A. Buchanan, *Secession: the Morality of Political Divorce from Fort Sumter to Lithuania and Quebec* (Boulder, Westview Press, 1991) 48.

29. In this respect, Israel provides one of the most striking contemporary examples of Romantic-collectivist nationalism in practice.

30. J. Mayall, *Nationalism and International Society* (Cambridge, Cambridge University Press, 1990) 55.

31. For an acute discussion of the problems of identifying the subject that could be supposed to exercise a right of national self-determination, see D. George, 'The Right of National Self-determination', *History of European Ideas* 16/4–6 (1993) 507–13. As George makes clear, these problems arise regardless of whether the nation is understood as a voluntary or involuntary group.

32. G. Graham, 'A Refutation of Nationalism', in *Politics in its Place* (Oxford, Oxford University Press, 1986) 125.

33. E. Kedourie, *Nationalism* 4th edition (Oxford, Blackwell, 1993) *passim.*

34. Graham, 'Refutation of Nationalism' 140.

35. D. Miller, 'The Ethical Significance of Nationality', *Ethics* 98/4 (July 1988) 647–62; 'In Defence of Nationality', *Journal of Applied Philosophy* 10/1 (1993) 3–16; 'The Nation-State: a Modest Defence', in C. Brown (ed.), *Political Restructuring in Europe: Ethical Perspectives* (London and New York, Routledge, 1993); *On Nationality* (Oxford, Clarendon Press, 1995). See also B. Barry, 'Self-Government Revisited', in D. Miller and L. Siedentop (eds), *The Nature of Political Theory* (Oxford, Oxford University Press, 1983) 141; Y. Tamir, *Liberal Nationalism* (Princeton, Princeton University Press, 1993).

36. For a similar argument but radically different conclusions, see Tamir, *Liberal Nationalism* 117–39.

3. Democratic theory: government by the people

> A democratic society requires a certain kind of unity, because its people supposedly form a unit of collective decision... They have to be able to trust one another and have a sense of commitment to one another, or the whole process of common decision will be poisoned by division and mutual suspicion. (Charles Taylor)[1]

Who are 'the people' whom democrats regard as sovereign? Modern democratic theory comes in a great many different versions, giving rise to a vast literature and a highly sophisticated discourse, but all of it is in some sense concerned with 'the people'. Whether what is talked about is government by the people, popular participation in decision-making, representing the people or making rulers accountable to the people, 'the people' are ubiquitous. One might expect, therefore, that any hidden assumptions about this 'people' must have been thoroughly exposed long before now. But this is not the case. Democratic theorists regularly make such tacit assumptions: in particular, they almost always assume that a 'people' can be taken as given. Let us look more closely at what this involves.

If a theory about the relation of government to the people is to make any sense, it must among other things include some guidance about three problematic aspects of 'the people':

1. Do they have geographic boundaries? Is democratic theory concerned with the whole of mankind or with smaller 'peoples'? If the latter, what counts as a 'people'?
2. Supposing that particular geographic limits can be established, what makes an individual within those boundaries part of the people? What are the qualifications for citizenship?
3. What makes those specified a collective 'people' able to take decisions and undertake long-term commitments, rather than a collection of persons?

I shall argue that the answers to these three questions are interconnected.

THE GEOGRAPHIC LIMITS OF THE PEOPLE

For the purposes of democracy, how are we to tell where one 'people' stops and another starts? The reader may object that geographic boundaries do not necessarily matter; after all, the members of an organization may be spread all over the world but may yet (with the help of modern technology) take decisions democratically. But this does not get round the problem of limits. For one thing, the more extended a democratic organization is, the more it needs precise criteria for membership. For another, our increasingly global interdependence does not alter the fact that political communities are typically territorial. The vast bulk of political decision-making in which 'the people' may or may not be involved concerns matters within a geographically limited entity of some kind. The reader may say that this supplies the answer: the people concerned are those inside the territorially limited political entity that happens to be there, typically a state with internationally recognized borders.

Unfortunately the inadequacy of this answer has been amply demonstrated by events following the collapse of communism in Yugoslavia and the Soviet Union. We cannot afford to take for granted that every inherited set of political boundaries contains a 'people' for democratic purposes, and the reason we cannot do so lies in the logic of democracy itself: given the opportunity, sections of the population may themselves challenge this convenient assumption. If democracy is (in however qualified a sense) about giving those at the grass-roots power to express their preferences, then it is not surprising that preferences about allegiance are just as likely to be expressed as preferences about policy. As Michael Walzer puts it, 'bring the "people" into political life and they will arrive, marching in tribal ranks and orders, carrying with them their own languages, historic memories, customs, beliefs, and commitments.'[2] After all, if we are to have some say in public affairs, the most fundamental issue for decision is the question of which public arena we are to participate in, and of what polity we are to be members.

Clearly, democrats cannot assume either that the boundaries between polities are unimportant or that contingent historic borders can be taken as given. It might seem that there is a simple answer to this problem, which is to settle the boundaries democratically: 'let the people decide!' But as Frederick Whelan has pointed out, this solution begs the question. Before 'the people' can vote in their referendum on where the border shall run, decisions must first be reached about the limits of the relevant population. For example, one of the points most at issue in Northern Ireland, preventing democratic settlement of the dispute, has long been the disagreement between unionists and republicans about the constituency that is entitled to be consulted about the border.

Whelan observes that 'boundary-drawing, and the determination of political membership, are perhaps the most fundamental political decisions. Democratic theory ... cannot simply take the matter for granted.'[3] One might therefore expect that theorists of democracy would have something to say about it. Not that one would expect detailed policy prescriptions from thinkers who may quite properly see themselves as concerned primarily with what democracy would be like if it were fully realized, but it seems not unreasonable to expect some consideration to be given to the limits of the people in any democratic theory that has claims to be political thought. And yet one can search book after book in vain. By way of illustration, let us look at one or two examples, selected more or less at random.

Giovanni Sartori's *The Theory of Democracy Revisited* is a comprehensive work by a distinguished scholar who has been thinking about democracy for thirty years. Furthermore, it contains a section on 'The Meaning of *People*' which explicitly draws attention to the need for clarity in the use of this slippery term, and elucidates many of its ambiguities. Nevertheless, there is no discussion of the issue of physical boundaries: geographically, 'peoples' are taken as given.[4] Another well known student of democracy, Barry Holden, waited until the second edition of his second book on the subject to acknowledge that although the question of territorial boundaries is 'a troublesome issue', 'democratic theorists...tend to ignore it, and take the unit as given.' After a brief recognition of the difficulties he concludes with an almost audible sigh of relief that 'the problem is not one for democratic theory *per se*; and it will not be considered further here.'[5] Keith Graham's *Battle for Democracy* starts more promisingly as he explains that the book is divided into two parts:

> In Part One I try to develop a theory of democracy relatively free of constraints imposed by particular facts about the circumstances in which we live or about human nature. In Part Two I then consider the modifications which may be necessary, from a variety of different perspectives, if that original theory is to have any influence in real life.[6]

We turn to Part Two in the hope of some discussion of the question of boundaries – only to be disappointed.

It seems, in other words, that many discussions of democracy in current political theory assume that existing state boundaries can be taken as given, and (a very questionable assumption) that those same state boundaries would not be called into question by the implementation of democracy. Although, as Whelan says, boundaries that are not seriously in question must be a prerequisite for democracy to flourish,[7] it is widely taken for granted that for the purposes of democracy, each existing state contains a people.

MEMBERSHIP OF THE PEOPLE

Our second problem is a closely related one. Supposing that a particular set of geographical borders can be taken as given, which persons within those borders count as citizens for the purpose of forming part of the democratic 'people'? Aspects of this problem have always been discussed by democratic theorists because so many historic political struggles have concerned the extension or restriction of citizenship. Athenian democracy excluded women, slaves and foreigners; successive Reform Acts in Britain in the nineteenth and twentieth centuries extended 'the people' to cover the poor, women and eighteen year olds while still excluding children, criminals in gaol, the insane and most foreigners.[8]

Recently, however, political theorists have begun to realize that there are problems of inclusion or exclusion quite a lot trickier than the question whether voting should start at seventeen or eighteen. These concern resident foreigners, particularly immigrants like the Turks in Germany or the Algerians in France, and whether or not they should be considered part of 'the people' for democratic purposes. As we saw in considering the previous question, the existence of a 'people' is taken as given: the problem debated is how generously or restrictively its boundaries should be drawn. Lurking behind such discussions is the more fundamental question, what makes human beings a 'people'? And although the instinct of the liberal-minded may be to say that all those inside the borders of a given state who are of sound mind at the time of an election must count, current dilemmas in a number of would-be democratic states demonstrate that when we think of 'the people', we mean something more than a simple aggregate of individuals. We mean some kind of collective body of which individuals can be members, with a corporate identity which can call on their allegiance and long-term interests which individuals can share.[9]

Consider, for example, the dilemmas faced by newly-democratized Estonia and Latvia about whether their large Russian communities should be entitled to full citizenship. If a democratic 'people' were simply an aggregate of the individuals within a given set of borders, there would be no justification for hesitating to award citizenship to all on equal terms. Similarly, if the Russians resident in the Baltic states were mere transients, they would have no claim to be members of a people that is necessarily more than just an aggregate. The conundrum arises precisely because, though originally invading foreigners and transients, many of the Russians have become to some degree rooted in the country and have at any rate some claim to form part of the collective people. What is at issue is how that collective people should be defined, and the extent to which qualifications for membership should be ethnic or linguistic.

The difficult issue of the proper boundaries of citizenship is beyond the scope of the present discussion. The purpose of raising it here, alongside the issue of geographical boundaries, is to make a point that many theorists of democracy have been reluctant to acknowledge, namely that the 'people' must have some degree of collective identity if democratic aspirations are to make sense.

COLLECTIVE IDENTITY

Within the English-speaking tradition of political thought collective entities are a touchy subject. Any notion that 'the people' might have to be regarded as something more than a collection of individuals is likely to set off nightmares about the *Volksgeist* and other Teutonic monsters.[10] But the notion that we can do without a 'people' with some degree of collective identity is an illusion made plausible only by the peculiarities of the English language. As we saw earlier, 'people' is ambiguous between individualist and collectivist senses, and even when we use the term in a collectivist sense to refer to a nation we give it a plural verb: 'the Scottish people demand independence', not 'the Scottish people demands independence'.[11] Since 'people' also means 'persons', it is not surprising if we often fail to notice that democratic legitimacy depends upon its collectivist sense.

But we need only translate 'the Scottish people have a right to rule themselves' into 'Scottish persons have a right to rule themselves' to see that in the former expression some kind of corporate identity is taken for granted, and that without this we have a prescription for anarchy, not democracy. If the 'people' are to be able to act, they have to be able to bind their present and future members: democracy presumes precisely that the people can take decisions that stick, pass laws that will hold and enter into binding commitments. For a salutary reminder of the problems of trying to take political action in the absence of any such firm collective identity, consider the recent failure of the ironically-named European Union and United Nations in Bosnia and elsewhere.

The same point is reinforced when we think about what is involved in representation. Modern theorists who have written about this topic have usually been most interested in the relation between representative and constituent and the problem of how individuals can make their wishes and interests felt at the level of decision-making. But an older and more fundamental sense of representation, which cannot be dispensed with even in the most democratic system, concerns the way in which a representative can speak for a community or institution and enter into commitments on behalf of its members, making contracts, accepting charges and so on. Even the smallest and most participatory of democratic organizations cannot avoid the collective commitments that go along with representation. If a tennis club elects a committee and empowers them to arrange for the tennis courts to be resurfaced, the contract undertaken imposes obligations upon the club as a whole. Where politics is concerned, a 'people' cannot have any effective existence unless it can generate representatives who are able to take binding decisions on its behalf, such as negotiating a peace treaty setting the boundaries of the people's state.

In the course of an interesting discussion of representation in *The New Science of Politics* Eric Voegelin points out that the first requirement for any political society to exist and act is that it should be sufficiently organized to produce representatives 'whose acts are not imputed to their own persons but to the society as a whole'. Representation of the polity preceded by many centuries the idea of representing people as individuals. In medieval political thinking, the king represented the realm, and members of Parliament represented local communities. Modern popular representation is according to Voegelin a further refinement on the basic idea of representing a political entity. In democracy, 'The government represents the people, and the symbol "people" has absorbed the two meanings... the "realm" and the "subjects".'[12]

Now, readers suspicious of the collective entities beloved of the German philosophical tradition may feel that to bring in Voegelin at this point is to go much too fast. Yes, in a sense any organization that has 'members' (that linguistic relic of organic metaphors) must have a collective identity of a sort: but this need be only the very thin kind of collective identity possessed by modern institutions from firms to charities, which does not seriously compromise methodological individualism.[13] Our tennis club, for example, may be able to act as a unit and undertake commitments through its representatives, but since it is a democratic association those representatives must be directly authorized by the individual members, who cannot acquire commitments against their will because they have chosen to join and can leave if they see fit. In other words, the notion of democracy is strongly associated in our tradition of political thought with assumptions of footloose individualism.[14] I shall argue that this association is mistaken: that democracy actually has much more stringent requirements in the way of collective identity than more repressive forms of polity, and that the reason this is so seldom noticed is that democratic theorists take for granted a political community that is already there.

Following a tendency that has been apparent in Anglo-American political thought ever since Locke, modern democratic theorists are inclined to blur the differences between polities and voluntary associations, and to represent the democratic polity as a kind of expanded tennis club.[15] However, this kind of analogy is gravely misleading. Not only is a polity something that contin-

ues over time, into which we are born, inheriting the commitments undertaken by the whole body; even more to the point, it is not something that we
can simply opt out of when we choose. We may be fortunate enough to be in
a position to move from one polity to another, but membership and its
commitments remains the norm. Polities claim the loyalty of their members,
especially in times of crisis and danger for the whole body. If a confirmed
individualist asks why individuals should heed such demands for loyalty, the
simplest answer is that a polity which cannot successfully command the
loyalty of its members will sooner or later be replaced by one that can, on
terms decided by the latter.[16]

Polities that are going to survive, let alone be able to take action, have to be
able to maintain some degree of unity and stability in face not only of the
competition from other polities but of entropy resulting from the plurality
and mortality of human beings. In a world where new people, all with their
axes to grind, are continually replacing one another, the problem of maintaining unity and stability has always been at the root of politics, and what is
interesting for our purposes is that it has historically been harder to solve on
democratic than on non-democratic terms. Much the most common solution
has been rule by one man at the head of an army, buttressed by as much
support from religion as could be mustered. As the seventeenth-century theorists of absolute monarchy made clear, the practical function of kingship was
above all to create political unity, which was not something that could be
taken for granted. In the words of a royalist broadside from the English Civil
War,

> A Monarchy's that Politick simple State.
> Consists in Unity (inseparate,
> Pure and entire); a Government that stands
> When others fall, touch'd but with levelling hands;
> So Natural, and with such Skill endu'd,
> It makes One Body of a Multitude.[17]

In view of the immense historic success of sacred monarchy as a form of
political system it is well worth considering the advantages it offered even
those of sceptical mind. For Hobbes, as the frontispiece to *Leviathan* shows
in graphic form, its great virtue was indeed its capacity to form a single body
politic out of the multitudinous natural bodies of its subjects.[18] A disadvan-
tage of monarchy was that kings are mortal, too. But as Ernst Kantorowicz
showed in his great book on *The King's Two Bodies*, the notion that the king
had a 'body politic' as well as a 'body natural' was devised by theologically-
minded lawyers in order to overcome the danger to political unity and stability posed by the mortality of the ruler. The physical unity provided by the
king was turned into an abstract, institutional unity.[19]

In the modern world that abstraction developed into the institution of the bureaucratic state, something which is by no means omnipresent but which is sufficiently common for us often to assume that the old political problem of maintaining unity and stability has been solved. We shall have occasion later to consider whether liberals in particular tend to take this too much for granted, but the salient point just now is that the statist solution to the problem of political order cannot be much comfort for democrats. One of the fundamental claims of any version of democratic theory is that the existence of a professional bureaucratic state is not enough for political legitimacy, and that it should be *our* state: that political institutions should belong to and express the *people*. And the catch here is that the more democratic the state is to be, the more need there is for the people to have some bond of unity other than that provided by common subjection. As Hobbes saw, if Leviathan is there to provide unity by bearing the person of every man,[20] it does not matter that the subjects are separate and mutually hostile. By the same token, however, there is no collective 'people' to whom Leviathan can be answerable. If the people were themselves to be sovereign, then (as Rousseau saw) they would need a corporate identity.[21]

The connection between popular power and collective identity is something that was clearly apparent in earlier times to opponents and supporters of popular rule alike. Both Filmer during the English Civil War and Burke during the French Revolution poured scorn on the idea of transferring power to a 'people' that was a mere collection of ever-changing individuals.[22] Within the classical republican tradition, where popular power was taken seriously, there was an obsessive concern with the need for unity among a people thought of in openly collectivist terms, together with a pessimistic recognition that unity was not easy to achieve or to maintain. In practice, the nemesis of popular republics was faction, failure of public spirit and unwillingness to sacrifice private interests for the good of the whole. Daniel Waley describes the elaborate corporate institutions of the medieval Italian communes, their symbols of unity and their intense civic patriotism, but chronicles their continual infighting, remarking that 'as hungry men dream of food and frozen men of warmth, so the men of the Italian republics dreamed of concord.'[23] When the effort to keep the people together failed, unity was invariably imposed by a *Signore*.

Practical experience of the fact that unity and stability are much harder to achieve in combination with popular power than with despotism was reflected in the emphasis placed on unity by classical republican thinkers. Within the tradition, popular self-rule was associated not with individualism but with civic virtue: the cultivation of intense forms of collective identity and of a willingness on the part of citizens to sacrifice themselves for the whole. Not for nothing was Sparta (rather than Athens) the admired ideal, and Rousseau was authentically classical when he spoke of the need for a 'people' to be created out of a collection of individuals by a lawgiver who would need to use all the resources of religion and education.[24]

Given this kind of background, an interesting conundrum presents itself: if (as both theory and experience suggest) popular self-rule is made possible only by the rare presence of a 'people' with a strong collective identity, why is it that modern democratic theorists are so silent on the subject? For it is a curious fact that even when they appear to be on the verge of doing so, they somehow evade the topic. Let me give some recent examples of admirable works that nevertheless contain this lacuna. Christopher Berry's *The Idea of a Democratic Community* is concerned with the idea of 'democratic commu- nity' used by critics of liberal capitalist democracies, and sets out in Berry's words to 'examine the assumptions that it makes'.[25] However, the nature of collective identity, with its bonds, its boundaries and its criteria for member- ship, does not figure in the book.

Carol Gould's book, *Rethinking Democracy*, looks promising for our pur- poses because it is specifically concerned with 'the analysis of the ontologi- cal foundations of democracy, that is, of the nature of individuals as agents and of their social relations, as well as of the nature of society and of institutions as constituted entities.'[26] In spite of her stress on ontological presuppositions, however, Gould does not discuss 'the people' as a continu- ing body, and even dismisses the notion that institutional terms such as 'the state' (let alone 'the people') could refer to anything other than individual officials.[27] We find what appears on the face of it to be a much greater awareness of democracy's need for collective identity in Keith Graham's *The Battle of Democracy*, but he too shies away from considering what is actually involved in a political community of that kind: what are its bonds of unity, its boundaries or its qualifications for membership.[28]

Why is it that (in sharp contrast to their predecessors in the civic republi- can tradition) even those democratic theorists who lament what they see as the absence of 'community' in the modern world do not actually focus their attention on the nature and conditions of political community? How is it that the need for a defined and united 'people' as the basis of democracy is not even noticed in the bulk of the literature? The explanation is, I suspect, that the theorists in question live in comparatively stable, well-established states that had early experience of nation-building and have for centuries contained 'peoples' with a significant degree of collective identity. If this is so, how- ever, it raises disturbing questions about the many locations around the world where the existence and boundaries of 'the people' can most definitely not be taken for granted, as for example in the former Yugoslavia. What purchase can democratic principles have in such situations?

Questions of this kind must be postponed until later. For the moment, let us turn from the tacit presuppositions of democratic theory to debates about social justice. What kind of assumptions do their practitioners make?

NOTES

1. C. Taylor, *Reconciling the Solitudes – Essays on Canadian Federalism and Nationalism*, ed. G. Laforest (Montreal and Kingston, McGill-Queen's University Press, 1993) 197.
2. M. Walzer, 'Notes on the New Tribalism', in C. Brown (ed.), *Political Restructuring in Europe – Ethical Perspectives* (London, Routledge, 1994) 188.
3. F.G. Whelan, 'Democratic Theory and the Boundary Problem', in *Liberal Democracy*, ed. J.R. Pennock and J.W. Chapman, *Nomos* XXV (New York, New York University Press, 1983) 13.
4. G. Sartori, *The Theory of Democracy Revisited* (Chatham, N.J., Chatham House, 1987) 21–5.
5. B. Holden, *Understanding Liberal Democracy* second edition (New York, Harvester Wheatsheaf, 1993) 11.
6. K. Graham, *The Battle of Democracy: Conflict, Consensus and the Individual* (Brighton, Wheatsheaf, 1986) 2. Other recent wide-ranging books on democratic theory that do not discuss the boundary question include J.W. Chapman and I. Shapiro (eds), *Democratic Community*, *Nomos* XXXV (New York and London, New York University Press, 1993) and D. Copp, J. Hampton and J.E. Roemer (eds), *The Idea of Democracy* (Cambridge, Cambridge University Press, 1993). Robert Dahl is unusual in acknowledging that 'advocates of democracy – including political philosophers – characteristically presuppose that "a people" already exists.' (R.A. Dahl, *Democracy and its Critics*, New Haven, Yale University Press, 1989) 3.
7. Whelan, 'Democratic Theory and the Boundary Problem', 41.
8. Holden, *Understanding Liberal Democracy* 7–9; Graham, *Battle of Democracy* 13–16.
9. On the long debates over this question within two contrasted national traditions, see R. Brubaker, *Citizenship and Nationhood in France and Germany* (Cambridge, Mass., Harvard University Press, 1992).
10. For an attempt in an earlier generation to cope with this difficulty, see Ernest Barker's 'Introduction' to O. Gierke, *Natural Law and the Theory of Society 1500–1800* trans. E. Barker (Boston, Beacon Press, 1950) in which Barker struggles to articulate a conception of group-personality that is 'something above a fiction or a collection, and yet less than a super-person' (lxx). Writing in the context of Fascist ideas, Barker was worried by the political implications of accepting Gierke's uninhibited affirmation of the reality of group-personality, remarking that, 'if we once accept the theory of the real personality of groups, we are bound to see behind the state the figure of the greatest and the most real of all groups – the figure of the nation and Folk itself.' (lxxxiv).
11. Cf. Sartori, *Democracy Revisited* 22; M. Canovan, 'People, Politicians and Populism', *Government and Opposition* 19/3 (Summer 1984) 312–27.
12. E. Voegelin, *The New Science of Politics* (Chicago, University of Chicago Press, 1952) 37–8. On medieval representation and the unreflective assumption that local communities and the community of the realm could be represented as wholes, see S. Reynolds, *Kingdoms and Communities in Western Europe, 900–1300* (Oxford, Oxford University Press, 1984) *passim*. Thinkers within the individualistic Anglo-American tradition tend to avert their eyes from this collective aspect of representation (e.g. A.H. Birch, *Representation*, London, Pall Mall, 1971). Hanna Pitkin, in her excellent *Concept of Representation* (Berkeley, University of California Press, 1967), does acknowledge and pay some attention to what she calls the 'authorization view' of representation (38–55), and she seems to concede that 'all governments represent in the formalistic sense that their actions not only

bind their subjects but are attributed *to* these subjects. The Government acts, and we say that the nation has acted' (228). However, her main interest lies in distinguishing 'representative government' from other forms, and she assumes the existence of 'states', 'nations' and 'peoples' without enquiring further into their corporate existence. Compare John Dunn's observation that 'the possibility of representation stops at the boundary of the moral community', in 'From Democracy to Representation: an Interpretation of a Ghanaian Election', in Dunn, *Political Obligation in its Historical Context* (Cambridge, Cambridge University Press, 1980) 154. See also S. Khilnani, 'India's Democratic Career', in J. Dunn (ed.), *Democracy: the Unfinished Journey* (Oxford, Oxford University Press, 1992) 205.

13. Legal theory has had a long-standing interest in the notion of corporate personality and the sense in which corporate bodies are real or fictitious entities. See e.g. F. Hallis, *Corporate Personality: A Study in Jurisprudence* (Oxford, Oxford University Press, 1930).

14. Barry Holden mentions the possibility of a 'corporate' conception of 'the people', but sees this as something characteristic of 'Continental', i.e. Rousseauist, theory. (B. Holden, *Understanding Liberal Democracy* 83–4).

15. For a cogent critique of that approach and an interesting exploration of the implications of 'membership' of a polity, see J. Horton, *Political Obligation* (Houndmills, Macmillan, 1992) 42–50, 145–71.

16. Compare Alasdair MacIntyre's suggestion that 'good soldiers may not be liberals' (A. MacIntyre, 'Is Patriotism a Virtue?', Lawrence, University of Kansas Department of Philosophy, 1984, 17).

17. W.H. Greenleaf, *Order, Empiricism and Politics* (London, Oxford University Press, 1964) 47. Cf. Nannerl Keohane, 'the will and power of the king provide the cement and structure for society'. (N.O. Keohane: *Philosophy and the State in France: The Renaissance to the Enlightenment*, Princeton, Princeton University Press, 1980, 18, 253).

18. T. Hobbes, *Leviathan*, ed. M. Oakeshott (Oxford, Blackwell, 1960) 112.

19. E.H. Kantorowicz, *The King's Two Bodies: A Study in Medieval Political Theology* (Princeton, Princeton University Press, 1957).

20. Hobbes, *Leviathan* 107, 112, 114. Cf. J. Dunn, 'Conclusion', in Dunn (ed.), *Democracy* 247.

21. J.J. Rousseau, *The Social Contract and Discourses*, trans. G.D.H. Cole (London, J.M. Dent, 1913) 32. Cf. P. Riley, 'Rousseau's General Will: Freedom of a Particular Kind', *Political Studies* XXXIX/1 (1991) 55–74.

22. According to Filmer, what is forgotten by those who 'talk big of the people' is that 'the whole people is a thing so uncertain and changeable, that it alters every moment, so that it is necessary to ask of every infant so soon as it is born its consent to government, if you will ever have the consent of the whole people'. (R. Filmer, ed. P. Laslett, *Patriarcha and Other Political Works*, Oxford, Blackwell, 1949, 252, 211). Cf. E. Burke, 'An Appeal from the New to the Old Whigs', *The Works of the Right Hon. Edmund Burke* (London, Holdsworth and Ball, 1834) Vol. I, 524–5.

23. D. Waley, *The Italian City-Republics*, second edition (London, Longman, 1978) 126.

24. Rousseau, *Social Contract* 32–5.

25. C. Berry, *The Idea of a Democratic Community* (Hemel Hempstead, Harvester Wheatsheaf, 1989) ix.

26. C. Gould, *Rethinking Democracy: Freedom and Social Cooperation in Politics, Economy and Society* (Cambridge, Cambridge University Press, 1988) 2.

27. According to Gould, to say (for example) that 'the United States sent an envoy' means only that the *President* sent an envoy, and 'to speak otherwise is to reify or to hypostatize the abstract entities in the sense of regarding them as having the properties of concretely existing individuals' (103). Gould does not consider what it means to say (for example) that 'the United States has signed a treaty and undertaken obligations', the point of which is that the individuals who represent the US in such circumstances bind not only themselves and their individual successors but the entire polity.

28. Graham, *Battle of Democracy* 96, 235, 242.

4. Social justice: looking after our people

'The idea of distributive justice presupposes a bounded world within which distribution takes place'. (Michael Walzer)[1]

I have argued that underneath the discourse of democratic theory, presupposed by talk of people, representation and citizenship, lie assumptions about the existence of bounded, unified political communities that seem suspiciously like nation-states. This section will be concerned with similar presuppositions within the discussions about social justice that have been so prominent a feature of the political philosophy of the last quarter century. In the course of those discussions the topic has been approached from different angles, some more liberal and others more socialist. It is not surprising, given the communitarian traditions of socialism, that thinkers toward that end of the political spectrum should have been readier to acknowledge the need for political community, and even (in some cases) to defend the nation-state itself as a setting for the advancement of social justice. However, I shall try to show that the ghostly presence of a political community that appears to be a nation-state can also be detected in theories that are more liberal and apparently universalist in approach.[2]

In view of the 'communitarian' focus of much current debate, it must be stressed that our concern here is not with the question whether or not liberal theories rely on an impoverished conception of the individual as an 'unencumbered self', and whether instead individuals are or should be embedded within communities.[3] That debate is less concerned with politics than with the nature of modern (and particularly American) selfhood, as the vagueness of its references to 'community' makes clear.[4] What is at issue here, by contrast, is a much more political question: what sort of polity would have to exist for contemporary ideas about social justice to make sense? Would it have to be a state that was also a community? And is a state that is a community in fact a nation?

The arguments for the inescapability of political community as a condition of social justice are partly a matter of logic and partly to do with the nature of *political* thought. Let me summarize them briefly before going on to explore them in more depth. Logically, any theory about the proper distribution of social goods must include some specification of the boundaries within which distribution is to go on, and some reason why the goods inside those boundaries should be regarded as shared assets. These minimal requirements are necessary if a theory is to be able to identify cases of justice and injustice and to guide conscientious persons in judging where action is needed to bring situations closer to the ideal. At the level of moral principle, there is no reason why the boundaries of justice should not be as extensive as the human race, or indeed wider still. However, theories of social justice are usually assumed to be political as well as moral theories, carrying specifically political implications, implying (as Rawls says) that 'laws and institutions... must be reformed or abolished if they are unjust.'[5] It is more difficult in the case of political than of moral obligations to avoid questions of power, its foundations and its costs. The demand that society must be made just by political means requires the political power to carry out the necessary redistribution of goods. If (as seems to be universally assumed within recent academic discourse) Leninist levels of coercion are ruled out and justice is to be achieved by relatively consensual means, social justice will be politically feasible only in a polity with a high degree of communal solidarity. Most contemporary theories of social justice carry within them a tension between universalist moral principles and particularist political commitments, a tension that has been concealed from many participants in the discourse by the tacit agreement to take nation-states as given. In what follows I shall develop these claims.

BOUNDARIES AND BONDS

The question of boundaries is easily overlooked by theorists who approach questions of justice in abstract and universal terms while tacitly taking for granted the territorial and legal limits of the state within which they happen to be writing. Those who do pay explicit attention to this issue and confront the difficult problems it creates in political theory and practice are liable to meet disapproval for apparently leaving the high ground of moral universalism. Nevertheless, a few theorists have been sufficiently intrepid to do so, including Michael Walzer. As he observes, 'when we think about distributive justice...we assume an established group and a fixed population, and so we miss the first and most important distributive question: How is that group constituted?' *Membership* of the group within which rights and obligations are going to be shared out is, as Walzer says, 'the primary good that we distribute to one another.'[6]

Clearly, this is a crucial point. If we are to talk sense about social justice we must know what the relevant social and geographical boundaries are. Are we talking about fair shares within a family? A club? Scotland? The United Kingdom? The European Union? The human race? The ecosystem? It may of course be reasonable to think in terms of different boundaries for different purposes, but we cannot talk sense at all unless we know what the boundaries are. Furthermore, unless we are talking about a voluntarily undertaken system of mutual cooperation, we need some reason why resources inside those boundaries should be regarded as a common possession to be shared out according to some principle of justice. It would be very odd to suggest (for example) that the passengers who happen to be on a cross-Channel ferry on a particular day constitute a group whose luggage ought to be redistributed according to Rawls's principles of justice (unless some catastrophe had turned them into a community of fate). Implicit in the notion of social justice, and helping to determine the relevant boundaries within which it applies, is some presupposition about a community of obligation. Certainly the *practice* of social justice is likely to demand mutual commitment: as Walzer says, justice presupposes 'a group of people committed to dividing, exchanging, and sharing social goods'.[7] But even if we stick to strictly logical considerations, justice presupposes a group who *ought* to share in this way, and therefore requires us to give some reason why these people have these obligations.

As both communitarian and libertarian critics pointed out, this was a weak spot in John Rawls's *Theory of Justice*. Michael Sandel identifies a contradiction between Rawls' 'difference principle' and his anti-utilitarian insistence that individuals should not be used as means to other people's ends. 'The difference principle, like utilitarianism, is a principle of sharing. As such, it must presuppose some prior moral tie among those whose assets it would deploy and whose efforts it would enlist in a common endeavour. Otherwise, it is simply a formula for using some as means to others' ends, a formula this liberalism is committed to reject'.[8] Evidently some sort of community of obligation is assumed to exist, although, as Sandel observes, there is nothing in the logic of Rawls' theory that enables us to identify its members. Rawls has subsequently spelled out this tacit condition by stating that for the purposes of his theory he assumes the deliberate abstraction of a 'closed society' whose 'members enter it only by birth and leave it only by death', but he does not discuss the basis on which the borders of the closed society might be determined. Although he also considers the question of 'just relations between peoples', he seems to assume that 'peoples' can be taken as given.[9]

Tacit assumptions that goods are collectively owned and available for redistribution have triggered the fears of libertarians like Nozick and Hayek. Nozick argues that any patterned distribution is inconsistent with individual rights,[10] while Hayek warns that the notion of social justice is always implicitly socialist in that it takes for granted that goods are the common possession of a unified society with common aims.[11]

These objections from both libertarians and communitarians are not necessarily fatal to the notion of social justice, but they do strongly suggest that those who want to use the notion need to give more thought than most of them have done to questions of the boundaries and bonds of community. Socialists have of course been readier than liberals to argue that individual assets are indeed part of a social product, and that society is a common enterprise that should be conducted so as to secure justice for all. Most of them, however, have been just as vague as liberals about the boundaries of the community in question and the bonds that hold it together. Typically, theorists in both camps start by apparently aiming their prescriptions at humanity as a whole, and then slip almost imperceptibly into talking about the particular nation-state of which they are members. Even Michael Walzer, who explicitly discusses membership and defends the notion that the proper setting for distributive justice is 'the political community', is surprisingly cursory in his discussion of this 'political community' and how far it coincides with the territorial state.[12] However, some political thinkers have recently been prepared to defend openly what others have tended to assume tacitly, namely that the area within which notions of social justice have most scope is the nation-state. Their arguments take us beyond the logical requirements of social justice to its political preconditions, namely social solidarity and effective government.

SOCIAL SOLIDARITY AND EFFECTIVE GOVERNMENT

It must be conceded that attempts to implement social justice do not necessarily presuppose the conjunction of both these conditions. Empirically, either on its own can be effective up to a point. At one end of the spectrum, universalist principles and general human solidarity enable non-governmental organizations like Oxfam to carry out a certain amount of redistribution of goods, most of it across state frontiers. At the other end, authoritarian governments in communist states have carried out far-reaching redistributions under conditions of social hostility and fragmentation. If we assume, however (as theorists of social justice usually do) that justice requires a scale of redistribution beyond the powers of voluntary organizations, and furthermore that it should be brought about by compulsory but consensual means, then what is required is a political community, that is to say, a polity whose inhabitants share sufficient sense of mutual trust and obligation to generate and support effective sharing. We need only consider the political difficulties created within the European Union by comparatively limited redistributive policies that share 'our' fishing grounds with foreign fishermen and that transfer 'our' taxes to 'them' to see the point. For national leaders within the EU to attempt a more thoroughgoing redistribution would be to invite a populist reaction within the donor states and to imperil the degree of sharing that does exist.

The problem for socialists is that this political precondition for social justice contradicts their sense of obligation to mankind in general. 'National socialism' as a theoretical position is comfortable only for those who feel themselves to be the historic victims of imperialism, not for its historic beneficiaries. Nevertheless, pragmatic considerations may point in that direction, for there can be no doubt that measures of social redistribution and welfare provision are much more likely to be feasible where social and political solidarity already exists, and where there is a sense of obligation to look after '*our* people'.[13] During the surge of patriotism engendered by the Second World War, the Beveridge Report, bible of the British welfare state, observed that while citizens share a common interest in the prevention of want, 'it may be possible to secure a keener realization of that fact in war than it is in peace, because war breeds national unity and readiness to sacrifice personal interests to the common cause.'[14]

The link between redistribution and nationhood has been made most persuasively by David Miller in a series of recent writings. As he makes clear, Miller does not propose that we should ignore duties to the rest of humanity and adopt a 'narrow-minded and exclusive nationalism', though he does argue 'against a naive form of internationalism'.[15] Furthermore, the understanding of nationhood he uses is a sophisticated one which does not identify nationhood with ethnicity.[16] His point is that the mutual trust between fellow-citizens that follows from shared identity and shared loyalty is especially important for the politics of social justice. 'Redistributive politics of the kind favoured by socialists are likely to demand a considerable degree of social solidarity if they are to win popular consent, and for that reason socialists should be more strongly committed than classical liberals to the nation-state as an institution that can make such solidarity politically effective.'[17]

Miller arrives at this position by working through the implications of two stipulations that are now widely accepted on the Left, firstly that socialist institutions, once in place, should enjoy democratic support, and secondly that keeping them in place should require no more coercion than under present-day capitalism. In other words, they should be widely regarded as legitimate. Rejecting the notion that all that is needed to achieve this state of affairs is rational argument, Miller points out that our notions of distributive fairness depend heavily on our perceived relations with others. Those who lose in the redistribution are much more likely to accept this with a good grace 'if they regard themselves as bound to the beneficiaries by strong ties of community: the stronger the ties, the more egalitarian the distribution can be.'[18] Many socialists would agree that a strong sense of community is indeed desirable, but would hope to build one with an international scope, and would in the meantime wish to weaken national ties. Miller argues, however, that communities cannot be simply invented, and are particularly hard to come by in the context of modern industrial society, so that those that do exist 'must be husbanded with care.' Since 'a realistic form of socialism must start out from actually existing communities', it follows that 'the nation as a form of community must have a privileged position in socialist thought.'[19]

It may perhaps be objected that in the contemporary context of global markets, which set severe limits to the control that can be exercised by any government over any national economy, there is no such thing as 'a realistic form of socialism'. Another objection, raised by Bhikhu Parekh, is that (as the case of the US shows) a strong sense of nationhood can in some cases go along with a rooted hostility to redistributive policies.[20] In any case, we shall see later in this book that there are difficulties with any argument framed in general terms in favour of nation-states. What we are concerned with here, however, is simply the fact that the (usually unacknowledged) presence of nation-states looms larger in contemporary political theory than most of its practitioners seem to realize. For our purposes, therefore, what is even more interesting than Miller's explicit defence of the nation-state is the way that it somehow creeps into apparently universalist theories by the back door. The most illustrious example here is Rawls's *Theory of Justice*.

Rawls initially presented his theory as an attempt 'to generalize and carry to a higher order of abstraction the traditional theory of the social contract as represented by Locke, Rousseau, and Kant'.[21] That tradition had always involved abstracting men from their actual social and political locations and placing them as nameless individuals in a hypothetical state of nature, but Rawls gave the process of abstraction a further twist by placing his individuals behind a 'veil of ignorance', and stipulating that they should arrive at principles of justice without knowing how they personally would be affected by the principles they chose. No one is to know his or her place in society, his natural talents, his preferences and his convictions. As communitarian critics have pointed out *ad nauseam*, the theory starts, apparently, from the 'unencumbered self'. Rawls is particularly anxious to rule out advantages and disadvantages that depend on mere chance, such as the chance of birth into a fortunate or unfortunate social situation. He observes of aristocratic and caste societies, for example, that 'the basic structure of these societies incorporates the arbitrariness found in nature.' This is unjustifiable because 'the social system is not an unchangeable order beyond human control...in justice as fairness men agree to share one another's fate. In designing institutions they undertake to avail themselves of the accidents of nature and social circumstance only when doing so is for the common benefit.'[22]

This is a noble vision, and must have seemed a particularly inspiring one to anyone who happened (by the accident of nature and social circumstance) to have been born on the wrong side of a crucial frontier such as the Rio Grande. The arbitrariness found in nature distributes to those born into the families of US citizens rights and opportunities denied by fate to those born Mexicans. Given the generality and abstraction of Rawls' approach, one might reasonably expect that political frontiers, with all their implications for differential rights and benefits, must be one of the main sources of injustice with which he is concerned. However, this expectation is disappointed. Not only does it eventually emerge that Rawls is assuming for the purposes of his theory 'the notion of a self-contained national community';[23] more seriously, he makes no attempt to justify this concession to sheer contingency or to explain why co-nationals should have special claims upon one another whereas (for example) fellow members of a superior caste do not.[24]

Rawls has made clear in subsequent writings that his theory was not intended to have the universal scope it appeared to have, and that what it proposes is a 'political conception of justice', intended to apply to 'the "basic structure" of a modern constitutional democracy'. This conception may or may not have relevance 'for different kinds of societies existing under different historical and social conditions'.[25] Although he continues to talk in general terms of constitutional democracies, it seems fairly clear that he has the existing US in mind when he observes not only that his conception of justice arises from a particular political tradition but that his purpose is to formulate principles implicit in 'our public political culture itself, including its main institutions and the historic traditions of their interpretation.'[26] Evidently the existing borders of states are simply given; within the boundaries of the US, citizens are to live together on terms of fair cooperation, but no explanation is given why the moral relations between individuals inside those borders should be different from their relations with individuals who happen to be outside. This omission is all the more striking because Rawls reiterates the principle that mere good fortune is not a sufficient justification for social privilege: 'one of our considered convictions, I assume, is this: the fact that we occupy a particular social position is not a good reason for us to accept...a conception of justice that favours those in this position.'[27] *Political Liberalism*, in which Rawls develops what he takes to be a more 'strictly political' theory, does not address this anomaly. While Rawls worries about stability and justice among citizens with different beliefs, he assumes that these problems are to be solved inside a 'closed society' recruited by birth. Although (in parenthesis) he specifically leaves aside 'the problem of justice between nations', the existence of nations and the stability and justice of the borders between them is simply taken for granted.[28]

What is even more remarkable than Rawls's incongruous tacit assumption is that so little of the voluminous criticism of his theory has focused on this particular weak spot.[29] Evidently most of those participating in the debate (including those who bewail the absence of 'community' in the modern world) share the same unconsidered assumptions. Let us try to elicit more

clearly what it is that is being assumed. Rawls takes for granted the continuing existence of modern territorial states such as the US, complete with
secure borders. The people inside those borders, far from being 'unencumbered selves' or rootless individuals, are to be regarded as 'fully co-operating
members of society'.[30] They have a collective identity, collective possessions
and collective obligations: 'we' share traditions and convictions, resources
are 'our' assets, to be shared according to principles that 'we' accept. Above
all, membership of this fellowship of social justice is not normally a matter of
individual choice: individuals happen to belong to 'us' for the most part by
the chances of birth. Lurking behind the apparently universalist terms of
Rawls' theory, in other words, so much taken for granted that it never comes
up for inspection, is a territorial political community that is a community of
fate, not choice, and that seems remarkably like a nation.[31]

In contrast to Rawls and most of his commentators, some theorists of
social justice have been prepared to confront and reject nationhood and to
present more genuinely universalist theories, thinking about justice in a global perspective. Thomas Pogge, for example, proposes to take Rawls's principles to their logical conclusion, arguing with considerable justification that,
from the point of view of Rawls's concept of justice, 'nationality is just one
further deep contingency (like genetic endowment, race, gender, and social
class), one more potential basis of institutional inequalities that are inescapable and present from birth', and which cannot in itself entitle anyone to
special favours.[32] Global thinking is widespread also in the discourse of
human rights.[33]

This fully universalist theory may appear to avoid the inconsistencies we
have been looking at, and to offer the possibility of a coherent theory of
social justice that does not rest on dubious national assumptions. But hopes
of this kind founder on the problematic relationship between moral and
political theory that we noted at the beginning of this chapter. If universalist
principles of justice were presented simply as a moral ideal (or even as a
political utopia) grubby questions to do with political power could be ignored
with a clear conscience. But the case is different if (as usually seems to
happen) such principles are presented as contributions to political theory and
intended to guide political action. For any theory that requires political action
presupposes the existence of some political body with the power to act, and
therefore presupposes the generation and maintenance of political power.
Theories that require *liberal* political action are especially demanding, since
tyrannical power will not do: such theories rely upon the generation and
maintenance of a particularly consensual, minimally coercive kind of political power. But power of that kind does not come naturally; it requires a
particular kind of political community. In other words, a universalist theory
presupposes a particularist home base. In the following chapter I shall argue

that even the most severely anti-communitarian versions of liberalism cannot avoid this logic, and appear to do so only because they too are sustained by the hidden foundations of the nation-state.

NOTES

1. M. Walzer, *Spheres of Justice – A Defence of Pluralism and Equality* (New York, Basic Books, 1983) 31.
2. For powerful arguments along similar lines, see Y. Tamir, *Liberal Nationalism* (Princeton, Princeton University Press, 1993) 117–21. Tamir's theory will be discussed below.
3. For a representative sample of the debate, see S. Avineri and A de-Shalit (eds), *Communitarianism and Individualism* (Oxford, Oxford University Press, 1992). For a useful survey, see S. Mulhall and A. Swift, *Liberals and Communitarians* (Oxford, Blackwell, 1992).
4. On this point see N.L. Rosenblum, 'Pluralism and Self-Defense', in Rosenblum (ed.), *Liberalism and the Moral Life* (Cambridge, Mass., Harvard University Press, 1991) 207–26.
5. J. Rawls, *A Theory of Justice* (Oxford, Oxford University Press, 1972) 3.
6. Walzer, *Spheres of Justice* 31.
7. Walzer, *Spheres of Justice* 31.
8. M. Sandel, 'The Procedural Republic and the Unencumbered Self', in Avineri and de-Shalit, *Communitarianism and Individualism* 22.
9. J. Rawls, *Political Liberalism* (New York, Columbia University Press, 1993) 12; 'The Law of Peoples', in S. Shute and S. Hurley (eds), *On Human Rights: The Oxford Amnesty Lectures, 1993* (New York, Basic Books, 1993).
10. R. Nozick, *Anarchy, State, and Utopia* (Oxford, Blackwell, 1974) 183–231.
11. F.A. Hayek, *Law, Legislation and Liberty* (London, Routledge, 1973) I 28, II 62–100.
12. Walzer seems to be talking about nation-states, and he evidently recognises that not all states come into this category. (*Spheres of Justice* 28–9).
13. This point is explicitly made by Brian Barry in 'Self-Government Revisited', in B. Barry, *Democracy, Power and Justice: Essays in Political Theory* (Oxford, Clarendon Press, 1989) 174–5. For a more defensive argument that nationalism is at any rate not inconsistent with socialism, see J. Schwarzmantel, *Socialism and the Idea of the Nation* (London, Harvester Wheatsheaf, 1991) *passim*. C.M. Vogler argues persuasively that (contrary to Marxist notions about proletarian internationalism) the working-class have a particularly large stake in the nation-state. (*The Nation-State: The Neglected Dimension of Class*, London, Gower, 1985). For a curious statement of revolutionary 'national communism', see the interview with Regis Debray, 'Marxism and the National Question', in the *New Left Review*, No. 105 (September–October 1977) 25–41.
14. Quoted in R. Goodin, *Reasons for Welfare: The Political Theory of the Welfare State* (Princeton, Princeton University Press, 1988) 78.
15. D. Miller, 'The Ethical Significance of Nationality', *Ethics* 98 (July 1988) 648.
16. D. Miller, 'In Defence of Nationality', *Journal of Applied Philosophy* 10/1 (1993) 6–8. This understanding of nationhood, and the wider implications of Miller's position, will both be discussed later.
17. D. Miller, 'The Nation-State: a Modest Defence', C. Brown (ed.), *Political Restructuring in Europe: Ethical Perspectives* (London and New York, Routledge, 1993) 159, note 7.
18. D. Miller, 'In What Sense must Socialism be Communitarian?', *Social Philosophy and Policy* 6/2 (1988–9) 59.
19. Miller, 'In What Sense must Socialism be Communitarian?', 68. Cf. D. Miller, *Market, State and Community: Theoretical Foundations of Market Socialism* (Oxford, Oxford University Press, 1989) 238. During one of the House of Commons debates on the

Maastricht Treaty and the European Union, a Labour Left-winger, Ken Livingston, M.P., explained that he opposed greater European integration for socialist reasons: the nation-state is in effect 'a mechanism for the redistribution of wealth' to a greater extent than the EU is likely to become. (Hansard, 4th November 1992, 255).

20. B. Parekh, 'The Politics of Nationhood', in *Cultural Identity and Development in Europe* ed. K. von Benda-Beckman and M. Verkuyten (London, University College of London Press, forthcoming).
21. Rawls, *Theory of Justice* viii.
22. Rawls, *Theory of Justice* 102.
23. Rawls, *Theory of Justice* 457.
24. Cf. Tamir, *Liberal Nationalism* 119; F.G. Whelan, 'Citizenship and Freedom of Movement: An Open Admission Policy?', in M. Gibney (ed.), *Open Borders? Closed Societies? The Ethical and Political Issues* (Westport, Conn., Greenwood Press, 1988) 10.
25. J. Rawls, 'Justice as Fairness: Political not Metaphysical', in Avineri and de-Shalit, *Communitarianism and Individualism* 187–8.
26. Rawls, 'Justice as Fairness' 192.
27. Rawls, 'Justice as Fairness' 202.
28. Rawls, *Political Liberalism* xv, 12, 136, 272; Cf. 'The Law of Peoples'.
29. For example, there is no reference to this topic in Mulhall and Swift, *Liberals and Communitarians*, nor in C. Kukathas and P. Pettit, *Rawls: A Theory of Justice and its Critics* (Oxford, Polity, 1990), nor in N. Daniels, *Reading Rawls* (Oxford, Blackwell, 1975), though see B. Barry, *Theories of Justice* (London, Harvester-Wheatsheaf, 1989) 189, 236–41.
30. Rawls, 'Justice as Fairness' 199.
31. Cf. Tamir, *Liberal Nationalism* 117. In *Social Justice in the Liberal State* (New Haven, Yale University Press, 1980) Bruce Ackerman does explicitly recognize the dissonance between his principle that no power or inequality should go unjustified, and the inequalities following from citizenship, which imply that some are apparently 'entitled to more simply because they were born on one side of an arbitrary geographic boundary' (256). In effect, however, he gives up on the challenge to his principle of consistency posed by 'the intractable difficulties of international relations', and concentrates on safeguarding 'the integrity of liberal politics on the national level' (257). For an interesting discussion of the issue focused specifically on the control of borders and immigration by the liberal state, see Whelan, 'Citizenship and Freedom of Movement', 16–34.
32. T. W. Pogge, *Realising Rawls* (Ithaca, Cornell University Press, 1989) 247.
33. E.g. H. Steiner, *An Essay on Rights* (Oxford, Blackwell, 1994).

5. Liberal universalism: a national heritage?

Cosmopolitanism is the privilege of those who can take a secure nation-state for granted. (Michael Ignatieff)[1]

We have seen that most theorizing about social justice takes political community for granted in the sense of aiming at fair shares *inside* the nation-state. Furthermore, I suggested that even those theorists who follow the logic of their universalist principles and aim at global justice still find themselves assuming the existence of at least one political community with the power to act on these principles. Some critics of American liberalism may regard this point as further confirmation of what they see as an alarming tendency to ideological imperialism, in which the universalist principles of liberal discourse hide an impulse to universal domination.[2] However, I shall argue in this chapter that less ambitious versions of liberalism cannot avoid making similar assumptions about power and political community. The most plausible candidate for a liberalism that would be genuinely free of any hint of communitarianism must be the kind of neo-classical version devoted to the traditional aims of limiting government power and political ambition, and protecting rights to life, liberty and property through the rule of law. As we shall see, however, even this apparently modest political agenda presupposes a kind of political community that is not easy to come by, and that has in practice been most closely approximated by certain nation-states.

A number of influential versions of neo-liberal thought are explicitly hostile to any conception of politics that has communal overtones. In particular, ever since the Second World War and the aspirations toward communal politics set off by wartime solidarity, there has been in Britain a group of sceptical liberal and liberal-conservative thinkers who have protested against the notion of politics as a collective project. Their guiding spirits, Friedrich Hayek and Michael Oakeshott, both argued in their different styles against rationalist and ideological politics and in favour of limited government. Both favoured a view of politics as what Oakeshott calls 'civil association',[3] meaning that instead of the state being thought of as the director of a common endeavour to achieve collective goals, it should be limited to providing a framework of laws and institutions designed to protect citizens from arbitrary power and allow them to pursue their own individual and group projects. According to this view, the bond between citizens is common allegiance to the law rather than any shared project or identity.[4] From the point of view of the generation to which Hayek and Oakeshott belonged it was socialism that was the main danger, threatening to enroll all citizens within a single mobilized 'society'. However, they were equally hostile to any other form of communitarian politics, including nationalism, and their ideas have recently been extended and developed by John Gray in ways that are (as we shall see) particularly interesting for our purposes, in that Gray has explicitly opposed any attempt to interpret modern states as nation-states. I shall try to show, however, that even these liberals cannot avoid relying on the existence of a political community.

One straw in the wind here, suggestive if scarcely conclusive, is that when efforts were made during the 1980s to translate vulgarized versions of neo-liberal thinking into practice, the politics of the New Right in Britain and America turned out to be an apparently incongruous combination of economic individualism at home and strident patriotism abroad. Without wishing to make too much of what was more a matter of pragmatism and muddle than a Machiavellian strategy, we should perhaps treat this as a reminder of the importance of allegiance, electability and popular mobilization as we consider something not often analysed: what political preconditions must exist if the liberal ideal of individual rights protected by the rule of law is to be possible?

Because the classical liberal view of the minimal state is often dismissed as a deplorably undemanding view of politics, it is generally assumed to be easy to attain: any fool can establish a nightwatchman state; the hard bit is to create participatory democracy or social justice. But the liberal ideal is in fact very demanding. Consider just a few of the conditions it requires:

–   laws that are impartial and fairly administered, and do not (for example) favour one religious, ethnic or status group over another;
–   a government that is strong enough to maintain internal order and external defence, but that is not arbitrarily coercive;
–   a public culture of impartiality and public spirit that restrains the rulers and officials from using their positions to further their private interests and those of their connections.

No doubt the conditions listed describe an ideal that is never met in full. But the important point to recognize is that it is rare both in contemporary and in historic polities for them to be met at all. The majority of governments suffered by the human race are and always have been arbitrary and coercive. Most of them have been corrupt, using government and law to serve the private interests of the rulers and their associates. Not only has the administration of justice usually been unequal, but the laws themselves have normally favoured some aristocratic, religious or ethnic groups at the expense of others.[5] A condition of equal subjection has been rare enough, let alone one of equal citizenship. If the political problem really were (as liberal social contract theories have often suggested) how to settle the terms on which identical rational individuals could agree to live together, then it would perhaps be soluble even if the parties to the contract were Hobbesian individuals or Kant's rational devils.[6] Truly 'unencumbered selves' could perhaps work out a *modus vivendi* that would be fair. But atomistic models of this kind are misleading precisely because of the lumpiness of human interaction. Politics is about relations not between individuals but between groups of many kinds, not just the parties and interest groups so prominent in contemporary democracies, but a host of much less manageable entities from kin groups, castes and patronage networks through religious and ethnic communities to militias and warlords.[7]

Liberal polities do not exist by nature, and when we think about these conditions we can see that they are made possible only by a series of rather difficult balancing acts. The state must be strong and effective without being excessively coercive: it must, therefore, be able to mobilize support from at least some large sections of the population. However, if it is also to administer equal justice to its citizens it cannot support itself (as so many governments have done) by helping one group to keep another in subjection. It must in general be trusted by all sections of its subjects. But if, sustained by a culture of bureaucratic professionalism, it tries (like the Habsburg Empire in some phases of its later existence)[8] to rule impartially over all groups, it is likely to find that it has the support of none. It is scarcely surprising that liberal polities are rare. What is it, then, that has made approximations to them possible in certain places at certain times? Some interesting reflections on this subject have recently been offered by Adam Seligman in an impressive book on *The Idea of Civil Society*.

'Civil society' is, as Seligman acknowledges, a protean term which is currently used in a great many different contexts. What particularly interests him, however, is its significance as 'an ethical ideal of the social order'[9] in which private and public, individual and social are linked. As an intermediate area between the individual and the state, civil society interests political thinkers in Western liberal democracies and in Eastern ex-communist states, but for opposite reasons. Communitarian critics of Western societies look to the notion to overcome the atomism of what they see as an excessively individualistic society, whereas for critics of communist repression and uniformity (as for the sceptical neo-liberals we are interested in) it represented freedom and pluralism. Superficially, convergence on the concept from West and East might seem to imply that civil society is indeed a golden mean in which the defects both of Western atomism and of Eastern repression can be overcome. But Seligman is less sanguine, arguing that civil society represents a delicate balance between individualism and communalism that has rarely occurred and that may in the long run prove self-destructive. His argument is complex and many-stranded, but an important element in it is his claim that what originally made the project of a civil society possible in the West was the formation of a particular type of nation that has no parallel in most parts of Eastern Europe.

Civil society involves a plural society in which much of the interaction between people goes on not at the level of the state but through informal organizations – political parties, trade unions, churches, voluntary organizations and the rest, all contained within a framework of impartial law. Seligman points out, however, that there are two preconditions for this kind of liberal pluralism, the existence on the one hand of autonomous individuals who feel themselves to be free from ascriptive identities, and on the other of generalized trust among the members of the society, whatever their group membership. These are not conditions that can be taken for granted. In many parts of the world identity and solidarity are overwhelmingly ascriptive and communal. Most individuals are born into a communal group of a religious or ethnic kind, and are likely to place their trust almost exclusively in fellow-members of their community. Attempts at pluralism in societies dominated by communal identities of this kind are not likely to produce the many overlapping groups and associations of liberal civil society, but only a collection of separate and mutually hostile worlds, like Northern Ireland but without the British state to hold the ring.[10]

Those who assume that liberal pluralism can be easily transplanted fail (according to Seligman) to recognize the specific and unusual history of Western Europe and its offshoots. In the wake of the Reformation, certain West European societies saw the emergence of the idea and the experience of autonomous individuals who were in a position to form free-standing associations on the basis of contracts. Simultaneously, nation-states emerged out of this tradition that embodied an unusual kind of 'social trust',[11] no longer limited to local, ethnic or religious communities but effective at a wider and more abstract level. Eventually, as the result of a long and highly contingent historical process which took different routes in different places, Western Europe benefited from '(1) the crystallization of a national identity out of different ethnic groups...and (2) the formalization and universalization of the criteria for membership and participation within this national identity...'.[12] Civil society was made possible, in other words, because individuals had been released from communal identities, and had instead become members of new, more abstract national communities that transcended ethnicity. Seligman argues that the 'generalization and universalization of trust'[13] involved in this nation-building has been a necessary condition for the kind of democratic legitimacy and conflict management required by civil society. The ability to cope with disputes between plural groups depends upon this overarching solidarity, and cannot easily be achieved where it is absent.[14]

Seligman's purpose is not simply to congratulate Western nations on their fortunate inheritance, for, as he points out, the notion of civil society is also being invoked by those who find these polities excessively individualistic. He suggests that the process of abstraction and universalization that created the Western liberal nation and made possible the autonomous individual and civil society may in fact be continuing to destroy social bonds to the point of undermining itself. Perhaps it is the case that 'the very universalization of trust... vitiates the mutuality and communality upon which trust must be based.'[15] Seligman's tone is pessimistic and he does not propose solutions. But his picture of civil society depending on a kind of nationhood which is precariously balanced between the Scylla of ethnic communalism and the Charybdis of atomistic dissolution does have important implications for liberalism, suggesting not only that it is linked with specific and historically restricted traditions rather than being the natural inheritance of all mankind, but also that it may require a kind of national solidarity that liberalism itself tends to undermine. Roger Scruton, defending a nationalist version of conservatism, has made a similar point more starkly: 'More than any other system of government, the liberal rule of law depends upon the renewal of public spirit, and therefore on patriotism.'[16]

Is it the case, then, that liberalism, for all its apparent universalism, is parasitic upon a pre-existing political community, relying on bonds of trust and loyalty that are an unusual and precious national heritage? Notice that two different sorts of issues are involved here, one more philosophical, the other more political. The first concerns the philosophical status of liberal universalism, about which a number of post-modern thinkers have recently expressed doubts. But the second (with which this book is more particularly concerned) is to do with the tacit political conditions of power and solidarity built into liberal principles, and this second question is relevant whichever way the philosophical question of foundationalism versus relativism is decided. Naturally enough, philosophical controversy tends to focus on whether liberal universalism has theoretical foundations. But even if that question is answered affirmatively, there remains the political question, 'where could the power come from to implement liberal principles, and what are the implications for those principles of the need to generate and sustain the right kind of power?'

John Gray's thought is particularly relevant here because he is interested in both questions, philosophical and political. Furthermore, he is very much in sympathy with Seligman's sceptical and pessimistic approach,[17] yet he is determined to resist Scruton's linkage between liberalism and nationhood. Gray is as critical as the communitarians of ideological versions of liberalism that present it as a foundationalist doctrine claiming universal truth.[18] His own version is 'a form of post-modern individualism that is fully conscious of its own historical particularity.'[19] He argues that liberal ideas arose out of practices and traditions that had become established in particular places (notably England) at a particular time, and that although they were then turned into a doctrine with universal pretensions, these pretensions are unpersuasive. Denying that liberal values should be assumed to be valid for all mankind, he argues that it is dangerous to attempt to apply the doctrinal version of liberalism even in the countries that have inherited liberal institutions, like Britain and the US. 'The danger we confront in the established civil societies of the West is that of the corrosion of liberal practices by liberal ideology.'[20]

To Gray as to Oakeshott and Hayek, the great sin of modern politicians and political philosophers alike is hubris: they expect too much of politics, and thereby run the risk of destroying the limited blessings that civil association can bestow. But if he is worried by the dangers of what he calls 'fundamentalist liberalism',[21] he is equally critical of the characteristically modern 'heresy', adhered to by conservative as well as Marxist critics of liberalism, 'that political orders ought to embody or express the cultural identity of homogeneous moral communities'.[22] Gray challenges Roger Scruton's attempt to connect conservatism with a form of Romantic integral nationalism,[23] asserting that in the circumstances of contemporary multi-cultural societies nationalism is damagingly unrealistic, whereas the traditional institutions of limited government become more relevant than ever.

> Where moral solidarity is lacking, where (as in all modern societies) there is cultural diversity rather than seamless community, the role of government is first and last that of preserving liberty in civil association under the rule of law.[24]

Gray's argument is impressive, but (as he himself acknowledges) it leads him into something of an impasse. He is well aware of the difficulty of holding a polity together by formal rules alone, and castigates elements in the New Right for being led astray by the 'unrealisable and dangerous utopian project of a minimal or neutral state enforcing a regime of common rules that is not underwritten by a fund of common culture'.[25] He even criticizes his mentor Oakeshott for assuming too easily that a polity needed nothing more than allegiance to procedural rules to hold it together, and observes that that particular aspect of the liberal tradition was an illusion which arose at a time when thinkers like Kant could take the common cultural identity of European

Christendom for granted[26] (although, significantly, he maintains that the culture that is necessary to sustain civil society is a 'culture of individualism' rather than a communal identity). [27]

If, as he recognizes, laws by themselves are not enough, and if, as he believes, attempts to mobilize national feeling in a multi-ethnic society can only be dangerous romanticism, where does Gray go from here? As he says, 'it is not clear what are the institutional forms appropriate to a state which respects cultural diversity and does not seek to bolster or embody any specific form of cultural identity.' In the past, states which have managed to command allegiance without such communal solidarity have been monarchies, empires or religious institutions. But the Habsburg Monarchy cannot very well be revived and was in any case unable to cope with ethnic diversity. Consequently there is, as Gray says, 'a dilemma of allegiance'. He casts longing glances in the direction of Hobbes's account of a state that is strong but concentrates on keeping the peace, but he also recognizes that it is very doubtful whether a Hobbesian state 'could command allegiance when it lacks the support of an inspiring mythology'. His solution to this dilemma is to fall back on what he calls 'a form of political solidarity that does not depend on shared moral community, but only on the mutual recognition of civilised men and women.'[28]

On the face of it, this sounds a pretty forlorn hope with which to confront the political catastrophes that Gray sees on the horizon.[29] However, he appears to believe that this civilized political solidarity actually exists in Britain. While denying emphatically that the United Kingdom is a nation-state,[30] he nevertheless claims that it is sustained by a political allegiance that 'may, and should, invoke a shared sense of Britishness, where this means a sense of fair play, of equality before the law, and a spirit of toleration and compromise on matters about which we have deep differences.'[31] Although the emphasis is on the 'culture of individualism', it is evident that 'Britishness' must incorporate the kind of mutual trust within an overarching loyalty that we saw Seligman discussing. In spite of the absence in Britain today, then, of 'a deep community of shared values',[32] there seems to be a thinner kind of political community with its own specific inherited character, with a good deal of mutual trust and with the ability to recognise not only a certain territory but a certain kind of politics as 'ours'. Indeed Gray seems to be edging ever-closer to appreciating the value of nationhood in sustaining a liberal-conservative polity. For all his doubts about the nation-state, he has gone so far as to acknowledge that it is now the only political institution with authority and legitimacy.[33]

The fact that Gray arrives at this position in spite of his explicit resistance to communitarian politics does seem to back up the argument that a political community of some sort is presupposed by contemporary political theorists.

Gray might concede this point, however, while denying that this thin version of political community can in any sense be considered a nation, for (like some supporters and many opponents of nationalism) Gray understands nationhood in terms of ethnicity and/or common values. Clearly, this matter cannot be debated until we have examined what nationhood actually is, and I shall argue in the next section that its complexity has been generally underestimated. Before we move on, however, it may be helpful to sum up the argument so far.

POLITICAL THEORY, POLITICAL COMMUNITY AND NATIONHOOD

I have argued so far that the discourses of liberalism, social justice and democratic theory rely upon tacit assumptions about the existence of political community. Let us recall briefly what the key assumptions are:

− Even anti-communal versions of *liberalism* assume the existence of a polity resting upon sufficient generalized trust to outweigh the bonds of kin, caste, religion or ethnicity and to make possible equal laws, public probity and government that is effective but impartial.
− Discussions of *social justice* assume all this, but add the requirement of a bounded political community with collective resources and communal solidarity.
− *Democratic* discourse requires not only trust and common sympathies but the capacity to act as a collective people, to undertake commitments and to acquire obligations.

Although the aspect of political community required is rather different in each case, it is easy to see that the three are connected and mutually supportive. In spite of the efforts of neo-liberals to restrain democracy[34] and to resist considerations of social justice, it is hard to see how generalized trust and equal laws could exist in the absence of some measure of both. It was not by accident that classical liberalism acquired democratic and social agendas.[35] What we are talking about, therefore, is not really three distinct political agendas, but rather variations on the theme of the liberal-democratic welfare state that provides the agenda for contemporary political theory. We could have arrived at similar conclusions by examining discussions of citizenship, which assume some principle of social closure,[36] or of political obligation, which makes no sense without some conception of membership.[37]

So far, the argument has been concerned chiefly with spelling out what *would* have to be the case for these theories to hold. The claim that a presupposed political community is implicit in the discourse of contemporary political thought does not in itself tie that thought down to the messy realities of actual nation-states, for it is of the essence of theory to go beyond the merely existent. Nevertheless, it may be instructive to stand back for a moment from contemporary concerns and to turn our thoughts to Rousseau, to whom all the various strands of thinking we have been considering are indebted, because when we compare his thoughts on political community with those of contemporary thinkers an interesting paradox emerges.

The concept of the General Will, into which Rousseau packed so much meaning, unites crucial ideas of each of the three topics we have been considering: participatory democracy; justice achieved by exalting the common good over individual interests; general laws that apply to all equally, in contrast to the privileges of the old regime. Looking back at Rousseau, however, what is interesting is the depth of his pessimism. While describing an ideal of democratic participation, communal sharing and the rule of law, he assumed that his ideals were totally unattainable in states on the scale of France, and unlikely even in a city-state because of the level of unity, public spirit and common identification required of citizens.[38] While Rousseau may have been temperamentally pessimistic, neither republican theory nor past historical experience gave good grounds for optimism. It is therefore a strange paradox that in the two centuries since Rousseau's death his ideal has come to be seen as something that does bear some relation to actual polities, and, furthermore, to large states, not just face-to-face communities.

One of the reasons for this, clearly, is economic growth, which softened conflicts of interest and thereby made possible (though by no means certain) less coercive forms of government. But we can perhaps see another reason if we consider the way in which Rousseau's French Revolutionary followers unconsciously translated his terminology. For Rousseau's 'people', which (he assumed) needed to be welded into a collective entity by a charismatic lawgiver, was effortlessly construed as 'the nation': a historic entity that could be assumed to be already in existence. As the revolutionaries found, of course, it was easier to talk about this nation's 'one and indivisible' sovereignty than to find unity in practice.[39] Over the longer time span, however, what is remarkable is that in some cases, large scale polities really have shown so much cohesion that it has been possible for large populations to recognize the state as 'our' state, for the notion of a common good within the borders of that state not to seem merely laughable, and for the equality of citizens before the law to be more than an utterly utopian dream.[40] So much has this come to be assumed within Anglo-American political thought that theorists rarely even stop to think about the sources (or the limits) of this remarkable cohesion. Unlike Rousseau, they tend to assume that it can be taken for granted. Later on in this inquiry we will consider some of the rethinking that might be necessary if political theorists were to recognize how shaky the hidden foundations of many of their debates actually are.

This complacency on the part of most political theorists about the existence of political community is particularly odd in view of the fact that the requirements of theory are necessarily more stringent than those of practical politics. Political scientists have devoted a good deal of time to considering the circumstances in which liberal democracy is likely to flourish, and have often suggested that nationhood is a favourable indication, whereas ethnic divisions are not.[41] However, getting some semblance of modern Western politics to work in practice, hard as it may be in many situations, is significantly less demanding than realizing the ideals of contemporary Western political theory. In the practical politics of what passes for the liberal democratic welfare state, theoretical principles, while influential, are mingled with copious doses of improvisation, bargaining and coalition-building. 'Democracy' as popular sovereignty gives ground to the play of parties and pressure-groups; 'social justice' becomes bargains struck between powerful interests; 'the rule of law' tends to be deflected by political considerations. Even in the empirical world, politics of this imperfectly liberal-democratic kind seems usually to be easier to sustain within the framework of a nation state than without one; however, deals are regularly struck to conciliate potentially fractious groups, including regions or ethnic groups outside the national core; in some fissiparous states, membership of the European Union provides an anchor against currents of separatism; while the occasional successful cases of 'consociationalism' show that the practice of political bargaining itself can sometimes serve to hold together a fragmented polity that lacks any significant sense of overarching national identity.[42]

In the unredeemed world of empirical politics, then, political community may sometimes be recognizable only as the minimal community of those involved in horse-trading. But political theory is more demanding. At the level of theory, government by the people is supposed to mean more than trade-offs between factions; social justice is concerned precisely to silence the clamour of special interests; law is supposed to be impartial, and the public interest something other than the interest of the government of the day. It is these demands that make imperative the existence of political community, and while the community in question is no doubt always to some extent a Platonic ideal, the thesis proposed here is that contemporary political theory is saved from complete utopianism and linked to the tangled world of empirical politics only because the community it presupposes is an idealized version of a political community that really does exist in some places, namely the nation.

This is not a conclusion that many political theorists will find congenial, and if it is to be made plausible we will need to meet three different kinds of objections. In the first place (the critic will say) our argument jumps a vital step. It may be the case that political theorists do assume the existence of political communities; it may even be the case that they tend, like everyone else, to generalize from their own experience, which may be of nation-states. But the kind of political community strictly required by their theories need not and should not be national, but should be a different kind of political community without the obvious defects of nations. Secondly (the critic will add), to posit nations as a prior condition of liberalism, social justice or democracy is really quite bizarre in view of our experience of nationalism. Surely it is obvious that far from supporting these lofty ideals, nationalist politics destroys them, leading to civil war, ethnic cleansing and populist dictatorship? Anyway (he will cry triumphantly) what *is* a nation?

I will try to meet these objections, starting with the last and coming back to the other two later.

NOTES

1. M. Ignatieff, *Blood and Belonging: Journeys into the New Nationalism* (London, Vintage, 1994) 9.
2. See e.g. J. Gray, 'After the New liberalism', *Social Research* 61/3 (Fall 1994) 720–35.
3. M. Oakeshott, *On Human Conduct* (Oxford, Clarendon Press, 1975) 108–84. Cf. F.A. Hayek, Law, Legislation and Liberty, 3 vols, (London, Routledge and Kegan Paul, 1973–9).
4. e.g. Oakeshott, *On Human Conduct* 158; Hayek, *Law, Legislation and Liberty*, *passim*. Cf. A.E. Galeotti, 'Individualism, Social Rules, Tradition: the Case of Friedrich A. Hayek', *Political Theory* 15/2 (May 1987) 163–81.
5. On the historical normality of 'polyethnic hierarchy' see W.H. McNeill, *Polyethnicity and National Unity in World History* (Toronto, University of Toronto Press, 1986), *passim*.
6. *Kant's Political Writings* ed. H. Reiss (Cambridge, Cambridge University Press, 1970) 112.
7. Liberals are not the only people who have tended to overlook this point in recent times. For some astringent comments on the failure of communitarian thinking to address the problems of plural societies, see J. Dunn, 'Political Obligation', in D. Held (ed.), *Political Theory Today* (Cambridge, Polity, 1991) 29.
8. For a useful corrective to the assumption that sheer longevity of a state is enough to hold it together and perpetuate its existence, see O. Jaszi, *The Dissolution of the Habsburg Monarchy* (Chicago, University of Chicago Press, 1929).
9. A.B. Seligman, *The Idea of Civil Society* (New York, Free Press, 1992) x.
10. This is scarcely news to political sociologists, who have long been interested in the difficulties of getting liberal democracy to work in plural societies. (See e.g. A. Lijphart, *Democracy in Plural Societies*, New Haven, Yale University Press, 1977). But political theorists have been oddly reluctant to face up to the implications of communal identity, except to see it as a base for claims for group rights – which of course assumes the existence of a framework of impartial law and thereby begs the question (e.g. W. Kymlicka, *Liberalism, Community and Culture*, Oxford, Oxford University Press, 1989).
11. Seligman, *Idea of Civil Society* 147.
12. Seligman, *Idea of Civil Society* 160.
13. Seligman, *Idea of Civil Society* 179.

14. On the historic link between liberalism and nationhood, see L. Greenfeld, *Nationalism: Five Roads to Modernity* (Cambridge, Mass., Harvard University Press, 1992), discussed in Chapter 6 below. The arch-individualist Hillel Steiner has acknowledged that 'as a matter of empirical fact, the historical advance of classical liberal or libertarian principles was…on balance aided by the development of the strong nation-state'. ('Libertarianism and the Transnational Migration of People', in B. Barry and R. Goodin (eds), *Free Movement: Ethical Issues in the Transnational Migration of People and of Money* (New York, Harvester Wheatsheaf, 1992) 93.

15. Seligman, *Idea of Civil Society* 184.

16. R. Scruton, 'In Defence of the Nation', in Scruton, *The Philosopher on Dover Beach* (Manchester, Carcanet, 1990) 319.

17. See Gray's review of Seligman in the *New York Times Book Review* (September 13, 1992).

18. J. Gray, *Post-Liberalism: Studies in Political Thought* (New York and London, Routledge, 1993) 284.

19. J. Gray, 'The Politics of Cultural Diversity', *The Salisbury Review* (September 1988) 40.

20. Gray, *Post-Liberalism* 327.

21. Gray, *Post-Liberalism* 327.

22. Gray, 'Politics of Cultural Diversity' 38.

23. J. Gray, 'Conservatism, Individualism and the Political Thought of the New Right', in J.C.D. Clark (ed.), *Ideas and Politics in Modern Britain* (Houndmills, Macmillan, 1990) 89–90.

24. Gray, 'Politics of Cultural Diversity' 42.

25. Gray, 'Conservatism, Individualism and the New Right' 88.

26. Gray, *Post-Liberalism* 45.

27. Gray, 'Conservatism, Individualism and the New Right' 96.

28. Gray, 'Politics of Cultural Diversity' 43–4.

29. Gray, *Post-Liberalism* 327.

30. 'The sovereign state of the United Kingdom is precisely that, a kingdom encompassing four nations, and not a nation-state.' Gray, 'Politics of Cultural Diversity' 41.

31. Gray, *Conservative Disposition* 20.

32. Gray, *Conservative Disposition* 20.

33. J. Gray, *Beyond the New Right: Markets, Government and the Common Environment* (London, Routledge, 1993) 149, 151.

34. Hayek, *Law, Legislation and Liberty* Vol. 3; cf. Gray, *Post-liberalism* 203, 210.

35. On the links between civil, political and social rights see T.H. Marshall, *Citizenship and Social Class* (Cambridge, Cambridge University Press, 1950) 1–85.

36. R. Brubaker, *Citizenship and Nationhood in France and Germany* (Cambridge, Mass., Harvard University Press, 1992) 21–8.

37. J. Horton, *Political Obligation* (Houndmills, Macmillan, 1992) 158–70; Y. Tamir, *Liberal Nationalism* (Princeton, N.J., Princeton University Press, 1993) 130–39.

38. J.J. Rousseau, *The Social Contract* (Harmondsworth, Penguin, 1968) 84–9, 96, 124, 131, 134, 138.

39. J. Hayward, *The One and Indivisible French Republic* (London, Weidenfeld and Nicholson, 1973) 6.

40. Cf. T.H. Green, *Lectures on the Principles of Political Obligation* (London, Longmans, 1941) 130–31; R. Bellamy, *Liberalism and Modern Society: An Historical Argument* (Cambridge, Polity, 1992) 38.

41. Cf. A.H. Birch, *Nationalism and National Integration* (London, Unwin Hyman, 1989) 40, 221; A.A. Mazrui and M. Tidy, *Nationalism and New States in Africa* (London, Heinemann, 1984) xii, 373–7; A. Ware, 'Liberal Democracy: One Form or Many?', and L. Whitehead, 'The Alternative to "Liberal Democracy": a Latin-American Perspective', both in D. Held (ed.), *Prospects for Democracy* (*Political Studies* Special Issue, XL, 1992) 141, 144, 157; R.A. Dahl, *Democracy and its Critics* (New Haven, Yale University Press, 1989) 254; C. Young, *The Politics of Cultural Pluralism* (Madison, University of Wisconsin Press, 1976) 516–17.

42. Birch, *Nationalism and National Integration* 170–82, on Canada; P. R. Brass, *Ethnicity and Nationalism: Theory and Comparison* 168, on India; A. Lijphart, *Democracy in Plural Societies* (New Haven, Yale University Press, 1977) *passim.*

6.   What is a nation?

Many attempts have been made to define nations, and none have been successful. (H. Seton-Watson)[1]

As all commentators on nations and nationalism agree, this is a subject on which it is extraordinarily hard to get a conceptual grip. Not that defining political phenomena is ever easy: any attempt to encapsulate a complex and variable phenomenon in a definition invites counter-examples, while the form of words chosen often has controversial political overtones. But the bulk of the literature on nationhood breathes an air of frustration that seems to have two sources, a sense that there is something peculiarly elusive about nations, reinforced by the feeling that they are in any case such ramshackle constructions of myth and illusion that they scarcely deserve serious analysis.[2] This sense that there is something particularly odd about nationhood can only be increased by the perspective that I have so far adopted, since I have been implying on the one hand that its capacity to generate the political power presupposed by liberal democratic political theory makes nationhood highly significant, and on the other hand that this vitally important political phenomenon is nevertheless so unobtrusive that most political theorists somehow fail to notice it. I shall argue that all these peculiarities are interconnected, that the power of nationhood is indeed linked with its elusiveness, and that nations are exceedingly complex phenomena, the key to which lies in their ability to mediate between different aspects of social and political life.

In order to bring out the complexity and the mediating role of nationhood I shall not start with a definition, but will instead employ a more dialectical approach. This chapter will work towards an understanding by considering five well-known approaches, each of which contains some truth but leads ultimately into a blind alley. In the next chapter I shall try to advance beyond these in a way which will (I hope) illuminate the significance of nationhood for political theory. The five approaches seek to understand nations as follows:

- as states
- as cultural communities
- in terms of the subjective identities of individuals
- as ethnic groups
- as products of modernization

NATIONS AS STATES

Time and again we find that the concept "nation" directs us to political power.
(Max Weber)[3]

When the victors of the Second World War set up a forum in which the leaders of the world's states could meet, they called it 'the United Nations'. To have called it 'the United States' would no doubt have invited confusion, but the precedent of the League of Nations in any case suggested that sovereign states and nations could be regarded as interchangeable.[4] There is certainly a great deal in English usage to support this identification. In American English, of course, where 'state' usually refers not to a sovereign entity but to the components of the union, the US itself as actor on the world stage is often referred to as the 'nation'. No doubt this has helped to give rise to a discourse in which relations between sovereign states are 'international' relations. Within that familiar discourse, states have 'national' anthems, played when the 'national' team wins an Olympic medal; possessors of state passports have a 'nationality', and appropriation of industries by the state is called 'nationalization'. Rulers like to think of themselves as representatives of nations, because (unlike 'state') the term suggests some degree of popular support.[5] In other words, our ordinary use of language encourages us to think of states and nations as equivalent, and not only politicians and journalists but political scientists and political theorists often use the terms interchangeably, unless their attention is specifically focused on nationhood.

The virtue of this approach is that it does remind us that nations are political phenomena – a truth which (as we shall see) sometimes gets obscured by over-emphasis on other aspects of nationhood. Part of what is involved in belonging to a nation is some conception of citizenship, however attenuated: some notion that a nation is a *people*, all members of which are politically connected with one another in a way that lords and subjects in pre-national societies were not.[6] This is a point to which we shall return later: for the moment, it is important to keep the political dimension in mind, precisely because the first move serious analysts of nationhood tend to make is to distinguish between nations and states, pointing out that the two cannot be the same thing. Many states have existed and still do exist which are not nation-states: neither the Soviet Union nor Liechtenstein could be regarded as a nation-state, while many ex-colonial states would claim to be engaged in a process of 'nation-building' that is usually incomplete and sometimes an obviously lost cause. Conversely, some nations have existed and still do exist without corresponding to states. Any attempt to specify contemporary cases is inevitably controversial, but it is easy enough to see that (for example) a Polish nation still existed after the Nazi conquest of Poland, and had existed for some time before the establishment of the Polish state following the First World War.

If some of the 'United Nations' are not really nations at all, only states, what is it that they lack? What *is* a nation? one of the most venerable answers focuses on culture.

NATIONS AS CULTURAL COMMUNITIES

Wherever a separate language is found, there a separate nation exists. (Fichte)[7]

When the French Revolutionary armies swarmed across Europe carrying their political understanding of nationhood as citizenship, they provoked German intellectuals like Fichte into articulating a Romantic counter-nationalism that focused on culture and particularly on language.[8] A hundred years later, Friedrich Meinecke formalized the contrast with a distinction between 'political nations' that had been formed from above through the unifying influence of rulers, and 'cultural nations' formed from below through the growth of a national literature and other cultural expressions.[9] Many of the nationalist movements of the nineteenth century followed the German Romantics in being particularly concerned to preserve and celebrate cultural heritages such as languages, folk tales and traditional music, while more recently, as modernization has carried American English, Coke and Big Macs across the globe, there has in some quarters been a renewed stress on safeguarding what are seen as unique and threatened national cultures.

Understandings of nationhood in cultural terms have been reaffirmed recently both by supporters and by opponents of nationalism, and it is undeniable that some national identities are experienced primarily in terms of cultural distinctiveness.[10] For all the persuasiveness of this approach, however, any generalized attempt to use 'culture' to identify nations rapidly gets into difficulties. The German Romantics believed that each language was the expression of a particular *Volksgeist*, which also produced characteristic styles of poetry, music and so on. But if distinctive national identity ever corresponded closely to language (itself a question-begging term),[11] it certainly does not necessarily do so now. Only consider the varied assortment of nationalists (American, Irish, Scottish, Indian and so on) who have eloquently expressed their grievances in English. If the language and spirit of a people really were so closely wedded, it is hard to see how this could be done. For every case (like Quebec, for instance) in which language is the central symbol of national identity, there is another where it is secondary.

Are we looking in the wrong place, though, in focusing on language as such? Should we take 'culture' to refer not so much to the medium of expression as to what is being expressed – say, a set of beliefs? John Gray, writing about 'The Politics of Cultural Diversity' and the imprudence of invoking nationalism in a culturally pluralist society, speaks of nationhood as implying 'membership of a single moral community'.[12] This suggests that members of a nation would have to agree (for example) on fundamental moral and religious doctrines. No doubt there is an element of truth in this, as we can see if we consider the anxious debates that have at various times been conducted within nations about whether Catholics could really be English, whether Communists could be American and whether Muslims can really be French.[13] But the stress in these cases is not so much on doctrine as on political loyalty: is the belief in question a sign of divided and insecure allegiance? It may be that in some other cases religious faith is indeed so closely entwined with nationhood that the two cannot be separated. Certainly nationalist groups have at various times maintained that only the Orthodox can be truly Greek or only the Catholic truly Irish. However, these confessional accounts of nationhood have been stoutly contested, and cannot in any case be generalized. Gray's suggestion that shared beliefs are at the heart of nationhood perhaps reflects the excessive stress on matters of intellect that is an occupational hazard of the academic life.

What if we try a looser conception of culture? Yael Tamir understands a nation as a form of 'cultural community', and claims that 'two people are of the same nation if, and only if, they share the same culture'.[14] At first sight, this is rather startling. Did Michael Oakeshott and some semi-literate skinhead in a Union Jack tee-shirt really share the same culture? But were they not both English? (British too, of course: we shall be considering the relation between the two identities later). But Tamir is in fact using a conception of 'culture' more like the anthropologists' sense, 'embodying patterns of behaviour, language, norms, myths and symbols that enable mutual recognition.'[15] This is more plausible, but it is also circular: 'the set of specific features that enable members of a nation to distinguish between themselves and others is culture.'[16]

In other words, we cannot use sharing the same culture as a criterion of nationhood, because it is precisely the fact that features are specific to a particular nation that makes those features count as 'culture'. Writing in 1941, George Orwell tried to pin down what was 'distinctive and recognizable in English civilisation...a culture as individual as that of Spain. It is somehow bound up with solid breakfasts and gloomy Sundays, smoky towns and winding roads, green fields and red pillar boxes....The suet puddings and the red pillar-boxes have entered into your soul.'[17] Looking back, we can still find the smoky towns and (some of) the green fields, but not much else, not the suet puddings, and certainly not 'the crowds in the big towns, with ...their bad teeth and their gentle manners'. If it were suet puddings, gentle manners or any other specific features of 'culture' that made English people English, the nation would have disappeared altogether. But it seems that what matters is not the features themselves, but the fact that, for the time being, they happen to be characteristic of a group of people who can recognize one another as belonging together even though their common features change.[18] Instead of looking for an identifiable culture as the mark of nationhood, then, why not concentrate on mutual recognition?

NATIONS AND SUBJECTIVE IDENTITY

National communities are constituted by belief: a nationality exists when its members believe that it does. (David Miller)[19]

Most modern literature on nationalism agrees that what makes a set of people a nation is not anything as objective as shared characteristics, whether those be political, cultural or biological. The crucial factor is conscious-ness. As Hugh Seton-Watson says, 'a nation exists when a significant number of people in a community consider themselves to form a nation, or behave as if they formed one.'[20] Benedict Anderson's account of nations as 'imag-ined communities'[21] has been widely accepted because it seems to capture a lot about the way nations exist: the fact that, being 'imagined' rather than face to face communities, they link together fellow-nationals who will never meet in person; the connection between the growth of national feel-ing and the development of printed vernacular literature, which enabled strangers to share that consciousness; above all, the fact that nations exist in the mind.

Long before Anderson showed us the need for nations to be imagined, Ernest Renan, who is also much quoted in recent literature on the subject, pointed out in 1882 that if a nation is to perpetuate itself it needs to be willed. 'The existence of a nation is...a daily plebiscite'.[22] Now, there can be no doubt that this stress on consciousness, imagination and will is indeed true to life, although (as we shall see later) different nations are imagined and willed in different ways. All the same, we need to be rather careful in following this approach, for it can, as Eric Hobsbawm observes, 'lead the incautious into extremes of voluntarism.'[23] Whereas stress on consciousness gave rise in the German collectivist tradition to the concept of the *Volksgeist*, within the tradition of Anglo-American methodological individualism it can encourage subjectivism, giving the misleading impression that since nationhood is all in the mind it is a matter of individual choice, and that national identities can be created and dissolved ad lib. There are two reasons why these subjectivist conclusions do not follow from the fact that nationhood depends on consciousness: because nations are collective products and because they are inherited from the past.

Admitting that nations are efforts of collective imagination does not mean bringing in the *Volksgeist* by the back door. It simply means that although a nation would cease to exist if all its individual members ceased to think in national terms, its existence confronts any particular member as part of objective reality. The nation I belong to may be all in the mind, but it is not all in *my* mind and I cannot alter the situation by an act of will. To argue otherwise is like arguing that since the value of coins and banknotes rests wholly upon convention, I can choose whether or not to give my consent to the use of money and the economic system it makes possible.[24] Any particular individual confronted by a well-established convention cannot will it away. It is true that shifts in the attitudes of a multitude of individuals continually alter these social facts, but whether or not banknotes are worth more than scraps of paper is not a matter of individual choice. Nations also grow, change and decay as a result of myriad acts and opinions, but this is not to say that individuals can simply opt in or opt out. Very often, of course, national consciousness is buttressed by institutional and legal forms, the apparatus of states and citizenship. But even where these are absent, national identities can confront individuals as solid and insuperable social realities. In the case of Northern Ireland, for example, where an Irish Republican national identity meets a stridently Unionist Britishness, the significant number of individuals who do not wish to identify themselves with the side of the national divide on which they are born may find it virtually impossible to escape such identification except by leaving the territory. What matters is not just how one chooses to identify oneself, but how one is defined by others.[25]

This example reminds us of the other feature of nationhood that makes it highly resistant to individual choice: the historical depth of nations, which may depend for their existence on consciousness now, but which are inherited from the past by members who are normally born into membership. Renan, whose remark about the 'daily plebiscite' is so often quoted, made quite clear that inheritance was as crucial as will.

> A nation is a soul, a spiritual principle. Two things, which are really only one, go to make up this soul or spiritual principle. One of these things lies in the past, the other in the present. The one is possession in common of a rich heritage of memories; and the other is actual agreement, the desire to live together, and the will to continue to make the most of the joint inheritance.[26]

An important implication of this point is that although the imaginings and commitments of the present generation are indispensable, nationhood is unusual and anomalous in the modern world in being primarily an ascriptive identity, not a matter of choice. It is of course true that many individuals do acquire new nationalities: some nations, such as the United States, define themselves in less ascriptive terms, and therefore make this much easier, than others, such as Germany. But nationals by choice are very much the exception. In the overwhelming majority of cases, if people belong to a nation it is because their parents did so. An individualistic modern society in which people expect to choose their own spouse, their job, their religion, their sexual orientation and so on can find the *natal* quality of nationhood hard to take. Thus Yael Tamir protests that 'individuals should not be seen as encumbered by duties imposed on them by their history and their fate'.[27] Trying to formulate a specifically '*liberal* nationalism', she insists that 'membership in a nation is elective', implying that 'this turns the adherence to a culture and the assumption of national obligations into voluntary acts rather than inevitable consequences of fate.'[28] However, since she admits that 'continuity and respect for the past are inherent in national cultural identity',[29] her claim that 'individuals have a right to choose the national group they wish to belong to'[30] can make any sense only on the assumption that very few individuals will actually exercise such a choice, choosing between national identities that are kept going by the majority who are simply born into a nation and pass it on from generation to generation.[31]

The cliché that nations depend on consciousness therefore needs to be qualified by the observation that this sort of imagined community is not constituted simply by individual choice in the way that (say) there may be an imagined community of supporters of a football team or fans of a pop group. Although nations exist in the mind, that apparently flimsy identification is usually passed down through families and experienced as fate. Benedict Anderson is himself well aware of this, saying that 'it is the magic of nationalism to turn chance into destiny.'[32] But if the consciousness that constitutes nationhood is collective and inherited rather than subjective and a matter of individual choice, does that mean that nations are indeed, as the Romantic nationalists maintained, primordial realities? If membership is normally a matter of birth, are nations essentially ethnic groups?

NATIONS AS ETHNIC GROUPS

> It is not our will that has made us French. We have not willed our nationality… the *patrie* is a *natural society* or, which comes absolutely to the same thing, a *historic* one. Its decisive characteristic is birth. We no more choose our *patrie* – the land of our fathers – than we choose our father and mother. (Charles Maurras)[33]

History is full of accounts of 'peoples' of one sort or another – Jews and Philistines, Romans and Etruscans, Angles, Saxons and Jutes, Huns and Mongols, Sioux and Zulus. Many modern states also contain groups of people distinguished from the majority population by descent, culture and identity, ranging from indigenous populations like the Aborigines in Australia to immigrants like the Turks in Germany. Both historic and contemporary cases are often regarded as examples of 'ethnicity', and one way of trying to understand nations is to see a nation as a 'politically conscious ethny'[34] and a nation-state as a state that is ethnically homogeneous. This approach has obvious continuities with the Romantic belief that humanity is naturally divided into peoples, each with its own *Volksgeist* creating its own culture, and each destined in the fullness of time to awake to political consciousness and claim its own state.[35] However, overtones of 'naturalness' and 'destiny' are not inevitable. Ethnic groups may be regarded as contingent products of history rather than natural data, but it may still be argued that they are massively solid features of the social landscape, perpetuated chiefly through descent. An 'ethnic' approach need not involve the claim that peoples are genetically distinct[36] but is likely to stress, as Donald Horowitz does, that ethnicity is usually transmitted through families and is a form of identity relying heavily on 'birth and blood'.[37]

Ethnic conceptions of nationhood have not been much favoured in the recent literature, partly because some contemporary societies that are clearly nations (such as Switzerland[38] and the USA) have been formed from ethnic groups that are still distinguishable, but also for more political reasons. At a time when many societies are becoming markedly less ethnically homogeneous, the notion that nationhood requires ethnic homogeneity is unwelcome. Nevertheless, Anthony Smith has argued persuasively that although modern nations are much more inclusive and heterogeneous than earlier ethnic groups, they have 'ethnic origins' in the sense of being built in each case around an 'ethnic core' that continues to perform a vital role in providing the nation with the historical depth that modern polities need if they are to function properly.[39]

The virtue of approaching nationhood from the angle of ethnicity is that one is able to give due weight to vital features, such as the fact that nationhood is usually inborn; the sense of kinship with fellow-nationals; the stress on inheritance, continuity, obligation to our ancestors. Modern liberals may find it hard to take seriously the belief that one's nation is a sacred entity that transcends mere individual life and calls for self-sacrifice, but evidence of the vitality of such beliefs is everywhere. However, any exclusively ethnic approach (something which Smith avoids) has severe limitations, distorting the nature both of ethnicity and of nationhood. For one thing, although ethnicity is often thought of as a simpler and more 'natural' form of identity than nationhood, it has its complexities too, and is not always as immemorial as is sometimes thought. There are, it is true, cases of impressively deep-rooted ethnicity to be found, cases where peoples who are distinguishable now can be traced back over centuries or even millennia, changing, to be sure, but preserving an identity largely through blood relationship. Consider, for example, the long histories of the Jews, the Armenians, the Japanese. Less dramatically, there are cases like the Tyrolean valley studied by John Cole and Eric Wolf, where German-speaking and Romance-speaking villages had existed within a mile of one another and under common rule since time immemorial, struggling with the same demanding environment but keeping intact their cultural distinctiveness, which seemed to approach the conventional stereotypes of Germanness and Latinness.[40]

However, ethnic identities and boundaries are rarely as clear-cut as these examples might suggest. There is always some degree of fluidity,[41] some possibility of escape from or recruitment to an ethnic group, some greater or lesser scope for redefinition of ethnic identities, and just who counts as a member and what membership involves depends partly on the incentives and sanctions available. Eugeen Roosens has pointed out that in modern multicultural societies there may be legal, economic and political benefits to be gained from membership of a recognized ethnic group;[42] Paul Brass has drawn attention to the ways in which élites struggling for political power use ethnic symbols to mobilize support, and sharpen or blur group differences for political reasons.[43] Neither suggests that ethnic groups can be created out of nothing – as Roosens says, 'the mobilization of ethnic groups is only possible because political leaders are able to rely on profound affective factors related to origin.'[44] But both give good reasons for viewing with considerable scepticism claims that most ethnic groups are primordial or fixed. Consequently, claims that nations are or should be the political organization of pre-existing ethnic peoples lose at least some of their persuasiveness.

In fact, as students of nationhood ever since Renan[45] have frequently pointed out, many of the most authentic modern nations were formed through the merging or assimilation of peoples who were originally distinct. There are only a few cases of nations that seem to be ethnically homogeneous – Iceland, perhaps? The French and English nations emerged out of populations deposited by successive waves of alien conquest, and it is perhaps particularly striking that five hundred years after the Norman conquest of England, which was quite as brutal and exploitative as many instances of twentieth century imperialism, the descendants of conquerers and conquered had merged into a single nation. Radical campaigns against 'the Norman Yoke' lingered on until after the French Revolution, but they called for abolition of the institutions of conquest, not for ethnic cleansing of the conquerors.[46] Unification was made possible by common settlement of the 'realm', the compact territory defined by the monarchy.

Common occupation of politically-defined territory is clearly very important. Sharing a homeland is, as Roger Scruton observes, a vital element in nationhood, together with the shared language, shared associations, shared history, shared culture and, indeed, shared kin that often accompany common settlement.[47] Note, though, that mere proximity within a single political unit does not necessarily produce a shared identity. Within the territories of the Habsburg Empire, Germans and Czechs, Jews and Poles, Magyars and Croats and many other 'peoples' preserved distinct identities through many centuries of common subjection.[48] Even in Britain, the persistence of the two communities in Northern Ireland, divided not only by religion and politics but by kinship ties and cherished historic memories, demonstrates how intractable identities may be. Renan was right to say that one of the essential factors in the making of a nation was a degree of historical amnesia,[49] allowing old defeats and victories to disappear into decent obscurity. One of the most effective ways in which this can happen is through mobilization against a common enemy. Long wars against France greatly aided the emergence first of an English and then of a British nation.[50]

While we may agree with Anthony Smith, then, that 'there is a remarkable continuity between nations and *ethnie*', we must immediately add, as he does, 'continuity, but not identity.'[51] One way of understanding nations is to say that they are political communities that are experienced as if they were communities of kin, but the 'as if' is vital. Within any given nation, many fellow-nationals really will be blood relations, and nations depend upon the symbolism of kinship for much of their emotional appeal. Nevertheless, much of that kinship is imagined kinship, and a good deal of it is always distinctly fictitious. As we shall see, the capacity to *seem* like ethnicity is both the strength and the Achilles' heel of nationhood.

If ethnic groups themselves are not actually primordial kin groups, but involve a greater or lesser element of fiction in their claim to common blood; if nations, though built around some core ethnic group, are built through the blurring of boundaries and the adoption of ancestors; if the political mobilization of populations through the use of evocative fictions is inescapable from nationalism, then should we perhaps be looking at a different, more sceptical account of nations, which understands them in terms of the use of myths to serve the functional requirements of modern society and the universal imperatives of economic change?

MODERNIZATION AND NATION-BUILDING

Nationalism is not the awakening of nations to self-consciousness: it invents nations where they do not exist. (Ernest Gellner)[52]

One account of nations and nationalism that is frequently advanced holds that the nation is a product of modernization, an ersatz community that comes into existence to meet the needs of modern society. According to this account nations are in their own terms entirely inauthentic, but are nevertheless indispensable because of the social and political functions they perform. Various versions of this general thesis emphasize different aspects:

- the functional needs of a modern economy
- the emotional needs of modernized populations
- the tactical needs of modern politicians.

The best known and most ambitious version of modernization theory is Ernest Gellner's attempt to explain the advent of nations and nationalism by means of a large-scale contrast between traditional agrarian societies and modern industrial societies. Gellner's theory (which is presented at a high level of generality) centres on the way in which the role of culture in society changed with modernization. In agrarian societies high culture was the preserve of a small élite, while (since the mass of the population was tied to hereditary occupations) an indefinite number of folk cultures could coexist in the same polity without causing economic or political difficulties. For modern societies, by contrast, culture is crucially important. The education that is necessary to produce modern employees must be conducted in one or another official language. Similarly, because modern states are much more intrusive than pre-modern polities they continually need to communicate with their subjects, with the result that language becomes inescapably politicized. 'Universal literacy, mobility and hence individualism, political centralization, the need for a costly educational infrastructure', all conspire to put questions of language and culture on to the political agenda of industrial society and 'impel it into a situation in which political and cultural boundaries are on the whole congruent.'[53]

Although this coincidence between political and cultural boundaries is what Gellner understands by nationhood, he pours scorn on the Romantic nationalist idea that culturally defined nations are already there in traditional society, waiting to be turned into states. On the contrary, the emergence of a nation involves the destruction of most of the myriad traditional folk cultures as they are absorbed into a new version suitable to be the official culture of a state.

> Nationalism is not the awakening and assertion of... natural and given units. It is, on the contrary, the crystallization of new units suitable for the conditions now prevailing, though admittedly using as their raw material the cultural, historical and other inheritances from the pre-nationalist world.[54]

In Gellner's view, then, 'it is nationalism which engenders nations, and not the other way round',[55] and he insists with obvious zest upon the artificiality, the deceptiveness and yet the inescapability of this aspect of modernization. Nationalists of course believe that what they are fighting for is the preservation of their ancestral traditions, but what they are really helping to bring about is the destruction of traditional society and 'the establishment of an anonymous, impersonal society'[56] held together by the artificial culture of the modern nation.

If nationalism is so phoney, why do ordinary people respond with so much enthusiasm to its appeals? Apart from pointing to situations where (for example) separatism may offer job opportunities to speakers of a minority language, Gellner himself does not pay much attention to this question, but an answer in terms of modernization is readily available, and plenty of writers on nationalism have supplied it. It is that, as Simone Weil put it, we have to love the nation because there is nothing else left for us to love.[57] The communities to which people were formerly attached, communities of kin, village, occupation, status and so on have been dissolved, leaving individuals with nothing to turn to except the imagined community of the nation.

> For a long time now, the single nation has played the part which constitutes the supreme mission of society towards the individual human being, namely, maintaining throughout the present the links with the past and the future.[58]

Furthermore, in a secular age the nation supplies a sacred authority that transcends the individual and can demand sacrifices from him. Many commentators on nationalism have remarked on its quasi-religious atmosphere, and Conor Cruise O'Brien, who has made the most thorough study of this aspect of nationhood, produces a quotation from the French nationalist historian Michelet that is particularly explicit:

> It is from you that I shall ask for help, my noble country: you must take the place of the God who escapes us, that you may fill within us the immeasurable abyss which extinct Christianity has left there.[59]

The entrepreneurs between the functional needs of modern economies and the emotional needs of modern populations are of course politicians, who see in nationalism a heaven-sent opportunity to mobilize a following for the capture of state power and the rewards that go with it: a capture, moreover, which can be presented as legitimate in the eyes of the world because of the currency of the ideology of national self-determination. John Breuilly is resolutely hard-boiled in his analysis of nationalist politics, maintaining that

> Nationalism is not the expression of nationality... Rather, an effective nationalism develops where it makes political sense for an opposition to the government to claim to represent the nation against the present state.[60]

There is much that is salutary in the astringent approach and debunking tone
of the theories of nationalism as modernization. It is particularly useful to be
reminded that it can often be in the interest of prominent persons to claim
national status for their states, movements and cultures. But scepticism can
cut both ways, and we may wonder whether those who take for granted the
connection between modernization and nationhood may themselves be too
ready to take 'nations' at their face value. Not only Gellner but many other
students of nationalism seem to assume that whatever may have been the case
in the past, in the contemporary world nations are ubiquitous.[61] But are there
not good grounds for scepticism about this? Are not many of the 'United
Nations' even more unconvincing than Gellner himself suggests? The implication of modernization theory seems to be that since there are no natural
nations to get in the way, the artificial process of nation-building ought to be
quite straightforward. Experience has shown, however, that this is not so, and
in particular that states engaged in such a process tend to meet resistance
based on ethnic identities that seem often to be deeper and more intractable
than Gellner's theory would suggest.[62]

Would it not be wise, therefore, to take on board Breuilly's point about the
incentives many politicians have to *claim* that they represent nations, and to
treat many of those claims with appropriate scepticism? (No doubt many of
their 'ethnic' opponents are equally self-serving, of course.) And once we
recognise that nations do not follow effortlessly from modernization and may
not be ubiquitous, we are in a position to raise another more fundamental
query. It is easy to see why there is a lot to be gained nowadays from trying to
construct nations or to pretend that they exist: but where did the idea come
from in the first place? If nations are to be worth imitating, must there not be
some genuine examples from which the fakes can borrow some reflected
authenticity? Might it not be the case, then, that nations are not actually a
universal result of universal socioeconomic processes, but contingent phenomena, the result of specific historical developments from a particular historical beginning? This is the thesis put forward by Liah Greenfeld.

NATION-BUILDING AND MODERNIZATION

> Rather than define nationalism by its modernity, I see modernity as defined by
> nationalism. (Liah Greenfeld)[63]

Where Gellner and others claim that modernization produces nations,
Greenfeld turns the tables by arguing that nationhood produced most of the
features that we know as modernity. It did so by generating a society in which
the traditional barriers between nobles and commoners were transcended in

common membership of a people, and that 'people' acquired enough solidarity to replace a king as the bearer of sovereignty. Consequently,

> Democracy was born with the sense of nationality. The two are inherently linked and neither can be fully understood apart from this connection. Nationalism was the form in which democracy appeared in the world, contained in the idea of the nation as a butterfly in a cocoon.[64]

The place where this happened was, according to Greenfeld, sixteenth-century England, and those chiefly responsible were the new nobility raised by the Tudor monarchs. Within the society of orders that was the norm throughout Europe, nobility was a status sharply distinguished from those lower down the hierarchy: to be noble meant to be distinct and superior. The remarkable thing that happened in England was that the new nobility asserted their status as an élite not by pushing the rest of the population down beneath them but by identifying themselves with a nation which was itself thought of as an élite. 'In a way, nationality made every Englishman a nobleman'.[65] It was the Reformation above all that made it possible for the English to see themselves as God's chosen people. An entire population, poring over the gruesome illustrations in Foxe's Book of Martyrs, could celebrate the special English witness to divine truth and echo the cleric who asserted that 'God is English' and called upon Englishmen to thank God seven times a day that they had not been born mere Italians, Frenchmen or Germans.[66]

Greenfeld argues that the English nation was born as a kind of vastly expanded nobility, with the entire population of the realm collectively elevated into an élite. Initially, of course, the monarchy provided the boundaries of the nation and its most obvious bond of unity, and during the reign of Elizabeth the queen was symbolically identified with the nation. Under the Stuarts, however, a rift opened up between king and nation, and during the Civil War it became apparent that the nation could be conceived of as a sovereign entity that might not even need a king to give it its existence, and that continued to be seen as God's elect and as the leader in commerce and knowledge as well as in religion and politics.[67] What had emerged was in fact a new kind of political community capable of mobilizing impressive resources of popular solidarity, a development of enormous political significance. According to Greenfeld, 'It is nationalism which has made our world, politically, what it is.'[68]

Greenfeld claims that the English nation was not only the first of its kind, but that it was also (with the possible exception of the Dutch) the *only* nation in existence for nearly two hundred years. It was, moreover, a nation with a highly specific character, an individualistic one in which collective national identity meant membership of a body distinguished by its heritage of Protestantism and liberty. The Englishmen who settled America took this nationhood with them, and it was, paradoxically, that same heritage that led them to secession and the formation of a new breakaway nation in defence of their inherited rights. English principles, detached from English soil, were universalized into the American creed of natural rights.[69] In a sense, there-fore, American nationhood was part of the unique English experience, as, presumably, are other English-derived nations. Other nations, according to Greenfeld, are different, in that all were influenced from the start by the existence of at least one prior example to emulate and resent. Controversially, she claims that even French nationhood is derivative, arguing that although a 'consciousness of being *French*'[70] had existed for centuries, it had been specifically attached to the monarch's realm (and for many centuries under-stood in terms of the special holiness of the French monarchy) and was transformed into national consciousness only in the eighteenth century, when the dissident nobility imported the idea from England. During the French Revolution, of course, the king was replaced by the sovereign nation – but a nation closely modelled on the monarchy it displaced, inheriting the concen-tration of authority, the sanctity, the passion for glory. French nationhood, in other words, was very different from English nationhood.

In further case studies, Greenfeld attempts to show that Russian and Ger-man nationhood were each different again, and that each was conceived by a discontented élite group (aristocrats in Russia, writers in Germany, each with more than half an eye on the established nations to the West) who found a way to enhance their status by identifying themselves with a supposedly uniquely gifted nation. Though very different from one another, both versions were collectivist, with a stress on the spirit of the people that made them in political terms élitist rather than democratic. Nationalism spread ever further around the world, borne by similar concerns with status vis-à-vis nations already in existence. According to Greenfeld, '*national identity is, fundamen-tally, a matter of dignity.*'[71] She stresses, however, that nations vary according to the particular historic circumstances of their birth. 'Nationalism is not a uniform phenomenon'.[72]

Greenfeld's book is combative and there is much in her analysis that is highly controversial. But however much argument there may be about spe-cifics, two fundamental pillars of her argument do seem sound. One is the claim that nationhood is not a uniform condition to be found everywhere in the modern world, but is a highly specific historical phenomenon that varies greatly from place to place and in many places may not exist at all. The other is the observation that the advent of the nation created a new kind of political community, one with enormous political significance. Let us now attempt (drawing on the various approaches we have explored) to sum up what is involved in nationhood.

NOTES

1. H. Seton-Watson, *Nations and States* (London, Methuen, 1977) 3.
2. Benedict Anderson remarks on this tone in the literature. (B. Anderson, *Imagined Communities: Reflections on the Origin and Spread of Nationalism* (London, Verso, 1983) 14–15.) For a particularly striking example see K. Minogue, *Nationalism* (London, Batsford, 1967).
3. M. Weber, *Economy and Society*, ed. G. Roth and C. Wittich (New York, Bedminster Press, 1968) Vol. I, 397.
4. Faced in 1919 with a suggestion that the incipient League of Nations should rather be called the League of States, 'Lord Robert Cecil replied that he thought the difference between the words "nations" and "states" was a very small one.' A. Cobban, *The Nation State and National Self-Determination* (London, Collins, 1969) 123.
5. F. Hertz observed in 1944 that the British were particularly prodigal in their use of 'national', applying the term not only to the 'national debt' but (in wartime) to 'the national loaf' and 'national butter'. F. Hertz, *Nationality in History and Politics: A Study in the Psychology and Sociology of National Sentiment and Character* (London, Kegan Paul, 1944) 3.
6. 'Whatever else it may be, what we mean by "national" identity involves some sense of political community, however tenuous.' (A.D. Smith, *National Identity*, Harmondsworth, Penguin, 1991, 9). On the contrast between uniform national citizenship and the highly particularistic rights and privileges characteristic of the Ancien Regime, see R. Brubaker, *Citizenship and Nationhood in France and Germany* (Cambridge, Mass., Harvard University Press, 1992) 35.
7. J.G. Fichte, *Addresses to the German Nation* (Chicago, Open Court, 1922) 215.
8. For a vivid account of the process, see L. Greenfeld, *Nationalism – Five Roads to Modernity* (Cambridge, Mass., Harvard University Press, 1992) Ch. 4.
9. As Meinecke pointed out, German cultural nationalism had interacted with Prussian political nationalism to produce the German state. F. Meinecke, *Cosmopolitanism and the National State* (Princeton, Princeton University Press, 1970) 234.
10. Y. Tamir, *Liberal Nationalism* (Princeton, Princeton University Press, 1993) 26, 58, 67–8; J. Gray, 'The Politics of Cultural Diversity', *The Salisbury Review* (September 1988) 38–45. Cf. J. Hutchinson, *Modern Nationalism* (London, Fontana, 1994) 41–63.
11. 'Languages' as opposed to families of dialects are of course literary creations, in many cases devised for specifically nationalist purposes. See E. Hobsbawm, *Nations and Nationalism Since 1780* (Cambridge, Cambridge University Press, 1990) 54–9.
12. Gray, 'Politics of Cultural Diversity', 41.
13. On Catholics and Britishness see L. Colley, *Britons: Forging the Nation 1707–1837* (New Haven, Yale University Press, 1992) 18–36, 324–34.
14. Tamir, *Liberal Nationalism* 68.
15. Tamir, *Liberal Nationalism* 68.
16. Tamir, *Liberal Nationalism* 67.
17. G. Orwell, 'England Your England', in *Selected Essays* (Harmondsworth, Penguin Books, 1957) 64.
18. 'Groups tend to define themselves not by reference to their own characteristics but by exclusion, that is, by comparison to "strangers".' (J.A. Armstrong, *Nations Before Nationalism*, Chapel Hill, University of North Carolina Press, 1982, 5). For a classic statement of this theory of boundary-maintenance with reference to ethnic groups, see Fredrik Barth's 'Introduction' to Barth, *Ethnic Groups and Boundaries: the Social Organization of Culture Difference* (London, George Allen and Unwin, 1969).
19. D. Miller, 'In Defence of Nationality', *Journal of Applied Philosophy* 10/1 (1993) 6.
20. Seton-Watson, *Nations and States* 5.
21. Anderson, *Imagined Communities*.
22. E. Renan, 'What is a Nation?', in *Modern Political Doctrines*, ed. A. Zimmern (London, Oxford University Press, 1939) 203.

23. Hobsbawm, *Nations and Nationalism Since 1780* 8.
24. Cf. J. Locke, *Two Treatises of Government*, ed. P. Laslett (Cambridge, Cambridge University Press, 1964) 318–20.
25. On the compulsive logic of conflicts over identity see M. Ignatieff, *Blood and Belonging: Journeys into the New Nationalism* (London, Vintage, 1994) *passim*.
26. Renan, 'What is a Nation?', 202–3.
27. Tamir, *Liberal Nationalism* 39.
28. Tamir, *Liberal Nationalism* 87.
29. Tamir, *Liberal Nationalism* 29.
30. Tamir, *Liberal Nationalism* 37. For critical comments on voluntarist conceptions of cultural identity see J. Gray, 'After the New Liberalism', *Social Research* 61/3 (Fall 1994) 725–6.
31. Tamir's observations about choice seem to be addressed particularly to the situation of those Jews who are able to decide whether or not to settle in Israel.
32. Anderson, *Imagined Communities* 19.
33. Quoted in Cobban, *The Nation-State and National Self-Determination* 107.
34. P.L. Van den Berghe, *The Ethnic Phenomenon* (New York, Praeger, 1981) 61. For an impressive account of the historical roots of proto-national group identities see Armstrong, *Nations Before Nationalism*.
35. On Herder's seminal views, see R.A. Ergang, *Herder and the Foundations of German Nationalism* (New York, Octagon, 1976).
36. Though for a defence of a sociobiological approach see Van den Berghe, *Ethnic Phenomenon*.
37. D.L. Horowitz, *Ethnic Groups in Conflict* (Berkeley, University of California Press, 1985) 51.
38. Being committed to the view that nations are ethnies and ethnies are extended kin-groups, Van den Berghe has to deny that the Swiss are a nation. *Ethnic Phenomenon* 61.
39. A.D. Smith, *The Ethnic Origins of Nations* (Oxford, Blackwell, 1986); *National Identity*. Smith takes the 'core' of ethnicity to lie in 'myths, memories, values and symbols' (21) and identifies six dimensions of ethnicity: a collective name, a common myth of descent, a shared history, a distinctive shared culture, an association with a specific territory and a sense of solidarity (22). But in his anxiety to avoid anything that could be construed as biological determinism he probably overemphasizes the cultural element and underemphasizes family ties. *Ethnic Origins*, 15, 22–30.
40. J.W. Cole and E.R. Wolf, *The Hidden Frontier: Ecology and Ethnicity in an Alpine Valley* (New York, Academic Press, 1974). Cole and Wolf reported that the German villagers thought their neighbours were disorderly, lazy, dirty and loquacious. The Romance villagers saw their counterparts as militaristic, over-disciplined, stingy, backward and excessively hard-working (272).
41. 'Group boundaries are made of neither stone nor putty. They are malleable within limits'. (Horowitz, *Ethnic Groups* 66).
42. Roosens compared the situation in Canada, where special legal status and respect for ethnic cultures has given many people of mixed blood an incentive to affirm their Indianness and rework their cultural tradition, with the situation in Bolivia, where the political environment rewards assimilation. (E.E. Roosens, *Creating Ethnicity: The Process of Ethnogenesis*. London, Sage, 1989).
43. P.R. Brass, *Ethnicity and Nationalism: Theory and Comparison* (London, Sage, 1991).
44. Roosens, *Creating Ethnicity* 15.
45. Renan, 'What is a Nation?' 188–91.
46. C. Hill, 'The Norman Yoke', in Hill, *Puritanism and Revolution* (London, Secker and Warburg, 1965) 50–122.
47. R. Scruton, 'In Defence of the Nation', in Scruton, *The Philosopher on Dover Beach: Essays* (Manchester, Carcanet, 1990) 314–15.
48. O. Jaszi, *The Dissolution of the Habsburg Monarchy* (Chicago, University of Chicago Press, 1929) *passim*.
49. 'To forget and – I will venture to say – to get one's history wrong, are essential factors in

the making of a nation' (Renan, 'What is a Nation?' 190). Cf. Hobsbawm, *Nations and Nationalism Since 1780*, 12: 'No serious historian of nations and nationalism can be a committed political nationalist… Nationalism requires too much belief in what is patently not so.'

50. Already in 1290 Edward I was mobilizing his subjects by telling them 'that the king of France had a detestable plan to wipe the English language from the earth.' S. Reynolds, *Kingdoms and Communities in Western Europe, 900–1300* (Oxford, Oxford University Press, 1984) 272.

51. Smith, *Ethnic Origins* 216.

52. E. Gellner, *Thought and Change* (London, Weidenfeld and Nicholson, 1964) 168.

53. E. Gellner, *Nations and Nationalism* (Oxford, Blackwell, 1983) 110.

54. Gellner, *Nations and Nationalism* 49.

55. Gellner, *Nations and Nationalism* 55.

56. Gellner, *Nations and Nationalism* 57.

57. S. Weil, *The Need for Roots – Prelude to a Declaration of Duties Towards Mankind* (London, Ark, 1952) 109.

58. Weil, *The Need for Roots* 95.

59. C. C. O'Brien, *God Land: Reflections on Religion and Nationalism* (Cambridge, Mass., Harvard University Press, 1988) 50. Cf. Anderson, *Imagined Communities* 18–19; Smith, *National Identity* 162–3; Hutchinson, *Modern Nationalism* 64–96.

60. J. Breuilly, *Nationalism and the State* (Manchester, Manchester University Press, 1982) 382.

61. Benedict Anderson remarks on 'the formal universality of nationality as a sociocultural concept – in the modern world, everyone can, should, will "have" a nationality as he or she "has" a gender..' (Anderson, *Imagined Communities* 14), and Anthony Smith concurs: 'Of all the collective identities in which human beings share today, national identity is perhaps the most fundamental and inclusive… if any phenomena are truly global, then it must be the nation and nationalism.' (Smith, *National Identity* 143, though cf. A. Smith, 'State-Making and Nation-Building', in J. Hall (ed.) *States in History*, Oxford, Blackwell, 1986, 232, on the *scarcity* of nations in the Third World.)

62. Smith, 'State-Making and Nation-Building', 240–44. In effect, Gellner brings in ethnicity again by the back door under the heading of 'entropy-resistant traits' which get in the way of smooth nation-formation. (Gellner, *Nations and Nationalism* 64–72).

63. Greenfeld, *Nationalism* 18.

64. Greenfeld, *Nationalism* 10.

65. Greenfeld, *Nationalism* 47.

66. Greenfeld, *Nationalism* 60, quoting John Aylmer, *A Harborowe of True and Faithful Subjects* (1559).

67. Greenfeld, *Nationalism* 65–78.

68. Greenfeld, *Nationalism* 21.

69. Greenfeld, *Nationalism* 423.

70. Greenfeld, *Nationalism* 91.

71. Greenfeld, *Nationalism* 487, Greenfeld's emphasis.

72. Greenfeld, *Nationalism* 490.

7. Power from the people: nationhood and political community

> We have given to our frame of polity the image of a relation in blood. (Edmund Burke)[1]

As we have seen, nationhood is a peculiar phenomenon, extraordinarily difficult to pin down, and apparently justifying the disdain of those political philosophers who dismiss the whole notion as confused beyond redemption. I will argue in this chapter, however, that its peculiarity is precisely what makes nationhood significant for political theory, because it is this that makes possible the kind of political community required by liberal democratic theories, and this that makes generating such a community seem effortless. I shall try to show, firstly, that the key to nationhood as a political phenomenon is *mediation*, mediation between different aspects of experience and between the members of the nation; secondly that this mediation enables nations to act as batteries generating popular power, and thirdly that in doing so, nations present an appearance of naturalness that is profoundly misleading, especially for political theory. I will end the chapter by exploring some of the implications of this argument in terms of a particular example, the curious case of English/British nationhood.

NATIONS AS MEDIATORS

When we look back at our survey of the various suggested accounts of nationhood we may be inclined to despair of ever achieving clarity. Consider the suggestions we encountered about what it is that makes a nation:

- the state, with its institutional and territorial structure
- a common culture
- will and choice, individual or collective
- ethnicity, with its shared kinship, ancestral traditions and sacred obligations
- artificial construction to meet the functional requirements of modernity
- specific historical contingency

On the face of it, one might suppose that the various theorists could not possibly be talking about the same thing. We seem to be confronted by a series of dichotomies. Is a nation essentially a political entity, typically a state? Or is it essentially a community held together by language and culture? Is it constituted by birth or by choice? Is it a politicized version of ethnicity, or a matter of individual identification? Are nations natural or artificial? Are they immemorial or recent products of modernization? On the one hand we are offered solid, objective features of the world like institutions and territories: on the other, ideas, imaginings, emotions. Here, cold, impersonal structures: there, warm, intimate community. On one side the humanistic voluntarism of will and construction: on the other, romantic submission to the fate that gave each of us a specific kinship and a specific location in space and time.

My suggestion is that these apparently fruitless debates themselves point to an answer: nationhood is a *mediating* phenomenon, the strength of which is that it holds together the various pairs of alternatives just listed. Thus, a nation is a polity that feels like a community, or conversely a cultural or ethnic community politically mobilized; it cannot exist without subjective identification, and therefore is to some extent dependent on free individual choice, but that choice is nevertheless experienced as a destiny transcending individuality; it turns political institutions into a kind of extended family inheritance, although the kinship ties in question are highly metaphorical; it is a contingent historical product that feels like part of the order of nature; it links individual and community, past and present; it gives to cold institutional structures an aura of warm, intimate togetherness. In other words, nationhood is hard to define not because it is confused and nonsensical, but because it is extremely subtle, and, moreover, because (as perceptive commentators have frequently observed) an element of myth is essential to it.[2]

A phenomenon as complex as this is extraordinarily hard to describe and analyse, and we cannot reasonably expect to capture it in a brief definition. It happens, however, that an account of the specifically English/British version was given two hundred years ago by that master of articulacy, Edmund Burke, as he strove to explain to the French revolutionaries and to his own fellow-countrymen what it was that was so distinctive and effective about the English/British style of politics. It is worth quoting at length.

...it has been the uniform policy of our constitution to claim and assert our liberties, as an *entailed inheritance* derived to us from our forefathers, and to be transmitted to our posterity... By a constitutional policy, working after the pattern of nature, we receive, we hold, we transmit our government and our privileges, in the same manner in which we enjoy and transmit our property and our lives... Our political system is placed in a just correspondence and symmetry with the order of the world, and with the mode of existence decreed to a permanent body composed of transitory parts; wherein, by the disposition of a stupendous wisdom, moulding together the great mysterious incorporation of the human race, the whole, at one time, is never old, or middle-aged, or young,... Thus, by preserving the method of nature in the conduct of the state, in what we improve we are never wholly new; in what we retain we are never wholly obsolete. By adhering in this manner and on those principles to our forefathers, we are guided not by the superstition of antiquarians, but by the spirit of philosophic analogy. In this choice of inheritance we have given to our frame of polity the image of a relation in blood; binding up the constitution of our country with our dearest domestic ties; adopting our funda-mental laws into the bosom of our family affections; keeping inseparable, and cherishing with the warmth of all their combined and mutually reflected charities, our state, our hearths, our sepulchres, and our altars.[3]

Proudly adopting that 'we', making himself the nation's spokesman, Burke brings out into the open the intricate web of custom, contrivance and fiction that allowed the polity to be experienced *as if* it were a community of kin (and an aristocratic family into the bargain). Notice that he does not claim that the nation is actually a natural entity with common blood and a *Volksgeist*. His account is much more sophisticated and less credulous than the national-ist ideology of many Romantics who thought they were his disciples. While clothing the institutions of the state in the awesome vesture of family, nature and sanctity, he also makes clear that there is contrivance here and that the appearance of kinship itself contains elements of choice. He speaks confi-dently of 'our forefathers', but not only is he himself, as an outsider,[4] part of that 'we' by adoption: he is also aware that no political collectivity is natural, and that any that is to survive must be able to transcend the fleeting existence of individual mortal men.[5] The veil of imagined kinship and pretended natu-ralness thrown over the constitution becomes for him a rational policy de-signed to solve the fundamental problem of any body politic, that it is 'a permanent body composed of transitory parts'. The most remarkable feature of this passage is that by means of the incantatory magic of his rhetoric, Burke is able to acknowledge the crucial role played by myth in constituting nationhood without at the same time *exposing* the pretence.

Bhikhu Parekh has rightly observed that 'all statements of national identity are partial and partisan', and this one is certainly no exception.[6] Like other politicians, Burke had his own axe to grind, and we will postpone for later consideration the objection that a political community more just and demo-cratic than the one he was defending would not need to be shrouded in mystifying rhetoric. Furthermore, different nations are experienced in differ-ent ways, and some aspects of Burke's account would have to be modified to suit (say) French nationhood. Be that as it may, he does succeed in conveying the complexity that has made the nation such a formidable political force. This is consistently underestimated because it is of the essence of nationhood to *look* simple and straightforward.

A polity that seems like the family inheritance of an entire population is actually a very unlikely artifact, but where nationhood exists, it looks 'natural', and as a result we fail to notice what a remarkable political phenomenon it is. The fusion of the political and the familial creates an enduring 'we' that can form the basis of a strong and stable body politic and give the state unity, legitimacy and permanence because it is 'our' state. The existence of a nation makes it possible for the state that governs, coerces and taxes to do so in the name of the same collective 'people' who have to put up with these ministrations. This central mediation between state and community is linked with other mediations between the individual and the collective, the mundane and the sacred, the present and the past. As members of a nation, individuals are tied into a collective order that is at one and the same time an intimate community of birth and something grander and more demanding, a transcendent entity that comes down from the past and can call for sacrifices to take it into the future. Again, the nation is modern, referring to the state and people here and now, but it is also immemorial; a human product, but one that seems natural.

NATIONS AS WORLDS

If nations weave their spell by mediating between different areas of experience, they constitute political communities by mediating between their individual members. What I mean by this is that instead of being collections of people who are (as individuals) similar in some respect, nations hold their members together by lying outside and between them. To borrow Hannah Arendt's useful terminology, they are phenomena of the public 'world', which is 'between those who have it in common, as a table is located between those who sit around it; the world, like every in-between, relates and separates men at the same time.'[7]

This point is worth stressing because the dominant mind-set of contemporary culture makes it easy to miss the way in which a nation mediates between and holds together the diverse people who belong to it. In a philosophical milieu increasingly preoccupied with matters of personal identity, it is not surprising that those political theorists who take a relatively sympathetic view of nationhood tend to analyse it in personal terms, so that (like 'the gay community', for instance) a nation is taken to consist of individuals who have certain common characteristics. Since these theorists are far from being vulgar nationalists, the characteristics they point to are not physical features such as colour, but cultural traits, particular ways of thinking and feeling. This view is clearly stated by David Miller:

National divisions must be natural ones; they must correspond to real differences between peoples. This need not, fortunately, imply racism or the idea that the group is constituted by biological descent. The common traits can be cultural in character: they can consist in shared values, shared tastes or sensibilities.[8]

But to attempt to define nationhood in terms of the cast of individuals' minds is almost as misguided as to try to define it in terms of the colour of their bodies. What unites co-nationals is less the characteristics they possess as individuals than the inheritance they share as members, typically a heritage compounded of ethnic, political, cultural and other elements. National heritages differ a great deal in their composition and emphases, and some are much more obviously objective than others, being more clearly located in the world rather than simply in the minds of members of the nation. Thus we are British not in virtue of conforming to some particularly British way of thinking but because (either by inheritance or by adoption) we jointly own the complex legacy of the nation, from institutions like Parliament and the BBC to less tangible legacies ranging from Shakespeare's plays and a history of overseas empire to traditions of gardening and agitating against cruelty to animals – all of which are 'our'[9] heritage as British people even if we detest the lot of them. The point that needs to be stressed is that we are united into a nation by shared ownership of something *outside* us, not by similarities *inside* us. Our common inheritance unites us, whether we embrace it with open arms or angrily repudiate it. The most striking testimony to the collective identity constituted by nationhood comes from those who deplore the activities of their predecessors, but nevertheless feel co-responsible with them. When Christopher Hill observes that 'we have a great deal to be ashamed of in our history. We promoted and profited by the slave trade; we plundered India and Africa...'[10] he is bearing witness to the fact that it is *our* history whether we like it or not, and whatever the 'values, tastes and sensibilities' with which we approach it.

NATIONS AS BATTERIES

From a political point of view, the most important thing about nationhood is precisely those revealing pronouns, 'we', 'us' and 'our', usable not just by members of a party or those who are agreed on a policy but by a much wider, more variable and more enduring set of people. What nationhood does is to constitute a collective political subject – a 'we' – with the capacity to act collectively over long periods of time. In doing so, it acts as a reservoir of political power, providing a strikingly effective solution to the most fundamental of political problems. If we wanted to be hyperbolic, indeed, we might, paraphrasing Marx, say that the nation is 'the riddle of politics solved'.

For at the root of politics lies a problem far deeper than issues of policy, deeper than questions about the form of the state or how its power should be used. This is the problem of how stable political power is possible at all in a world where mortals are continually passing on and off the human stage, and where acquiescence in whatever arrangements happen to exist is not obviously in all their interests. Given the instability inherent in the human condition,[11] how does any political entity come to have enough unity to be able to generate the power to act and maintain itself, let alone enough permanence to outlast the life-span of a war-lord or charismatic leader? In particular, how can the relatively non-coercive political power that we associate with civilized politics be generated on a permanent basis?

No answer to this question can be found in the contractarian tradition of political thought. It is notoriously difficult to provide a plausible transition from contracting individuals to any polity at all, let alone one that can outlive its individual members and command their allegiance to the point of death. Yet the fact is that collective existence is an indispensable feature of any polity. To exist at all, and to provide even minimal political stability, a body politic must have an existence of its own over and above the separate existences of the inchoate individuals and groups within its territory, so that it can act as a unity in space and time, transcending the plurality of its members and surviving their mortality. And beyond the matter-of-fact, organizational transcendence which firms and other corporations possess, a body politic needs to be able to call on active support and allegiance, and to be able to count on at least some of its members to value its life higher than their own. Political order (and particularly political order that aspires to be relatively non-coercive) requires the integration and power made possible by collective existence.

There are of course other modes besides nationhood in which people can be mobilized to generate collective power. As contemporary experience reminds us, religion can be a particularly formidable agent of mobilization, while similar results have been achieved by movements and by ideological parties. The Communist Party of the Soviet Union generated and structured power for seventy years (albeit with the help of terror, arguably replaced in the latter years by Russian nationalism). But the advantage that nations have over alternative sources of collective power is that they can lie dormant without being defunct. A movement must keep its momentum if it is to generate power, and a party retain its structure intact, while religious mobilization relies on active faith. But nationhood, once established, functions like a battery, a reservoir of power that can slumber for decades and still be available for rapid mobilization: the flag remains, and the people can be rallied to it. Furthermore, by comparison with the ideological commitments that restrict the choices of religious or political movements, the power generated by nationhood is relatively flexible and all-purpose, particularly in long-established nations. While national feeling can itself be mobilized for ideological purposes, this need not be the case.[12]

This capacity for long-term mobilization is also, I suggest, the best available test of whether or not a nation actually exists. Some readers will by this time be irritated by my unwillingness to provide a definition of nationhood, and particularly by my failure to specify criteria for distinguishing between genuine nations and false claimants to the title. This quest for clear criteria stems partly from an understandable commitment to analytical clarity, but also from a habit of talking about nationalist claims in terms of the validity or otherwise of a right to national self-determination. Evidently, if genuine nations do indeed have a right to self-determination, then criteria for nationhood are crucial. For reasons which will become apparent later, I do not believe that it makes sense to talk in terms of rights to national self-determination, and the impossibility of providing appropriate criteria is one of the relevant considerations. However, theorists need to beware of the tendency to assume that phenomena which cannot be clearly defined must be insignificant. It is true that nationhood is an inherently fuzzy phenomenon, and that its existence or non-existence will in some cases always be disputable. But even if it is possible only in retrospect to be sure of the presence of a nation, the long-term mobilizability for collective power that is the chief evidence of its existence remains hugely important for politics, and not least for political theory.

If nationhood is a political phenomenon that can create and empower a stable, lasting collective subject, without needing to be kept in a frenzy of mobilization or saddling that subject with ideological commitments, then it is scarcely surprising that liberal democratic political theory should display a kind of elective affinity with it. Although political thinkers in recent times have rarely reflected upon the fact that their various projects presuppose the existence of a strong and stable political collectivity, able to incorporate the polity's inhabitants and to call upon their loyalty and support, I have argued that what they have actually taken for granted is the nation-state. To the question, 'Why has so little explicit attention been paid to this?', the answer must, I believe, be found in the intricacies of mediation that we looked at earlier. Part of the magic wrought by nationhood is to make the 'we' that it constitutes seem as natural as a family group. The peculiarity of established nationhood is that it not only solves the fundamental political conundrum, but does the trick so effortlessly that the problem disappears: stable polities experienced as political communities seem to exist by nature, and it is only departures from this norm that attract attention. But the illusion of naturalness that is the peculiar triumph of mature nationhood is, unfortunately, a dangerous illusion, giving the impression that political power is to be had as easily as pressing a switch.

Because of this deceptive appearance of naturalness, both those who take nations for granted and those who denounce national loyalties (in some cases the same people) tend to underestimate the complexity, specificity and fluidity of nationhood. To conclude this chapter I shall illustrate these points by looking more closely at a case of nationhood that has a particularly intimate connection with liberal democratic traditions of political thought: the strange case of English/British nationhood. It must be emphasized that this case is not intended to represent a model of *the* nation (an entirely mythical beast), nor even to represent a particular *type* of nation. Attempts are often made to sort nations into types for the purposes of analysis, and the distinction between 'civic' and 'ethnic' nations is particularly favoured in the literature.[13] What this tends to produce, however, is a set of ideal-types that take little account of the real differences between such supposedly 'civic' nations as Britain, France and the US (to which we shall need to pay some attention later). The case of English/British nationhood will illustrate the fluidity of nationhood and its capacity for expansion far beyond any sort of primordial ethnic core, and will to that extent suggest that its link with liberal democracy is not only intelligible but relatively comfortable. However, we will also see grounds for uneasiness about the link, both on account of contingent challenges to the nation-state itself and because of more deeply rooted tensions between the particularity of any nation-state and the universal principles of liberal democratic thought.

ENGLISH/BRITISH NATIONHOOD

The stake is England! Britons rise!
Your foes are Gauls! Those foes chastise!
(Charles Burney, 1804)[14]

In recent years, wrapping oneself in the Union Jack (literally or metaphorically) has been a political tactic associated particularly with chauvinists hostile to the European Community without and to immigrant communities within the United Kingdom. We therefore tend to think of British national loyalty as a particularly narrow and exclusive form of identity, insular in all senses of the word. This is a pity, because English/British nationhood is a phenomenon of great complexity that has until recently attracted far too little attention from students of nationalism.[15] It may be, of course, that (for good reasons) inarticulacy is as characteristic of English/British nationhood as continual debate and restatement are to the identities of the French and the Americans. But the history of English/British nationhood is a history of inclusion as much as of exclusion.

Contrary to the widespread and often-repeated assumption that nations are a purely modern phenomenon, it seems clear that *English* nationhood was well established by the end of the Middle Ages if not before.[16] Not that there was anything inevitable about this. As Hugh Kearney has pointed out, it is only in retrospect that there seems anything 'natural' about the boundaries within the British Isles and between them and France on the one hand and Scandinavia on the other. The early middle ages in particular was a time of conquest and subjugation, as the Norman invaders created 'a French-speaking ascendancy throughout the British Isles.'[17] On the basis of twelfth-century evidence, no-one could conceivably have predicted the emergence by the sixteenth century of an *English* nation that included Normans, Saxons, Danes and some Welsh while excluding Scots and Frenchmen. The growth of this nation was in no sense a reflection of primordial ties of blood.

While historians may argue about how far back into the Middle Ages English nationhood can be traced, there seems no doubt at all that the Reformation in the sixteenth century saw the emergence of a strident English nationalism closely connected with the sense that Protestant England had a special divine calling.[18] Neither was this self-conscious pride in Englishness confined to the religious dimension of identity. In a remarkable study of Elizabethan culture, Richard Helgerson has shown what a central preoccupation national identity was to writers in fields ranging from poetry to geography, from law to commerce and exploration. Alongside the Book of Martyrs stands, for example, Richard Hakluyt's 'Principal Navigations, Voyages, Traffiques and Discoveries of the English Nation.'[19]

As we recoil from the exclusive chauvinism of many of the expressions of early English nationhood we can easily fail to notice the *in*clusiveness of this identity, which took in not only the scions of Norman, Saxon and Welsh stock but also (and, at the time, more significantly) nobles and commoners. As we have seen, Liah Greenfeld argues that the overcoming of vertical status differences was in fact the crucial move in the formation of national identity. In her view, English nationalism was mobilized in the sixteenth century by a new élite who found a new way of asserting their own dignity – not by following the familiar path of marking themselves off from the common people, but by associating the people with them in English superiority to the rest of the world.[20] One thing to bear in mind here is that inclusion of this sort need not mean equality. When, later on, American and then French identity underwent revolutionary mobilization, the idea of equal citizenship was central, and commentators have often assumed that it is essential to nationhood.[21] But the English example shows that this is not so. Although English nationalism did indeed at various times form the basis for populist attacks on the monarchy or the aristocracy or both together,[22] a strong sense of national identity was for centuries compatible with a hierarchical society in which gentlemen and commoners were unequal, but equally English.

By the seventeenth century, *English* nationhood was already inclusive in the sense of encompassing ethnic and status distinctions that had in earlier times been acute. The subsequent expansion of English into *British* identity carried the nation even farther away from anything resembling primordial ethnicity. The relation between the two national identities is extraordinarily confused, baffling and controversial. To the irritation of Scots, Welsh and Irish, modern English people, including academics, rarely notice whether they are talking about England or Britain (or indeed the United Kingdom of Great Britain and Northern Ireland) and use the names and their corresponding adjectives interchangeably. This imprecision has a very long history, predating the Act of Union with Scotland in 1707, for the kings of England had for centuries claimed the whole island of Britain as their own.

The inheritance in 1603 by James VI and I of both the Scottish and the English Crowns and the incorporation of both kingdoms, a century later, into a Union dominated by England allowed the gradual expansion of Englishness into a wider identity.[23] (I leave on one side the contentious history of Scottish nationhood.) Linda Colley has traced the emergence in the course of the eighteenth century of a new 'British' nation composed of English, Scots, Welsh and (some) Irish and stressed the dialectical relationship between cohesion within the kingdom and confrontation without. Almost continuous warfare against Catholic France, culminating in national mobilization against the threat of Napoleonic invasion, was by far the strongest unifying force. Nevertheless, there were plenty of other ties to hold the new nation together and to encourage a consciousness of *British* identity in the late eighteenth century, such as the enormous number of Scots serving in the British army and navy, the building of roads into Wales and Scotland along which there were large-scale migrations, and the wide circulation of newspapers. Colley shows that British nationalism grew from below rather than being deliberately manufactured by the state.[24]

England was always the dominant partner in the Union, and there was in some quarters a Little-England reaction against the wider British identity, particularly against the influx of Scots into London.[25] What more commonly seems to have happened, however, was that the boundaries of Englishness became elastic and the difference between 'English' and 'British' largely imperceptible. From the point of view of a Scottish, Welsh or Irish nationalist this demonstrates the arrogance of the English, who seem rarely to have noticed the existence of their fellow-Britons. But this explanation is too simplistic. No one could have been more sensitive to the precise use of words than Edmund Burke, and as an Irishman as well as a great writer, Burke might be expected to be particularly alive to the linguistic nuances. But although, in *Reflections on the Revolution in France*, he refers to 'England' and the 'English' nation, throne, etc. most of the time, he also uses 'Britain' and 'British', apparently without any distinction of meaning. The impression that 'English' had stretched to accommodate a wider identity is given some support by the Scottish M.P. who declared in the House of Commons in 1805, 'We commonly when speaking of British subjects call them English, be they English, Scotch or Irish'.[26]

This is not of course to deny the persistence of half-buried tensions between Englishness and Britishness. Hugh Cunningham points out that (in the nineteenth century as in the twentieth), the Conservatives were largely an *English* party, sometimes stridently so.[27] No doubt it was that sort of insensitivity that prompted an advertiser in the Personal Column of the Times newspaper in November 1914, a time of national crisis, to this exhortation:

> Englishmen! Please use 'Britain', 'British' and 'Briton', when the United Kingdom or the Empire is in question – at least during the war.[28]

Whether this injunction was followed is uncertain. If it was, there was certainly some backsliding later, as on the occasion in 1924 when Stanley Baldwin gave a speech on 'England' to the Royal Society of St. George, and expressed his thankfulness 'that I may use the word "England" without some fellow at the back of the room shouting out "Britain".'[29] What is undeniable, however, is that English/British national identity had become remarkably inclusive by the twentieth century compared with English nationhood in the Elizabethan age. One of the most striking changes was of course the fading of the virulently anti-Catholic Protestantism which had for so long been right at the heart of the nation's identity, and which had made impossible the incorporation of Catholic Ireland on comparable terms to Scotland or even Wales.[30] The expansion of Englishness shows itself in the genuine confusion of most English people about what the boundaries of their national identity actually are, in spite of the strength with which that identity is felt. That confusion has of course been compounded by the rise and fall of the British Empire and the shadowy survival of the Commonwealth.

Some students of these matters, urgently seeking clarity, deal briskly with this confusion, arguing that there is not and never has been any such thing as a British nation: there are simply four nations inside the United Kingdom. Bernard Crick maintains, for example, that whereas there is an English nation, Britishness is 'a political and legal concept best applied to the institutions of the United Kingdom state' which does not 'correspond to any real sense of a nation.'[31] In support of this view, it may be pointed out that Britain sustains four separate international football teams: only when the English side is playing particularly badly is it ever suggested that they should be amalgamated into a single British team. It is also true, though often forgotten, that the monarchy has until recently played a vital role in holding together the United Kingdom while soothing the sensibilities of Scots and Welsh and allowing their own national traditions to be honoured.[32] But the claim that the UK consists of four nations and one state is too simple, for the crucial aspect of the amorphous identity of Britishness is not so much that Scots or Welsh feel British as that the *English* do. When they use the terms interchangeably they are not so much betraying arrogant unconcern for their non-English fellow-subjects as showing a sense of kinship, at any rate with the Scots and the Welsh. It is certainly remarkable that overrepresentation of Scotland at Westminster and subsidies to Scotland and Wales (the stuff of nationalist politics elsewhere) have not so far become issues in English politics.

In some ways the example of English/British nationhood may seem quite encouraging to liberal democratic political theorists. If the national political community on which many of them have been unconsciously relying does not necessarily have to be ethnic in form, but can actually be quite expansive and inclusive while continuing to be experienced as 'natural', then why should there not in the course of time be further expansion and the formation of an English/British/European nationhood, and even, eventually, an English/British/European/Global nationhood? Concentrating on the first of these projects, we cannot rule it out as totally impossible over the long term, however unlikely it may seem at present. The existence of European institutions may eventually attract loyalty, rather as the institutions of the British state did in earlier times: especially if Europe should be united (as the United Kingdom was) against a common enemy.[33] All the same, liberal democratic political theorists still have good reasons for worrying about their links with nationhood, whether the English/British variety or any other on offer. For one thing, various contemporary developments are subjecting nation-states such as Britain to severe strains. More fundamentally, there are serious problems in trying to reconcile the universal principles of liberal democracy with *any* particular loyalty.

To take the first of these points, any theory that recognizes the political significance of nationhood must also pay attention to contemporary developments that seem to call into question the persistence of the nation-state. Where Britain in particular is concerned, the specific form of the state is under threat from several quarters. Northern Ireland seems to be becoming ever more detached from mainland Britain; demands for devolution and even independence for Scotland are becoming more strident,[34] while the issue of Britain's integration or non-integration with the rest of the European Community not only threatens to split the Conservative Party, but also, by directing political attention to questions of nationhood, to tear off the comfortable blanket of silence in which the ambiguities of English/British identity have been cloaked for the past two centuries. These potential crises remind us that nationhood is always fluid, and that a history of integration and expansion is no guarantee against a future of disintegration and collapse.

Apart from these local difficulties, however (some of which have analogues in other established nation-states), a number of late-twentieth-century developments may seem to indicate that the days of the nation-state are numbered. Global markets, satellite television, huge movements of people and the internationalization of military and technological risk (not to mention the extension of humanitarian sentiment) seem to suggest that the political future lies with international organizations of various kinds. A nation on the scale of Britain or her European partners cannot control its own economy or defend itself without allies, while in the face of demographic imbalances and migrations too rapid and large-scale for gradual assimilation, nations that had been imagined (however mythically) as kith and kin are reverting to the condition of polyethnicity that has (as William McNeill points out) been the norm for civilized countries throughout history.[35]

Liberal political theorists accustomed to think in terms of universal human rights may be inclined to welcome these developments, and to feel that the nation-state is outdated as well as being unsavoury. This is an issue to which we shall need to return later, but the point that needs to be underlined is that contemporary trends toward globalization do not solve the crucial question of how power is to be generated. The feebleness on the international stage of the United Nations and even of the European Union highlights the way that the logic of politics runs athwart the logic of modern technology, modern markets and modern humanitarian sensibility. Political power, especially liberal-democratic political power, depends on the constitution of a 'we', and while there are plenty of signs of the growth of smaller, fissiparous, often fanatical collective identities which can attract loyalty, there is little evidence of the constitution of effective collective political identity at a level larger than the nation.[36]

It is this matter of collective political identity that is the real problem for liberal democratic political theory. For, as we have seen, there is a fundamental tension in such theory between universalist commitments and reliance on the existence of particularist loyalty to constitute the required body politic. But the fact that established nations are under strain, and that (as we shall see later) nation-states are not in any case a realistic possibility in many areas of the world, is not good news for liberal democrats unless there is some alternative, some other form of political community more acceptable than the nation. Is a non-national patriotism perhaps the answer to this problem? This is the subject of the next chapter.

NOTES

1. E. Burke, *Reflections on the Revolution in France* ed. C.C. O'Brien (Harmondsworth, Penguin, 1968) 120.
2. E. Renan, 'What is a Nation?', in *Modern Political Doctrines* ed. A. Zimmern (London, Oxford University Press, 1939) 190; D. Miller, 'In Defence of Nationality', *Journal of Applied Philosophy* 10/1 (1993) 9.
3. Burke, *Reflections* 119–20.
4. C.C. O'Brien, *The Great Melody: A Thematic Biography of Edmund Burke* (London, Sinclair-Stevenson, 1992) 13, 90–91. Cf. A. MacIntyre, 'Poetry as Political Philosophy: Notes on Burke and Yeats', in *On Modern Poetry: Essays presented to Donald Davie*, ed. V. Bell and L. Lerner (Nashville, Vanderbilt University Press, 1988) 147–52.
5. Cf. *Reflections* 193, 194–5; 'An Appeal from the New to the Old Whigs', in *Works of the Right Honourable Edmund Burke* (London, Holdsworth and Ball, 1834) Vol. I 524–5.
6. B. Parekh, 'National Identity and the Ontological Regeneration of Britain', in P. Gilbert and P. Gregory (eds), *Nations, Markets and Cultures* (London, Avebury, 1994) 107.
7. H. Arendt, *The Human Condition* (Chicago, University of Chicago Press, 1958) 52. Arendt does not herself speak of nations in this way, though the distinction she makes between Western nation-states and the 'tribal nationalism' of Eastern Europe depends on connected ideas. See *The Origins of Totalitarianism* (London, Allen and Unwin, 1967) 229–32; cf. M. Canovan, *Hannah Arendt: A Reinterpretation of her Political Thought* (Cambridge, Cambridge University Press, 1992) 246.
8. Miller, 'In Defence of Nationality', 7.
9. Just who is included in that 'we' is an inescapably contentious practical matter, not to be settled by theoretical stipulation. No nation has clear and unambiguous boundaries – one of many reasons for rejecting the notion that nations have a *right* to self-determination.
10. C. Hill, 'History and Patriotism' in R. Samuel (ed.), *Patriotism: The Making and Unmaking of British National Identity* Vol. I (London, Routledge, 1989) 3.
11. Cf. Arendt, *Human Condition* 55.
12. For a comparison of national and religious mobilization, see J. Hutchinson, *Modern Nationalism* (London, Fontana, 1994) 68–96.
13. Friedrich Meinecke's seminal distinction between 'political' and 'cultural' nations (F. Meinecke, *Cosmopolitanism and the National State*, Princeton, Princeton University Press, 1970, 10) reappears in a rather different form in Anthony Smith's categories of 'Western, civic, territorial' and 'non-Western, ethnic' nations (A. Smith, *The Ethnic Origins of Nations*, 135). Elsewhere, Smith adds two further types, 'the immigrant' (e.g. the US, Argentine, Australia) and 'the colonial' (e.g. most African states) (A. Smith, 'State-Making and Nation-Building' 241–2). For a protest from a Polish perspective against the tendentious association of civic nationhood with Western Europe and ethnic nationalism with Eastern Europe, see A. Walicki, *Philosophy and Romantic Nationalism: The case of Poland* (Oxford, Oxford University Press, 1982), *passim*.
14. Quoted in O. Dann and J. Dinwiddy (eds), *Nationalism in the Age of the French Revolution* (London, Hambledon Press, 1988) 63.
15. Cf. G. Newman, *The Rise of English Nationalism: A Cultural History 1740–1830* (London, Weidenfeld and Nicholson, 1987) xviii.
16. On the modernity of nations, see e.g. E.J. Hobsbawm, *Nations and Nationalism since 1780* (Cambridge, Cambridge University Press, 1990) 14. Susan Reynolds argues strongly for the earlier date (S. Reynolds, *Kingdoms and Communities in Western Europe. 900–1300*, Oxford, Oxford University Press, 1984, e.g. 272).
17. H. Kearney, *The British Isles: A History of Four Nations* (Cambridge, Cambridge University Press, 1989) 63.
18. C. Hill, 'The English Revolution and Patriotism', in Samuel, *Patriotism*, Vol. I 159–68.
19. R. Helgerson, *Forms of Nationhood: The Elizabethan Writing of England* (Chicago, University of Chicago Press, 1992).

20. L. Greenfeld, *Nationalism – Five Roads to Modernity* (Cambridge, Mass., Harvard University Press, 1992) 47.
21. e.g. A.D. Smith, *National Identity* (London, Penguin Books, 1991) 10.
22. Tom Nairn denied this in *The Break-Up of Britain* (London, New Left Books, 1977, 292), but there are plenty of examples, ranging from the radicals of the English Civil War via Wilkes in the mid-eighteenth-century to Orwell in the mid-twentieth (Greenfeld, *Nationalism* 73–6; Newman, *English Nationalism*, 35, 57, 127; G. Orwell, 'England Your England', *Selected Essays*, Harmondsworth, Penguin Books, 1957, 79, 90).
23. The image of 'Britannia', an ancient Roman personification, was revived under James I and VI and first appeared on coins of the realm in 1665 (M. Dresser, 'Britannia', in Samuel, *Patriotism* Vol. III 30; P. Furtado, 'National Pride in Seventeenth Century England', in Vol. I, 49). Britannia appeared frequently in eighteenth-century prints as a personification of the nation, but whether that was England or Great Britain varied according to context and seems not to have been a matter of concern. Eighteenth-century students of national genealogy seem to have been similarly confused about whether what they were tracing was an 'English' or a 'British' race (Newman, *English Nationalism* 77–8, 117).
24. L. Colley, *Britons – Forging the Nation 1707–1837* (New Haven, Yale University Press, 1992) *passim*; L. Colley, 'Whose Nation? Class and National Consciousness in Britain 1750–1830', *Past and Present*, No. 113 (Nov 1985), 97–117.
25. Colley, *Britons*, 105.
26. Colley, *Britons*, 162.
27. H. Cunningham, 'The Conservative Party and Patriotism', in R. Colls and P. Dodd (eds), *Englishness: Politics and Culture 1880–1920* (London, Croom Helm, 1986) 293.
28. Cunningham, 'Conservative Party', 294.
29. Cunningham, 'Conservative Party', 294.
30. As British identity has expanded to include Catholics, the cost has been a shrinkage, in that Ulster Protestants now find that the traditional Protestant Britishness to which they have been loyal has slipped away, leaving them stranded. See M. Ignatieff, *Blood and Belonging: Journeys into the New Nationalism* (London, Vintage, 1994) 169–70.
31. B. Crick, 'The English and the British', in Crick (ed.), *National Identities – the Constitution of the United Kingdom* (Oxford, Blackwell, 1991) 97.
32. T. Nairn, *The Enchanted Glass: Britain and its Monarchy* (London, Radius, 1988) 227.
33. Recent 'Fish Wars' suggest that most English people find more plausible a wider identification with a version of the old imperialist ideal of an 'English-speaking union'. In any case, from the point of view of liberal internationalism it is not clear why European nationhood should be regarded as an improvement on British nationhood, since both are particularistic. Cf. V. Harle, 'Nationalism – No! Metanationalism – Yes!', *History of European Ideas* 15/1–3 (1992) 39–46.
34. Cf. A. Marr, *The Battle for Scotland* (Harmondsworth, Penguin Books, 1992).
35. McNeill points out that the historical norm has been polyethnic *hierarchy* – i.e. not exactly what supporters of 'multiculturalism' have in mind (W.H. McNeill, *Polyethnicity and National Unity in World History*, Toronto, University of Toronto Press, 1986, especially 59-85). On trends that seem to threaten the nation-state, see also Hutchinson, *Modern Nationalism* 134–63; H. Goulbourne, *Ethnicity and Nationalism in Post-Imperial Britain* (Cambridge, Cambridge University Press, 1991); T. Hammar, *Democracy and the Nation State: Aliens, Denizens and Citizens in a World of International Migration* (Aldershot, Avebury, 1990), especially Part I.
36. See e.g. W. Wallace, 'Rescue or Retreat? The Nation State in Western Europe, 1945–93', in 'Contemporary Crisis of the Nation State?', *Political Studies* 42 (1994), Special Issue, ed. J. Dunn, 52–76. Cf. Hutchinson, *Modern Nationalism* 134–63.

8. Nationhood, patriotism and universalism

> In a despotism...the requisite disciplines are maintained by coercion. In order to have a free society, one has to replace this coercion with something else. This can only be a willing identification with the polis on the part of the citizens, a sense that the political institutions in which they live are an expression of themselves. (Charles Taylor)[1]

The argument presented so far, that most contemporary political theories unconsciously rely upon nation-states to provide them with the strong and stable political communities that would be needed for such theories to be realized, is not a comfortable one. Much liberal democratic political theory aspires to universalism and is addressed to all humanity, whereas nationhood is inescapably particularistic, constituted by limited loyalties to one's own people. Furthermore, national particularism has ethnic overtones (however fictive), making it even less attractive as a bedfellow for contemporary liberal democratic thought.

The question arises, therefore, whether there is any *necessary* relationship between the two. A critical reader might concede that as a matter of historical contingency liberal democracy (as theoretical ideal and as less-than-ideal practice) has been associated with certain nation-states, but maintain that the problem of constituting and maintaining a body politic could in principle be solved in a way more consonant with universalism, perhaps by substituting for national loyalty some form of liberal or republican patriotism. Despite the prevailing neglect in political philosophy of questions to do with the generation of power and political solidarity, a number of notable theorists have been thinking about such matters in recent years, often prompted to do so by dilemmas arising out of their own experience of national tensions. In this chapter I will consider some of their ideas, although I will conclude that it is doubtful whether patriotism in its various versions can solve the problems that make nationhood objectionable, and that it does indeed give rise to difficulties of its own.

STATES WITHOUT NATIONS

The modern state is a self-sufficient institution. (Bhikhu Parekh)[2]

Questions about the sources of political cohesion in a free society have recently been addressed by Bhikhu Parekh in a robust attack on 'the politics of nationhood'. This was prompted by the publication of arguments in favour of national loyalties by a number of British political theorists, most of them on the right of the political spectrum, but some further to the left. Their apparent rehabilitation of nationalism seems ominous to Parekh in view of Britain's increasing cultural diversity and the fact that 'every form of nationalism is antipathetic to outsiders'.[3] Denying that nationhood is needed to provide modern populations with a sense of belonging, and that it is either a necessary or a sufficient condition for distributive politics, he contends that any benefits that may flow from nationhood are bought at too high a price in hostility to outsiders, particularly immigrants. The appeal to national unity is in any case unrealistic, since current levels of ethnic, social and cultural fragmentation mean that no modern state is a nation in the sense implied, certainly not Britain.

Parekh does not explicitly address the role of nationhood in generating political power, but this is perhaps implicit in his acknowledgement that in modern pluralist societies, 'the old question as to what holds the modern state together therefore acquires enormous importance.'[4] However, to try to find unity in some 'grand and overarching sense of national identity'[5] is in his view not only dangerous but unnecessary. Instead he suggests that the modern state can draw on two different sources of unity to keep it stable. One of his points is a pragmatic one, the empirical observation that there is no need for all citizens to have the same reasons for their allegiance, and that different groups of citizens do in fact have different sources of loyalty ranging from ancestral pride in the state to enlightened self-interest and gratitude for concrete benefits. Political unity is, in other words, 'complex, multi-stranded and multi-layered'.[6]

For political theorists, however, the more interesting of Parekh's two suggested sources of cohesion (and the one he himself discusses first) is 'the state itself'. His argument is that the modern liberal secular state that emerged out of earlier struggles over religion and authority does not rely on any extra-political solidarity, but carries its legitimacy within itself.

> ...the modern state is a self-sufficient institution. It has a commonly accepted structure of public authority, a set of procedures for taking collectively binding decisions, and a body of widely shared politico-legal values. To be its member is to acknowledge these and to abide by its laws. Nothing more is required of its members in order for it to remain united and stable.[7]

The 'politico-legal values' to which the state is committed include 'the rule of law, equality before the law, respect for human dignity and common citizenship'. This 'self-sufficient' state is of course, as Parekh admits, a contingent product of history, indeed 'the product of a long and painful evolution',[8] and he assumes that its borders and territorial unity can be taken as given. His claim is, however, that the state itself can unite in common allegiance the population of a given territory, without recourse to dangerous invocations of national sentiment.

The argument that a purely political solution can be found to the problem of political cohesion (often conceptualized in terms of 'patriotism' as opposed to 'nationalism') is a powerful objection to the thesis I have argued above. It can be developed along three different lines, intimations of which can all be found in Parekh's account of the 'self-sufficient state'. In the first place, and in keeping with Parekh's concern to lower the emotional temperature by keeping politics clear of matters of religion, culture and identity, the state may be seen essentially as a provider of services which can expect to attract loyalty as long as it satisfies its customers. Secondly, it may be seen in a less utilitarian way as the contingent expression of the 'politico-legal values' listed by Parekh, on the understanding that in the last resort loyalty is owed to the values themselves rather than to the institutions in which they are imperfectly incarnated. Thirdly (for Parekh does after all allow a role for more affective ties like pride, gratitude and love) the loyalty that binds citizens to the state may be interpreted (calling on the tradition of republican patriotism) as a more active form of political solidarity. I will discuss each of these in turn, and consider how they fare as non-national sources of political power to underpin liberal democratic ideals.

THE STATE AS A 'SERVICE STATION'[9]

Parekh is certainly right to point out that loyalty to liberal democratic states does in practice have many different sources, and one of these corresponds to the traditional liberal view that since the state exists to protect and serve its inhabitants, it is entitled to allegiance as long as it does so. With varying degrees of efficiency, modern liberal democratic states do provide a wide variety of services ranging from health care to farm subsidies, and many, perhaps most, of their populations do indeed have instrumental reasons for their support. From the point of view particularly of large numbers of expatriates, the state in which they happen to be living may be seen entirely from this consumerist point of view, and be regarded as 'our' state only in the minimal sense in which one can acquire a degree of attachment to one's favoured shop or restaurant. Attachment to the European Union is perhaps mostly of this instrumental kind.[10] At a more theoretical level, some liberal theorists in increasingly multicultural societies, prompted by similar concerns to Parekh's, have favoured the notion of a 'neutral' state standing outside and above communal attachments.[11]

The difficulty with this view is that consumer loyalty is not a strong basis for political power. As Parekh says, it is not necessary for all citizens to share the same commitment, and any modern state can afford purely instrumental allegiance on the part of some of its members: in good times it may not matter if this kind of attitude is widespread. In times of crisis, however, citizens of this sort tend to prefer exit over loyalty or voice.[12] If Alistair MacIntyre were right to claim that being called on to give one's life for the modern state is like dying for the telephone company, it would be hard to have much confidence in the survival of the modern state.[13]

One notable contemporary political theorist who has devoted a good deal of thought to this question is Charles Taylor, who writes as a Canadian and Quebecker deeply involved in Canada's continuing crises over identity and political cohesion. In writings shadowing political developments over many years, Taylor has articulated the very great complexities involved, and the difficulties of finding a version of political identity that all Canadians can embrace. As a country of immigration, and one, moreover, that has been blessed with unusual levels of peace and prosperity, Canada might seem a particularly favourable location in which what Taylor on one occasion calls the 'service-station' model of the state might work, and there are no doubt many there who are content to view it as such. However, the challenge to the integrity of the Canadian state posed by the powerful (because national) identity of Quebec illustrates the comparative political weakness of less visceral loyalties.[14]

Taylor has argued on a number of occasions that a free society cannot rely in the long run on 'fair-weather friends', 'who support a society because of the prosperity and security it generates',[15] but that it needs a much greater degree of commitment – patriotism, in fact. This is not just a matter of the traditional test of citizenship, being willing to give one's life for the *patria*. Referring to the US, often thought of as the paradigm case of the 'neutral' state, Taylor observes that if a free state is to be able to defend itself against (for example) the kind of corruption that gave rise to Watergate in the US, there must be a significant number of citizens attached to it by the kind of 'patriotic identification' that prompts them to care about the fate of their republic to the point of feeling 'citizen outrage'[16] when it is betrayed. Cooler versions of allegiance are not sufficient to generate the kind of energy needed to sustain republican institutions and to take responsibility for the fate of the polity.

It can plausibly be argued, then, that those people in modern liberal states who do indeed regard the state in the light of a service station are able to do so only in so far as a substantial number of citizens are more deeply committed. But does that deeper commitment need to be in any sense *national*? Cannot a purely political patriotism serve to sustain liberal states without the disadvantages of nationalist exclusiveness? Those who argue along these lines draw on two different understandings of patriotism which are often intertwined, but which lead in different directions. The more liberal of the two (and the one with more affinity to Parekh's position) is sometimes called 'constitutional patriotism'. This puts its emphasis upon the universal principles of liberalism, pledging loyalty to them as they are enshrined in the state's constitution. The other, more republican, version maintains that democratic participation in politics can itself forge amongst citizens a political unity that need not be tainted with the ethnocultural overtones of nationhood. As we shall see, however, it is doubtful whether either version can succeed in overcoming the objections that make most political theorists so suspicious of nationhood.

CONSTITUTIONAL PATRIOTISM

The term *Verfassungspatriotismus* or 'constitutional patriotism' was adopted in Germany to refer to a loyalty to the liberal democratic constitution of the post-war Federal Republic distinct from and opposed to a German nationalism that was freighted with territorial claims and identified with an illiberal political heritage.[17] For anti-nationalists like Jürgen Habermas, this loyalty to 'abstract procedures and principles' has been part of the post-war Germans' renunciation of their unfortunate political traditions in favour of an 'opening to the West'.[18] As we shall see, it is symptomatic, if apparently paradoxical, that such an overtly abstract and universalist form of loyalty should be appealed to as a response to circumstances that are not only highly contingent but probably unique. In the specific context of post-war Germany there have clearly been great advantages in this attitude to the state. Whether it is really independent of German nationhood, and whether it can (more generally) function as an effective substitute for nationhood within political theory is a different question.

In reaction against the exclusionary tendencies of nationhood, and particularly of German nationhood, theorists have often looked to the US as an example of a more inclusive polity. Hannah Arendt contrasted the US with European nation-states in this respect; Habermas refers to it as a long-standing example of a state animated by constitutional patriotism, and Parekh also mentions America as a case of a patriotic but non-national state.[19] Since the US (for all its divisions) presents spectacular evidence of the power that can be wielded if 'we, the people' can indeed be mobilized behind the banner of a state, this is a case that merits further consideration. But how convincing is this classification? Should we indeed see the US as a non-national state, or simply as a nation-state that (like all nation-states) has its own distinctive features, one of which happens to be that American nationhood is unusually ideological and bound up with the liberal principles of the constitution? This is certainly Charles Taylor's view of the matter, as seen from north of the border and by comparison with Canada. He observes that 'the United States seems to offer the example of a nation which owes its identity to the common acceptance of a political formula'.[20] It is interesting to compare the abstract ideal of constitutional patriotism with the more flesh-and-blood account of it offered by an American patriot, John Schaar, who comes to the subject from the American Left and is just as concerned as Habermas or Parekh to distinguish the loyalty he wants to defend from 'nationalism, patriotism's bloody brother'.[21]

UNIVERSAL PRINCIPLES AND PARTICULAR POLITIES

In his essay putting 'The Case for Patriotism', Schaar explicitly rejects 'nationalism', by which he means bellicose attachment to the interests of the nation-state. The core of patriotism for him is 'love of one's homeplace... we become devoted to the people, places, and ways that nurture us...'.[22] There is in this sentiment a strong element of natural piety. 'To be a patriot is to have a patrimony... the gift of land, people, language, gods, memories and customs' which the patriot inherits, and which 'defines what he or she is'. Receiving with reverent gratitude what has been handed down to him, the patriot is 'determined to defend the legacy against enemies and pass it unspoiled to those who will come after.'[23]

Schaar acknowledges that the attachment to ancestral lands or immemorial cities that was the stuff of classic patriotism is not available to a modern immigrant people like the Americans. Nevertheless, he suggests that there is a peculiarly American variety which he calls 'covenanted patriotism' and finds it in the speeches of Abraham Lincoln. This is 'actively guided by and directed toward the mission established in the founding covenant', and is a matter of accepting one's inheritance from the Founders of the Republic and carrying on their work. He maintains that this sort of patriotism 'decisively transcends the parochial and primitive fraternities of blood and race, for it calls kin all who accept the authority of the covenant.'[24]

Although Schaar repudiates any ethnic element in Lincoln's patriotism and claims that it amounts to 'a strictly political definition of our nationhood', his deeply felt stress on the pieties of home and inheritance, and implicitly on the very specific duties to which those who inherit American citizenship are called, sounds extremely Burkean. Furthermore, he is aware that instinctive patriotism has a dark side, giving rise to 'fear and distrust of the stranger'.[25] On the whole, however, he tends to heap on to the shoulders of 'nationalism' the blame for that narrow and chauvinistic side of group loyalty, claiming that his and Lincoln's 'patriotism is compatible with the most generous humanism'.[26] How is this possible? Because (Schaar explains) patriotism of this kind means loyalty to universal principles of liberty, equality and self-government.

The interesting thing about Schaar's account (which is probably closer to the animating forces of American patriotism than is the bloodless ideal of *Verfassungspatriotismus*) is that a patriotism explicitly based on principles turns out to be just as particularistic as a more overtly national attachment. In fact, where principles do play a large role as the cement of a political community, it seems that they function not just as 'the true principles' but as '*our* principles', handed down to us by our forefathers. It is in fact obvious that universal principles by themselves could not form the bond of a polity on a smaller scale than a global state: 'constitutional patriotism' assumes that the principles in question are represented by a political entity already in place with a definite territory and definite membership. Whether or not nationhood is understood in terms of principles or more ethnic criteria can of course make important differences where such matters as immigration policy is concerned, but however liberal the polity, its membership is still limited. Charles Taylor observes that it has been the good fortune of the US that 'from the very beginning, its patriotism welded together the sense of nationality with a liberal representative regime'.[27] To suppose that shared principles on their own would be enough to constitute a political community would be to miss 'common history' and 'a sense of shared fate'. The patriot, in other words, is 'not dedicated to defend the liberty of just anyone', but specifically of his compatriots.[28] The limitations of loyalty to a particular political community cannot be transcended by interpreting that community as the carrier of universal principles which are the true focus of the patriot's loyalty. Patriotism demands loyalty to a *patria*.

It may still be objected that at least a patriotism informed by principles that are universal and emancipatory must be an improvement on merely national attachments. But even that is disputable, since the fusion of ancestral with ideological passions can also be damaging, making it hard for patriots to see any difference between the interests of their country and the interests of humanity. Charles Taylor observes that having a 'political formula' at the heart of their allegiance 'has given American liberalism that militant quality which has produced the best and the worst in US history', including the effect on foreign policy of 'the rhetoric of moral universal'.[29] It is revealing that for all the generosity of his sympathies, John Schaar slips into this mode, observing that covenanted patriotism 'assigns America a teaching mission among the nations, rather than a superiority over or a hostility toward them'.[30]

In spite of the pains Schaar takes to stress that this kind of patriotism does not involve an imperialistic urge to impose one's principles on others, that 'teaching mission' does rather give the game away, at any rate to those on the receiving end of the instruction. For in spite of his claim that 'patriots do not comfortably support wars of expansion or wars of "principle"',[31] Schaar's attempt to reconcile modern universalism and ancient patriotism follows a familiar track. Over and over again, patriots of one sort or another have tried to overcome the limitations of their allegiance to one polity in particular by seeing it as the carrier of a universal message, a strategy which disguises the problem of limited loyalties without doing anything to solve it. Although Schaar seems to regard the American case as unique, it is actually very common, being directly descended, like other examples, from the sanctified patriotism that has sustained polities convinced of their status as God's chosen.[32]

One version of the kind of universalist patriotism that gives its bearers a 'teaching mission among the nations' animated defenders of the British Empire from its earliest years. A descendant of the earlier conviction that Protestant England had a special divine calling, it underwent a process of secularization in the early eighteenth century. During the reign of Queen Anne, long before John Stuart Mill defended Britain's role in teaching 'barbarians' the benefits of freedom[33] or Kipling urged his countrymen to 'take up the White Man's burden',[34] the poet Thomas Tickell spelled out quite clearly the terms of Britain's mission:

> Her guiltless glory just Britannia draws
> From pure religion and impartial laws
> ...
> Her labours are to plead the' Almighty's cause
> Her pride to teach the' untamed Barbarian laws.
> Who conquers, wins by brutal strength the prize,
> But 'tis a godlike work to civilize.[35]

We should not suppose that there is anything exclusively Anglo-Saxon about this kind of condescension. An even more dramatic transmutation of religious into political chosenness (by way of cosmopolitanism) occurred among the 'patriots' of the French Revolution, for whom the land of Joan of Arc and the 'most Christian king' became the land of universal liberty, equality and fraternity. Istvan Hont has shown that the Jacobins began as pure internationalists, deeply hostile to a nationalism modelled on monarchical reason of state, and determined to promote the interests of the people of all countries. It is all the more startling, therefore, that the interests of humanity should in their eyes have become so thoroughly identified with the interests of France, or that Jacobin citizens of the world should have turned so quickly into persecutors of foreigners and cosmopolitans.[36]

Those early French efforts to export the benefits of their revolution provide a cautionary tale of what can easily happen when (in a vain hope of overcoming the particularism inherent in political power) the patriotism of a particular country is infused with universal principles. 'Liberation' was difficult to distinguish from conquest, and (in the eyes of the French) those in the Netherlands and other 'liberated' countries who counted as 'patriots' were the collaborators with the invading French armies, often regarded as traitors by their own people.[37] In France, as in the US, this sort of crusading universalist patriotism lasted a long time. Gerald Newman quotes an unconsciously chauvinistic French historian of the late nineteenth century who congratulated his fellow-countrymen on their precocious cosmopolitanism: 'It is we who taught the nations of Europe to detach themselves from a narrowly national ideal and to march resolutely towards a human ideal'.[38]

It is easy to mock any such patriotic 'teaching mission', and national pride disguised under the banner of humanity is particularly infuriating to those cast as pupils, whether it is Dutchmen being taught cosmopolitanism by the French, Indians taught 'tolerance' and 'fair play' by the British,[39] or assorted denizens of the Third World bombarded by American troops in the name of freedom and democracy. Britain, France and America have been the carriers of different versions of liberal universalism, and while (for example) the principles of the French Revolution may have seemed universally self-evident to those who propagated them across Europe, they were made harder to swallow by appearing to others as 'French principles'. Similarly, the efforts first of Britain and more recently of America to spread what they believed to be the benefits of civilization have, understandably, been received as imperialist hypocrisy. The fusion of universalist communism with Russian chauvinism in the Soviet Union shows that no nation and no part of the political spectrum is immune to this temptation.[40]

This is not to say that universal principles are inevitably doomed to turn into embellishments for national flags, but it does suggest that attempts to base patriotism upon them are not necessarily preferable to less ideological forms of nationhood. In fact there seems to be something of a dilemma here for the ideal of 'constitutional patriotism'. Where universal principles can be linked with national traditions, the result is likely to be effective political mobilization, but with the danger that universalism becomes a captive of nationalism. But where no such marriage between principles and national identity can be arranged, the strength and staying-power of 'constitutional patriotism' as a substitute for nationhood must be open to doubt.[41]

Habermas's reflections on 'Citizenship and National Identity' are interesting here. Referring to Taylor's reflections on patriotism, Habermas accepts that abstract principles by themselves are not enough, but that they need the backing of collective identification with a political community. Unwilling (in the German case) to fall back on the nation as the *patria*, Habermas considers the possibility of looking in a different direction, toward 'the republican model of citizenship [which] reminds one that the institutions of constitutional freedom are only worth as much as a population makes of them', which means a population 'well-versed in adopting the we-perspective of active self-determination.'[42] Habermas's reflections on the problem of anchoring universal principles in a particular polity are complex and multifaceted, but this aspect of them illustrates what may appear to be an attractive possibility. If a patriotism purely of abstract principles is either too weak or else too liable to capture by nationalism, is there nevertheless another solution, a way of building political community through citizen participation itself, drawing on republican traditions that flourished long before nationalism was invented?

REPUBLICAN PATRIOTISM

Every patriot hates foreigners: they are only men, and nothing to him.[43]
(Jean Jacques Rousseau)

The language of patriotism comes down to us from the tradition of classical republicanism, and those who would like to revive that tradition today are rarely sympathetic to nations or nationalism. For Mary Dietz, who traces the use of the term in the politics of opposition in eighteenth-century Britain and America, 'patriotism' has an admirable history, associated with republican principles, 'love of liberty' and 'self-sacrifice for a common cause'. 'Nationalism', by contrast, is a more modern term referring to an uncritical 'collective spirit rooted in a sense of national supremacy',[44] associated with warfare and conquest.

Those who look to citizen participation in the defence of liberty in order to denounce the bloodthirsty intolerance of modern nationalism have to pass rather hastily over most of patriotism's historic record since ancient times. For one thing, it is clear that before the advent of nation-states patriotism was an exceedingly rare phenomenon, confined for the most part to small city-states in which it rarely survived the incessant squabbles between different factions.[45] In so far as it did exist, patriotism was very much more illiberal than modern republicans would be prepared to countenance, for harmonious public spirit inside the state was inseparable from hostility to outsiders. As Daniel Waley observes of the city-republics of medieval Italy, 'fully-grown civic patriotism was the product of enmity and warfare between cities.'[46] The original roots of patriotism in the ancient polis lay in the military solidarity of the warrior bands whose mutual dedication on the battlefield made possible their freedom, and the virtue celebrated by the republican tradition down to the eighteenth century was an essentially military virtue.[47]

One of the main advantages claimed for patriotism in recent times is that since (unlike national loyalties) it does not pretend that the bonds between citizens are natural, it can transcend narrow ethnic solidarities.[48] Citizens need not share common blood so long as they share participation in a common polity. Historically, however, the belief that patriotic citizens are not born but made seems to have had consequences that were actually less liberal than the implications of some versions of nationhood. Whereas the nationalist fiction that members of the nation naturally belong together can (at any rate in established nations) lead to a fairly relaxed attitude to allegiance, the classical republican tradition (for which polities were not presumed to be natural) displayed throughout its history an anxious concern with the deliberate formation of citizens, that is to say, their patriotic education and the control of all aspects of their lives to ensure their loyalty and commitment to the state. Rousseau was an authentic heir of the tradition when he observed in *Emile* that the purpose of education for citizenship should be to eradicate individuality and give the citizen wholly to the republic.[49]

In a book on *Citizenship and Community*, Adrian Oldfield has undertaken a rare 'exploration of what it would mean to take civic republicanism seriously in the modern world'.[50] As he observes, a good many aspects of this do not harmonize very easily with the modern tenderness toward the individual and his or her inclinations. For citizenship does not come naturally; it requires that human beings should 'be moulded and shaped' by civic education so that they acquire a shared identity and shared goals as part of an exclusive community.[51]

> The moral character which is appropriate for genuine citizenship does not generate itself; it has to be authoritatively inculcated. This means that minds have to be manipulated. People, starting with children, have to be taught what citizenship means for them, in a political community, in terms of the duties it imposes upon them, and they have to be motivated to perform those duties. This is successful when they perceive that the interests of the community are also their own.[52]

Most classical advocates of patriotism would have agreed, surprised only that such obvious implications of citizenship needed to be restated. This line of thought is very much less congenial to those for whom one of the attractions of patriotism is precisely that it is presumed to be less restrictive than national loyalty, more compatible with internal diversity and universal humanity. It may be objected, however, that Oldfield's account is a good deal too classical, and that the 'we-perspective of active self-determination' which

Habermas and others consider necessary for citizenship need not have much in common with such totalitarian nightmares. On this view, republican citizens are formed not by some approximation to the creative efforts of Rousseau's Lawgiver, but through the democratic process of political participation itself. By acting together in public people acquire habits of solidarity.

An eloquent articulation of this position has been provided by Benjamin Barber in his account of a version of democracy more satisfactory than the weak liberal democracy to which we are accustomed, what he calls 'strong democracy'. Writing in America before recent events there and elsewhere focused attention on questions of ethnic pluralism and national unity, Barber nevertheless devotes a good deal of thought to the kind of unity amongst citizens that can in his view be generated by political activity itself. One of his central claims is that no preexisting communal ties are necessary for democratic politics. 'Far from positing community *a priori*, strong democratic theory understands the creation of community as one of the chief tasks of political activity in the participatory mode.'[53] In the course of public discussion, according to Barber, opinions and preferences undergo transformation, and individuals come to see themselves as citizens in relation to their fellows.

> The leap out of privatism and self-interest that democratic participation promotes is a leap to embrace strangers whose commonality with us arises less out of blood or geography or culture than out of talk itself.[54]

Barber's ideal is an appealing one, particularly because in criticizing liberal democracy he also rejects the stifling classical tradition of 'unitary democracy' in which citizens were thought of as brothers and expected to think and act like clones.[55] He is certainly right to point out that sharing in political activity can itself be a powerful source of shared identity: the experience even of 'weak' democracies bears this out to some degree. Nevertheless, there are difficulties. For one thing, although Barber insists that political participation does not presuppose community, it is clear that (as we noted earlier when discussing democratic theory) acceptance of common territorial boundaries and common political institutions is indeed presupposed. Participation cannot very well get under way where (as in so many contemporary examples) the terms of political membership are themselves in dispute. But assuming that this hurdle can be overcome, another barrier stands in the way of regarding republican participation as the solution to the problems of nationhood.

The difficulty is that this participatory version of republican patriotism involves a high level of political mobilization, which has its own dangers and costs. While there are obvious virtues in the active participation of citizens in political activity, it also has snags, for participation may be hard to distinguish from populism. To those who distrust and fear national passions, and who look to the state to provide plural societies with a purely institutional form of unity, participatory politics can only mean waking the sleeping dogs of communal identity and mobilizing ethnic and religious differences. As Barber says, 'the citizen is by definition a "we-thinker"', and the 'us' that emerges from participation cannot avoid particularism of some sort, and is likely to be coloured by existing communal identities. In so far as such political mobilization does not tend to divide a plural society into multiple 'we's, it may serve to reinforce a sense of 'us' directed against outsiders.[56]

Concerns of this kind form an ironic shadow haunting Habermas's 'constitutional patriotism', for while he sees the force of the republican case for participation, and is in any case committed to 'radical democracy' as the contemporary agenda for the Left, he is understandably worried about what may come crawling out of the grassroots: German nationalism, in fact.[57] And this is a more general difficulty facing those who would like to dispense with nationhood by building republican communities through political activity itself. For citizens who engage in political activity will bring to it their own preoccupations and identifications, and these may be precisely what republican theorists would like to keep out of the public arena: either a nationhood mobilized against outsiders or (even worse) communal hostilities unmoderated by any sense of common nationhood.

Whether republican patriotism can really act as a substitute for national attachments therefore remains unclear. Certainly the accounts of it given by Taylor often sound indistinguishable from actively mobilized nationhood. For Taylor, patriotism is 'a common allegiance to a particular historical community',[58] a matter of common history, shared fate and ineradicable particularism. He acknowledges that in contemporary societies participatory institutions and traditional expressions of national identity may not go together, and sees this as a serious problem. 'How these two relate in any given society matters a great deal to the form, the health and ultimately to the survival of democratic regimes.'[59] The most promising cases are, he believes, those 'where participatory institutions are thought to be an integral part of the national culture', and where he is even prepared to acknowledge the value of 'a kind of happy chauvinism' in attachment to a national heritage of free institutions.[60] In other words, just as 'constitutional patriotism' seems to be most effective where the abstract principles involved are 'our principles', so the republican patriotism based on participation seems to work best where it is a matter of inheriting 'our democracy'. There seems to be no escape from particularism.

Accepting this general line of argument does not of course imply that patriotic loyalty must be blind to be effective. Stephen Nathanson argues reasonably that patriots can and should question their country's actions and commitments, and aim at 'patriotism within the limits of morality'.[61] Faced with Alasdair MacIntyre's provocative claim that (since loyalty to the *patria* is bound at some point to conflict with the demands of universal principles) 'good soldiers may not be liberals',[62] Nathanson maintains that 'patriotic people have both a right and a duty to judge their country's cause before supporting it in war.'[63] Writing as an American, however, in a massively secure national territory and with the distant Vietnam War in mind, he unconsciously assumes that no unjust war could actually put in question the survival and identity of his country, and thereby underestimates the problems of reconciling local loyalties with universal principles in less fortunate areas of the world.

Some critics would argue, indeed, that within a political discourse dominated by American experiences, liberals and communitarians alike dodge the hard questions involved in maintaining the existence of a political community. The conservative philosopher Roger Scruton argues not only that liberals delude themselves in supposing that they can do without nations, but that 'communitarians' are equally evasive about what 'community' really involves. Reflecting on the numerous political theorists who in various ways hanker after 'community' in the modern world, Scruton observes that 'none of them is prepared to accept the real price of community: which is sanctity, intolerance, exclusion, and a sense that life's meaning depends upon obedience, and also on vigilance against the enemy.'[64]

Scruton's words, from an essay 'In Defence of the Nation', may at first sight seem to imply that the existence of a political community is inseparable from precisely the kind of chauvinism that the contrast between patriotism and nationalism was designed to avoid. His provocatively anti-liberal tone and his willingness to use the term 'race' in discussing nationhood help to create the impression of an integral ethnic nationalism with all the qualities in the patriots' caricature. Nevertheless, the impression is misleading. There is, for example, a surprising amount of common ground between Scruton's 'nationalism' and John Schaar's 'patriotism'. Patriotism as promoted by Schaar may be thought of as essentially political rather than ethnic, but, as we have seen, it turns out to be a political inheritance linked to family ties. Nationhood as defended by Scruton may have been judged by his opponents to be racist, but it turns out on inspection that the kinship ties he invokes are elastic ones, mediated through territory, culture and institutions.[65] No doubt the precise mix of the political and the ethnic differs in the two cases, but this may be accounted for by the specific character of the nations in question.

The project of distinguishing between 'patriotic' and 'national' loyalties in the modern world depends heavily upon a process of oversimplification in which antagonists have often unconsciously colluded. In truth, just as 'patriotism' on the one hand cannot really be equivalent to universalist humanism, so 'national' loyalties on the other hand are not reducible to the primordial bonds of the caricature. The kind of polity to which thinkers on both sides find themselves drawn is actually neither pure state nor simple ethnic community: it is a polity that is *ours*, structured by all the subtle mediations that give nationhood its content and its power.

I have argued in this chapter that despite the attractions for contemporary political theorists of an account of political community that would be non-national, it is very doubtful whether such an account can be convincingly given. The kind of political cohesion indicated seems to be either too weak to sustain the aspirations of liberal democratic political theory, or else just as particularistic as nationhood, and with a strong propensity in any case to become intertwined with the latter. This is not to deny that (as Bhikhu Parekh rightly points out) at the level of empirical politics some liberal democratic polities stumble along more or less successfully on the basis of less demanding and more multifarious forms of support. The question of the relation between theory and practice is an important one, to which we shall return later. For the moment, however, my argument that political theory relies on nationhood raises two further problems. One concerns the obvious dissonance between the particularism of any national (or patriotic) loyalty and the universalism of liberal democratic principles; between, as Hannah Arendt put it, 'the nation-state' and 'the rights of man'.[66] The other, which may seem more obviously pressing, is the glaring unsuitability of most modern nationalism to function as any kind of support for a liberal democratic political agenda. I will consider the latter problem in the next chapter, postponing the former to the concluding chapter.

NOTES

1. C. Taylor, 'Cross-Purposes: The Liberal-Communitarian Debate', in N.L. Rosenblum (ed.), *Liberalism and the Moral Life* (Cambridge, Mass., Harvard University Press, 1989) 165.
2. B. Parekh, 'Politics of Nationhood', in K. von Benda-Beckman and M. Verkuyten (eds), *Cultural Identity and Development in Europe* (University College of London Press, forthcoming.
3. Parekh, 'Politics of Nationhood'.
4. Parekh, 'Politics of Nationhood'.
5. Parekh, 'Politics of Nationhood'.
6. Parekh, 'Politics of Nationhood'.
7. Parekh, 'Politics of Nationhood'.
8. Parekh, 'Politics of Nationhood'.
9. Cf. C. Taylor, 'Institutions in National Life', in Taylor (ed. G. Laforest), *Reconciling the Solitudes: Essays on Canadian Federalism and Nationalism* (Montreal, McGill-Queens University Press, 1993) 121.
10. A recent survey conducted in South-East Asia revealed that most of those who had heard of the EU thought that it was an insurance company – a guess that is perhaps not too wide of the mark.

11. See e.g. J. Rawls, *Political Liberalism* (New York, Columbia University Press, 1993) xviii–xxiv; R. Dworkin, 'Liberalism', in S. Hampshire (ed.), *Public and Private Morality* (Cambridge, Cambridge University Press, 1978) 127.

12. A.O. Hirschman, *Exit, Voice and Loyalty: Responses to Decline in Firms, Organisations and States* (Cambridge, Mass., Harvard University Press, 1970). That Parekh himself feels the force of such considerations is evident from another article, on political obligation, in which he speaks eloquently of members of a polity 'forming part of a collective "we" because of their shared heritage and future'. (B. Parekh, 'A Misconceived Discourse on Political Obligation', *Political Studies* XLI, 1993, 242).

13. According to MacIntyre, although the modern state is an essentially instrumental organization, it has to pretend to be a much more authentic political community in order to secure allegiance. A. Macintyre, 'Poetry as Political Philosophy: Notes on Burke and Yeats', in *On Modern Poetry: Essays Presented to Donald Davie*, ed. V. Bell and L. Lerner (Nashville, Vanderbilt University Press, 1988) 149.

14. Many aspects of the complex problems of Canadian and *Quebecois* identity are explored in Taylor, *Reconciling the Solitudes, passim.*

15. Taylor, 'Cross-Purposes' 175.

16. Taylor, 'Cross-Purposes' 173–4.

17. For *Verfassungspatriotismus*, see e.g. Habermas, 'Citizenship and National Identity', *Praxis International* 12/1 (1992) 7, 17; for the sceptical view that it is actually nationalism in disguise see C.W. Morris, 'On Contractarian Constitutional Democracy', in D. Copp, J. Hampton and J.E. Roemer (eds), *The Idea of Democracy* (Cambridge, Cambridge University Press, 1993) 342.

18. J. Habermas, *The New Conservatism: Cultural Criticism and the Historians' Debate* (ed. and trans. S.W. Nicholson) (Cambridge, Polity, 1989) 261; *Forever in the Shadow of Hitler?* (trans. J. Knowlton and T. Cates) (New Jersey, Humanities Press, 1993) 43.

19. Cf. M. Canovan, *Hannah Arendt: A Reinterpretation of her Political Thought* (Cambridge, Cambridge University Press, 1992) 245–6; Habermas, 'Citizenship and National Identity', 7; B. Parekh, 'Ethnocentricity of the Nationalist Discourse', *Nations and Nationalism* 1/1 (1995) 41.

20. C. Taylor, 'Alternative Futures: Legitimacy, Identity and Alienation in Late Twentieth Century Canada', in A. Cairns and C. Williams (eds) *Constitutionalism, Citizenship and Society in Canada* (Toronto, University of Toronto Press, 1985) 215. Cf. L. Greenfeld, *Nationalism: Five Roads to Modernity* (Cambridge, Mass., Harvard University Press, 1992) 402, 423.

21. J.H. Schaar, 'The Case for Patriotism', in Schaar, *Legitimacy in the Modern State* (New Brunswick, Transaction Books, 1981) 285.

22. Schaar, 'Case for Patriotism' 287.

23. Schaar, 'Case for Patriotism' 288.

24. Schaar, 'Case for Patriotism' 293. For sceptical comments on the notion that American identity has been essentially a matter of allegiance to political principles rather than of ethnic ties, see R. M. Smith, 'The "American Creed" and American Identity: the Limits of Liberal Citizenship in the United States', *Western Political Quarterly* 41/2 (June 1988) 225–51.

25. Schaar, 'Case for Patriotism' 297.

26. Schaar, 'Case for Patriotism' 293.

27. Taylor, 'Cross-Purposes' 280, note 2.

28. Taylor, 'Cross-Purposes' 167, 170, 166.

29. Taylor, 'Alternative Futures' 215.

30. Schaar, 'Case for Patriotism' 293.

31. Schaar, 'Case for Patriotism' 302.

32. For a fascinating exploration of this topic, see C.C. O'Brien, *God Land* (Cambridge, Mass., Harvard University Press, 1987). See also M. Walzer, *Nation & Universe* (The Tanner Lectures on Human Values, Brasenose College, Oxford, 1989).

33. J.S. Mill, *Utilitarianism, Liberty, Representative Government* (London, J.M. Dent, 1910) 73, 382.

34. *Rudyard Kipling's Verse*, definitive edition (London, Hodder and Stoughton, 1940) 323.
35. 'On the Prospect of Peace', *Poems of Thomas Tickell* 135–6, *The British Poets* Vol. XXVII (College House, C. Whittingham, 1822).
36. I. Hont, 'The Permanent Crisis of a Divided Mankind: "Contemporary Crisis of the Nation State" in Historical Perspective', *Political Studies* 42 (Special Issue 1994: 'Contemporary Crisis of the Nation State?', ed. J. Dunn) 202–22.
37. C.C. O'Brien, 'Nationalism and the French Revolution', in *The Permanent Revolution: The French Revolution and its Legacy 1789–1989*, ed. G. Best (London, Fontana, 1988) 38–43.
38. G. Newman, *The Rise of English Nationalism* 49. For a curious late example of French revolutionary messianism, see the interview with Régis Debray, 'Marxism and the National Question', *New Left Review* 105 (September–October 1977) 25–41. More recently, of course, French patriotism has clothed itself in the idea of European integration. See S. Hoffmann, 'Thoughts on the French Nation Today', *Daedalus* 122/3 (Summer 1993) 63–79.
39. For a contemporary reiteration of the idea that 'Britishness…means a sense of fair play…and a spirit of toleration…', see J. Gray, *A Conservative Disposition: Individualism, the Free Market and the Common Life* (London, Centre for Policy Studies, 1991) 20. For a sharp reaction to recent attempts by British politicians (in the wake of the Rushdie affair) to instruct Muslim immigrants in British values of freedom and tolerance, see T. Asad, 'Multiculturalism and British Identity in the Wake of the Rushdie Affair', *Politics and Society* 18/4 (1990) 455–80. Cf. M. Billig, 'Nationalism and Richard Rorty: The Text as a Flag for *Pax Americana*', *New Left Review* 202 (Nov–Dec 1993) 69–84.
40. Cf. Lenin's essay 'On the National Pride of the Great Russians', quoted in L. Greenfeld, *Nationalism: Five Roads to Modernity* (Cambridge, Mass., Harvard University Press, 1992) 270. For the earlier history of 'Holy Russia', see M. Cherniavsky, *Tsar and People: Studies in Russian Myths* (New Haven and London, Yale University Press, 1961).
41. C. Taylor, 'Alternative Futures' 214–15.
42. Habermas, 'Citizenship and National Identity' 7.
43. J.J. Rousseau, *Emile*, trans. B. Foxley (London, Dent, 1911) 7.
44. M.G. Dietz, 'Patriotism', in T. Ball, J. Farr and R.L. Hanson (eds), *Political Innovation and Conceptual Change* (Cambridge, Cambridge University Press, 1989) 187, 189. Stephen Nathanson draws a similar distinction but situates it within both patriotism and nationalism, so that 'moderate patriotism' is contrasted with the chauvinist kind, and some forms of nationalism are acceptable; S. Nathanson, *Patriotism, Morality, and Peace* (Lanham, Md., Rowman and Littlefield, 1993) 185–97.
45. See e.g. D. Waley, *The Italian City-Republics*, second edition (London, Longman, 1978) 94.
46. Waley, *Italian City-Republics* 81.
47. See the description of Sparta in P.A. Rahe, *Republics Ancient and Modern: Classical Republicanism and the American Revolution* (Chapel Hill and London, University of North Carolina Press, 1992). On republicanism and *machismo* see H. Pitkin, *Fortune is a Woman: Gender and Politics in the Thought of Niccolo Machiavelli* (Berkeley, University of California Press, 1984).
48. Schaar, 'Case for Patriotism' 293.
49. Rousseau, *Emile* 7.
50. A. Oldfield, *Citizenship and Community – Civic Republicanism and the Modern World* (London, Routledge, 1990) ix.
51. Oldfield, *Citizenship and Community* 8, 146, 153.
52. Oldfield, *Citizenship and Community* 164.
53. B. Barber, *Strong Democracy – Participatory Politics for a New Age* (Berkeley, University of California Press, 1984) 133.
54. Barber, *Strong Democracy* 189.
55. Barber, *Strong Democracy* 218.
56. Barber, *Strong Democracy* 153. According to the theory of 'consociational democracy', stable democracy in plural societies is more likely if levels of grassroots participation are

low and élites representing the various communities can make deals among themselves. See A. Lijphart, *Democracy in Plural Societies* (New Haven, Yale University Press, 1977) 49–50.

57. A fascinating discussion between Habermas and Adam Michnik in the aftermath of German unification ('Overcoming the Past', *New Left Review* 203, Jan/Feb 1994, 3–16) illustrates this ambivalence, and his hope that the *deus ex machina* of the European Union can save Germans from themselves. See also J. Habermas (interviewed by M. Haller), *The Past as Future* (Lincoln, Nebraska, University of Nebraska Press, 1994) especially 154, 165.

58. C. Taylor, 'Cross-Purposes' 176.

59. Taylor, 'Alternative Futures' 214.

60. Taylor, 'Alternative Futures' 214.

61. Nathanson, *Patriotism* 37.

62. A. MacIntyre, 'Is Patriotism a Virtue?' (The E.H. Lindley Memorial Lecture, Lawrence, University of Kansas Department of Philosophy, 1984) 17.

63. Nathanson, *Patriotism* 146.

64. 'In Defence of the Nation', in R. Scruton, *The Philosopher on Dover Beach* (Manchester, Carcanet, 1990) 310.

65. Scruton, 'In Defence of the Nation' 300, 305.

66. H. Arendt, *The Origins of Totalitarianism* (London, George Allen and Unwin, 1967) 267–302.

9. Nationalism versus liberal democracy?

Nationalism and liberalism far from being twins are really antagonistic principles. (Elie Kedourie)[1]

A possible objection to the thesis presented above would go something like this:

> The notion that liberal democratic political thought presupposes nationhood makes no sense, because nationalism is overwhelmingly associated with the destruction of liberal democracy. Nationalist politicians are chauvinist demagogues, nationalist movements breed terrorists, and successful nationalist leaders are often dictators. As the fate of Yugoslavia shows, nationalism leads to civil war and 'ethnic cleansing', not to liberal democracy.

This is a persuasive objection, and it certainly dampens any naive optimism about the likely outcome of 'national liberation' in many circumstances. Nevertheless, I hope to show that it does not invalidate my argument. In this chapter I shall explore four responses to it, arguing firstly that nations differ a great deal, so that some versions of nationhood are much closer than others to the presuppositions of contemporary political theory; secondly that the presence of nationalism sometimes indicates the absence of nations; thirdly that however much liberal democratic projects may rely upon the existence of nation-states, such states have not been established by liberal democratic means; and finally that under modern conditions, attempts at 'nation-building' do indeed tend to be self-destructive. Although these arguments do (I believe) answer the initial objection, their combined effect is not encouraging, since it makes the dependence of contemporary political ideals on an increasingly elusive nationhood even more problematic than before.

NATIONAL VARIATIONS

No two nationalisms are alike. (Bhikhu Parekh)[2]

I have argued above that nationhood is a necessary condition of the liberal democratic welfare state as envisaged in contemporary political theory, because that theory assumes the existence of a powerful political community for which no convincing non-national substitute appears to be available. However, a necessary condition is not a sufficient condition, and there is no suggestion here that the existence of a nation is enough in itself (either in theory or in practice) to ground liberal democratic politics. Nations, as we have already seen, are idiosyncratic beasts with very different characters. The ideals that inform contemporary political thought have a particularly close link with certain specific national traditions, notably those of Britain, the US and France. But these nations are themselves very different from one another, and also from those other versions of nationhood that may seem closest to them, such as the Dutch and Swedish versions. The nationhood that constitutes a people can be imagined in many different ways, and some form much firmer bases than others for the various parts of the liberal democratic package.

Where a nation of any sort exists this facilitates the mobilization of political power, but how that power is likely to be structured and for what purposes it is likely to be used may vary a good deal between national traditions, as well as in response to circumstances. Since nationhood forms the basis for a strong state, it can provide the potential for the effective law-enforcement that is an essential element in liberalism, but can equally provide the potential for populist mobilization behind an authoritarian leader. There is no guarantee that a strong national state will share the liberal concern for individual freedom and rights, and if it does not do so, the power generated by nationhood may itself take the state further from liberal ideals. Hitler without the backing of genuine popular power would not have been able to wreak as much havoc as he did. In many cases, including those of Germany and Russia, nationhood has historically been articulated in opposition to the West, and specifically in opposition to what was seen as the atomistic individualism of France, Britain and the US.[3] Nationhood is of course not immutable, and the traumas of Nazism, defeat and division seem to have changed the flavour of German nationhood, perhaps for ever. Russia is another question, and in view of the strength of nationhood and the character of Russian traditions, one possible scenario is the emergence there of a strong state with some degree of social solidarity and populistic democracy, but little that is liberal. There are many other similar cases.

A number of political thinkers have been wrestling recently with the uncomfortable possibility that since liberalism (despite its universalist pretensions) arose out of a specific historical background, it may not easily take root in societies with different traditions.[4] The relation between universalist liberalism and national allegiance is a difficult topic, to which I shall return in the next chapter. For the moment, however, I wish only to establish that the past and present existence of numerous illiberal nationalist movements does not disprove my thesis. Liberal democratic political projects may be dependent on the existence of nation states even though many nation states do not conduct themselves in a liberal democratic manner.

NATIONALISM AS POLITICS

> Nationalism has little to do with the existence or non-existence of a nation...
> Rather there were circumstances ... when nationalism was the most appropriate
> form political opposition could take. (John Breuilly)[5]

There is another reason for refusing to regard the activities of nationalist movements as a refutation, which is that the existence of a nationalist movement does not of itself prove the existence of a nation. As we saw earlier when discussing nationhood, there is no need to adopt an all-or-nothing approach to nations and nationalism. Despite a tendency in the literature to assume that supposed 'nations' must be all authentic or all shams, a phenomenological approach would be more discriminating, accepting that nations have come into existence at different times, do not exist everywhere, and are probably much less often to be found in the contemporary world than are the political actors who claim to represent them.

Sceptical students of nationalism have rightly warned against the temptation to take the pretensions of nationalist movements at their face value, pointing out that modern politics gives rise to many circumstances in which politicians find it worth their while to claim nationalist credentials.[6] For example, during the process of decolonization after the Second World War, all parties in the new states made use of the rhetoric of nationalism, but it would be very unwise to deduce from this that they spoke for nations. Once the ideology of nationalism was loose in the world, spreading the assumption that states ought to correspond to nations, the politically ambitious or disaffected were handed a useful language in terms of which their power struggles could be waged. To suppose that nationhood caused those struggles would be as naive as to suppose that religion 'caused' all the sixteenth-century wars that were legitimized in religious terms.

If a certain number of 'nationalist' conflicts should be seen in these terms, then some at least of the atrocities committed in the name of the nation can be put down to original sin rather than to nationhood as such, leaving untouched the link suggested here between nationhood and liberal democracy. However, we need not rely on this kind of cynical discounting of ideology to rebut the objection raised above. There are other responses that are more powerful, though also more disturbing.

THE MODERN PRINCE

War made the State, and the State made war. (Charles Tilly)[7]

The nation-states that loom unnoticed among the tacit presumptions of modern political theory are not given as part of the order of nature: how did they come into being? Notoriously, the classic thinkers of the liberal tradition liked to imagine political communities as being founded on individual consent, thereby glossing over their unsavoury histories. But even if the notion of consent within a given polity can be made plausible, there remains the problem of how that polity comes to be given. The most elaborate of the social contract theories never made much attempt to come to grips with the boundary problem, transparently assuming that history had delivered convenient divisions of humanity within which consent could be supposed to occur.

The first nations were built by kings, and the methods they used were not those of liberal democracy. England and France were royal creations, their territories built up by conquest and secured by perpetual warfare. The popular mobilization that sealed their nationhood was in its turn mobilization for war. Even American nationhood, which often seems more authentically a matter of choice, was severed from Englishness in a revolutionary struggle, and not completed until the choice of the South to secede had been prevented by force.[8] It is unfortunately the case that a nation that is peaceful, secure and a favourable site for liberal democratic politics *now* usually has a past that no liberal democrat can comfortably look into. Writing of Englishness in the 1940s, Orwell liked to think that for all their unavoidable involvement in war, the English were a gentle, unmilitaristic nation, whose patriotic poetry tended to celebrate unsuccessful military actions like the charge of the Light Brigade.[9] But Englishness had by then had plenty of time to mellow with age. The patriotism of the eighteenth century or earlier was quite as strident as that of younger nations in more recent times. Nationalism with all its faults (the most conspicuous being bellicosity and the mobilization of the in-group against the out-group) seems to be a necessary stage in the evolution of nationhood.

Machiavellian skeletons lurk in the cupboards of liberal democracies, embarrassing dissonances between the values of a civilized polity and the methods that brought that polity into being. Indeed, nation-states are haunted by two rather different sorts of spectres, those of state-making and of nation-building (to adopt Anthony Smith's terminology).[10] There is in the first place the problem so memorably addressed by Machiavelli concerning the conditions for the foundation of state power. Bluntly stated, it is that to clear a space for order and justice in the world it is necessary to use force and deceit. Does the end – strong statehood – therefore justify the means? Even harder, does the way states like Britain and France acquired their territories in the past justify the use of similar methods by (for example) Saddam Hussein of Iraq now?

Where states are concerned, most of us want to will the end (present-day borders) without willing the means used in the past. This dilemma is bad enough, but the evolution from states to nations adds another layer of difficulty. Nationhood once achieved solves some of Machiavelli's problems, since a state that is a nation-state can sustain itself internally by calling on the loyalty of its population instead of having to resort to terror and deceit. But the road to this happy condition is very bumpy, for it lies through political mobilization of the population – that is to say, through nationalism, and probably through violence. The particular irony is that even when that price is paid, the road to peaceful nationhood is not clear, and those who embark upon it are liable to find themselves in a trackless wilderness.

How is the population of a state to be turned into a nation? The obvious answer is, by mobilizing them for struggle, preferably against their former rulers. Reflecting on the situation in Algeria, and in post-colonial states more generally, Frantz Fanon confronted the problem of turning a heterogeneous collection of former subjects into a people and argued that this could only be done through violent revolutionary activity.[11] A similar point has recently been made with shocking frankness by John Hall, who remarks that

> In a horrible sense, Third World countries have not had enough war, or, perhaps enough war of the right type. They are quasi-societies, not nation-states. Their states desperately need to be strengthened so that they can provide that basic order which we have come to take for granted.[12]

Is nationalist violence then the Machiavellian price that must be paid for stable nationhood and the civilized politics that it makes possible? Such a claim may sound like the ultimate in hard-nosed realism, but unfortunately it errs on the side of optimism. There is certainly a connection of sorts between war and the mobilization of national solidarity, but it is very much less straightforward than the passage just quoted might suggest. War severely tests a state's potential for solidarity, and if in some cases it gives birth to an intensified national consciousness within given borders (often at the price of 'ethnic cleansing'),[13] in others it merely exacerbates internal divisions and makes nationhood harder to achieve.

Faced with these reflections we are likely to conclude that the price of nation-building is far too high. Even if we reluctantly accept Machiavelli's original point, that *states* cannot be founded or maintained without at least the possibility of resorting to force, we may well feel that the further blood-stained steps in the direction of *nations* are simply not worth taking. The price of states is quite high enough: even if it is empirically as well as theoretically the case that liberal democratic politics needs a nation to grow in, why should we consider the extra premium for nationhood worth paying?

The answer to this appears, unfortunately, to be the old Machiavellian answer: necessity. Once states were established they drove pre-state polities out of business, and nationhood seems to have had an analogously corrosive effect on non-national polities. It has been difficult in the modern world to decide not to pay the price of nationhood, although there is no assurance that if the price is paid the goods will be delivered. Both that necessity and that uncertainty result from a dialectic of nationhood that has undermined other forms of polity, but that also tends progressively to undermine attempts at nation-building. Let us now see how this happens.

THE DIALECTIC OF NATIONHOOD

> The structure of the international system forces all dissatisfaction to seek articulation, however inappropriate, through the obligatory pretence that each minority, each disgruntled group of people, are a nation in waiting ... (Sudipta Kaviraj)[14]

For most of their history, human beings have conducted their affairs within polities that took no account of nationhood in the modern sense. City-states, federations, above all monarchies and empires were until the twentieth century the most common forms; more recently they were joined by communist dictatorships. None of these political forms relied upon nationhood for its legitimacy, and (as critics of nationalism point out) anyone fortunate enough to live under a relatively stable and orderly version of any of the above should be thankful, for pursuit of national self-determination is unlikely to be worth the dangerous and unpredictable upheavals involved in the redrawing of borders. By challenging the very identity of the state, nationalist movements all too often let loose the forces that states usually manage to keep under control, and blur the distinction between war and politics. During the 1930s and 1940s, many inhabitants of East-Central Europe looked back nostalgically to what seemed in retrospect the halcyon days of the Habsburg Empire. Increasingly, the same is true even of the Soviet Union.

To suppose, however, that the collapse of such empires could have been avoided if only nationalist intellectuals had had more sense is clearly unrealistic.[15] The collapse of the beliefs that sustained them had a great deal to do with invidious comparisons with the freer, more democratic, more powerful and more prosperous states to the West. What was destabilizing was the sense that nothing except the existing regime stood in the way of a better kind of polity, and this is what was promised by a rhetoric of Western democracy that leaned heavily on unconscious assumptions about nationhood.

The key point is that (because of its capacities for mediation, and thereby for the building of popular power) nationhood made liberal democracy seem easy and natural. During the many centuries of monarchical rule in Europe there were always a handful of republican city-states whose citizens prided themselves on their freedom, but until the eighteenth century this coexistence did not destabilize monarchy. However much the king's subjects might envy citizens their freedom, no one could suppose for a moment that the establishment and maintenance of a republican polity was easy. Republics were small, weak and fragile, tender plants that appeared to thrive only under exceptional conditions. The natural form of government, the fall-back position that was the only feasible alternative to anarchy and civil war, was monarchy.

It was the advent of nations that made republics a realistic alternative to monarchies, by making it possible for the subjects of a realm the size of France to form a people that could be conceived of as governing itself. Why have a sovereign king when, as the French revolutionaries claimed, sovereignty belonged to the nation? It is true that the immediate experience of the French nation was not encouraging, serving to convince some subjects of the continuing need for kings to keep order. Over the last two centuries, however, the advantages of the nation-state have become obvious. States in which the government belongs in some sense to a nation rather than to a royal family, a party or a junta appear in general to be better governed and more prosperous as well as being freer and more democratic. Comparison with them has therefore tended to deprive other regimes of legitimacy. As a recent commentator has observed in the course of reflections on the demise of the Soviet Union, 'underlying any sense of legitimacy (and for that matter, of statehood) is a sense of identity, of peoplehood'.[16]

Hence the widespread assumption that all states are now destined to turn into nation-states. But there is a catch here. As we have seen, it is of the essence of nations to seem natural, although in fact they are not. Those who speak the language of liberal democracy therefore easily assume that nations are ready and waiting to be liberated. Remove the dictator, the communist party or the military junta, and what remains will be a *people*: that is, an entity with enough cohesion to sustain (at the minimum) stable frontiers and internal peace, and perhaps also to establish the rule of law, representative government and the economic prosperity that tends to accompany these political blessings. Unfortunately, as experience has continually shown, these expectations are unwarranted. Removal of one variety of repressive regime does nothing in itself to ensure that 'a people' will be there to take over. In case after case, national self-determination has led only to the reinstatement of repressive rule, often worse than before, since the shattered state has to be rebuilt by Machiavellian methods.

The first twist of the dialectic of nationhood, then, is the process in which non-national regimes are destabilized by unrealistic expectations about the ease with which repressive regimes can be replaced by something better. But is this not a matter of time? Will not the new regime solve the problem through nation-building? It is here, unfortunately, that the dialectic takes a further downward twist, encouraging governments to attempt nation-building but at the same time undermining their efforts and making it unlikely that many nations will be built.

Surveying the history of the British and French empires we can see the dialectic at work. Nationhood, and the capacity for military mobilization it implied, was an important factor in enabling these European states to conquer and control vast overseas territories, and yet the dissonance between nationhood at home and imperial rule abroad itself tended to destabilize the latter by provoking nationalist movements in the conquered territories. During the struggle for independence the contrast between colonizers and colonized was sometimes enough to unify the latter and create a brief illusion of nationhood. Once independence was achieved, however, the new state was faced with the problem of giving substance to that illusion, what Clifford Geertz calls the task of 'defining, or trying to define, a collective subject to whom the actions of the State can be internally connected ... creating, or trying to create, an experiential "we" from whose will the activities of government seem spontaneously to flow.'[17]

In the early days of post-colonial regimes, the task was often seen as a process of 'nation-building' in which petty differences would be replaced by a new overarching solidarity. President Sekou Touré of Guinea expressed this confident perspective in 1959, predicting that 'in three or four years, no-one will remember the tribal, ethnic or religious rivalries which, in the recent past, caused so much damage to our country and its population.' But as Crawford Young recently observed, in today's perspective, '"national integration" and "nation-building" have all but vanished from the repertory of progressive statecraft'.[18] On the face of it, what the new states were trying to do was no more than had been accomplished earlier in the nation-states of Europe. Nationhood had not come naturally to England or France, either, but was largely the result of the activities of centralizing monarchies: why should not the 'new nations' repeat the process, perhaps initially under quasi-monarchical rule? Reflecting on the potentiality for nationhood in ex-colonial states, Sami Zubaida asks precisely this question:

> if these processes of homogenization could be achieved historically in certain countries, can they not be achieved under modern conditions in countries such as Nigeria, with diverse populations? Surely, modern techno-cultural facilities of transport, communications and armaments should greatly facilitate processes of political and cultural integration.[19]

For all the attempts at 'nation-building', however, so far 'few, if any, nations have been built',[20] and this is not really surprising. For the concept of nationhood has done more than undermine imperial rule and set a new standard of political legitimacy for new states to aspire to; it has also hindered the efforts to build nations in those new states by provoking the mobilization of ethnic identities. As we saw, nationhood makes the state *our* state by turning it into an imagined community of quasi-kin: the magic lies in the combination of state and community, artificiality and apparent naturalness. But this is not a balance that can easily be struck. Attempts to strengthen the state by turning it into a nation involve playing on communal themes that may themselves provoke rival versions of nationhood.[21]

Clifford Geertz wrote persuasively about the way in which processes of modernization and homogenization set off ethnic conflicts. From the point of view of the state, nation-building was an 'integrative revolution' that sought to incorporate its subjects as citizens of a modern national community. An Indian nationalist from the 1950s quoted by Geertz argued against multilingualism, on the grounds that a unilingual state was bound to be more stable than the reverse:

A state is built on fellow-feeling...a corporate sentiment of oneness which makes those who are charged with it feel that they are kith and kin.[22]

Inevitably, however, each new state's choice of a language of government and education itself politicized linguistic differences, in many cases turning what had previously been a relatively private matter into a focus of intense political antagonism. Similarly, the modernized communications and universal suffrage that were supposed to be part of the process of nation-building made it possible for politicians to build followings by appealing to sentiments of identity connected to language, religion and ethnicity. As Geertz said, 'the integrative revolution does not do away with ethnocentrism; it merely modernises it.'[23]

'Nation-building', in other words, is a bit like running up the down escalator. The problem is not simply one of starting with relatively narrow traditional attachments and trying to replace them with a wider national solidarity: it is that the attempt to mobilize populations behind the banner of nationhood turns out in many cases to provoke the mobilization of ethnic groups instead. This does not invariably happen; not all ethnic, linguistic or religious differences turn into political fault-lines, but there can be no doubt that powerful forces push in that direction. In the admirably comprehensive study which he published in 1976, Crawford Young stressed the range of variation in the politics of cultural pluralism, and the fact that there were in some countries deep ethnic divisions that had so far been little politicized. Returning to the subject in 1993, he remarks on the spread of ethnic political mobilization into areas previously unaffected.[24]

This has at least as much to do with modern political dynamics as with primordial identities. Paul Brass stresses the role of politicians in mobilizing ethnicity, arguing that ethnic groups in the sense of conscious, solidary political entities are no more natural than nations, and are equally artifacts of political processes. The trouble is that the political processes set in motion by the dialectic of nationhood do tend to highlight such differences, because 'the ability to mobilize large numbers of people around symbols and values with a high emotional potential is a major resource for political parties and religious elites.'[25] Furthermore, this process tends to be self-reinforcing. As rival communities are mobilized and state authority weakened, a situation can easily be reached where previously broad-minded people are polarized by fear. Speaking of ex-Yugoslavia, Michael Ignatieff observes that ethnic hostility was as much the result as the cause of the state's collapse: 'ethnic hatred is the result of the terror which arises when legitimate authority disintegrates.'[26]

What emerges from this is that (contrary to the expectations of the 'modernization' school of theories about nationalism) there seems not to be any simple historical trend via nationalist mobilization toward the advent of genuinely integrated nation-states. In many cases, the same forces that give rise to the demand for such states also prevent the supply, so that the unfortunate populations concerned are liable to suffer civil war, dictatorship and 'ethnic cleansing' and be no nearer at the end of it to the 'ethnic tranquillity' which Anthony Smith mentions as a condition of successful nation-states.[27] The familiar evils associated with nationalism, in other words, cannot always be rationalized as a Machiavellian price to be paid for stable nationhood: often they are a sign that nationhood does not exist and is not in prospect.

NATIONS UNDER THREAT?

> The peculiar balance between homogeneity and diversity that a few west European nations were able to strike ... was a phase – a passing phase ... (William McNeill)[28]

If the possibility of 'nation-building' seems increasingly chimerical, a final twist of the dialectic is putting in question the very nation-states that previously served as models and destabilized empires. For the nationalist rhetoric of identity and self-determination has returned from its world-wide career to rebound on those states themselves. As we have already observed, nationhood is fluid and liable to change, and some of the nations that had seemed most firmly established are now showing signs of fraying around the edges under the impact of demands for secession and cultural pluralism: demands fuelled by the very politics of identity that had previously given those states their strength. In the face of these demands, numerous commentators point to a 'contemporary crisis of the nation state' or ask whether such states are now 'at bay'.[29] Such language is, perhaps, exaggerated: the notion that established nations like France or the US are likely either to disintegrate or to lose themselves in some higher identity seems implausible. What does seem predictable, however, is that they will increasingly have to cope with conflicts over political identity between a national core and a variety of other groups, and that a new-found sense of insecurity on the part of the national core is not likely to make the situation any easier.

Taking a much longer historical perspective, William McNeill has argued in a striking monograph that the era during which a single people could expect to own 'their' state was a passing phase in world history, as 'time-bound and evanescent' as 'the classical ideal of a heroic and homogeneous citizenry' in Athens or Rome.[30] McNeill suggests that this classical ideal itself contributed, along with unprecedented demographic expansion and a military technology relying on mass infantry, to the West European national ideal of a united population in charge of their state, a formula that seemed in its heyday 'the supreme secret of politics – the sure and attested way of attaining power and wealth.'[31] This phase was in his view a rare exception to the historically normal model of polyethnic hierarchy in civilized societies. 'Civilised societies have nearly always subordinated some human groups to others of a different ethnic background.'[32] As the power generated by nationhood enabled European nations to build empires, new polyethnic hierarchies were established around the world, and then eventually reestablished in the European nation-states themselves, as the aftermath of empire, declining birthrates and immigration brought greater ethnic diversity.

While McNeill tends to equate nations with ethnic groups and to pay too little attention to the expansive and inclusive capacities of nationhood, much that he says is persuasive, and his argument that nation-states are reverting to the historic norm is, as he admits, disturbing. 'For those of us who value civic freedom and equality...the testimony of the past...ought to be troubling. Other civilised societies have almost always accepted and enforced inequality among the diverse ethnic groups of which they were composed.'[33] The norm (in other words) has not been multicultural equality, but a hierarchy of different statuses for different peoples within one polity.

We could add that such polities have not in the past aimed at being liberal democratic welfare states: and this point underlines the dilemmas posed for contemporary political theory (and practice) by its reliance on nationhood. Liberal democratic ideals need the nation state to provide the power and solidarity to give them political substance: but nation-states do not exist by nature, and although the myth of popular identity that constitutes them is very effective in destabilizing other forms of polity, it is all too liable to undermine itself. Its rhetoric is a perpetual invitation to the mobilization of subnational communal identities. Meanwhile the liberal democratic political agenda of participation, rights and social justice itself raises the stakes of political conflict and makes such mobilization still more appealing, since its rewards can be great. In other words, if I am right to stress a link between contemporary political theory and nationhood, this is not a position that gives grounds for complacency. What implications should political theorists draw from this argument? This will be the subject of my final chapter.

NOTES

1. E. Kedourie, *Nationalism*, 4th edition (Oxford, Blackwell, 1993) 104.
2. B. Parekh, 'Ethnocentricity of the Nationalist Discourse', *Nations and Nationalism* 1/1 (1995) 44.
3. L. Greenfeld, *Nationalism: Five Roads to Modernity* (Cambridge, Mass., Harvard University Press, 1992) Chapters 3 and 4.
4. e.g. A.B. Seligman, *The Idea of Civil Society* (New York, Free Press, 1992) 147, 160, 179; R. Rorty, *Contingency, Irony, and Solidarity* (Cambridge, Cambridge University Press, 1989) 61, 68; J. Gray, *Liberalisms: Essays in Political Philosophy* (London, Routledge, 1989) 240; J. Gray, *Post-Liberalism: Studies in Political Thought* (London, Routledge, 1993) 284, 328.
5. J. Breuilly, *Nationalism and the State* (Manchester, Manchester University Press, 1982) 381.
6. Breuilly, *Nationalism and the State*; P.R. Brass, *Ethnicity and Nationalism: Theory and Comparison* (London, Sage, 1991) *passim*.
7. 'Reflections on the History of European State-making', in C. Tilly (ed.), *The Formation of Nation States in Western Europe* (Princeton, Princeton University Press, 1975) 42.
8. M. Curti, *The Roots of American Loyalty* (New York, Columbia University Press, 1946) *passim*.
9. G. Orwell, *The Lion and The Unicorn: Socialism and the English Genius* (London, Secker and Warburg, 1941) 19.
10. A.D. Smith, 'State-Making and Nation-Building', in J. Hall (ed.), *States in History* (Oxford, Blackwell, 1986).
11. F. Fanon, *The Wretched of the Earth* (Harmondsworth, Penguin Books, 1967) 73–4.
12. J.A. Hall, 'Nationalisms: Classified and Explained', in *Daedalus* 122/3 (Summer 1993, Special Issue on 'Reconstructing Nations and States') 21. Cf. in the same issue M. Kramer, 'Arab Nationalism: Mistaken Identity' 197.
13. On the '*terrible simplification*' that was perpetrated in East-Central Europe during and after the Second World War, and that had the effect of making the successor states much more homogeneous, see K. Kumar, 'The 1989 Revolutions and the Idea of Europe', *Political Studies* XL/3 (1992) 444.
14. S. Kaviraj, 'Crisis of the Nation-state in India', *Political Studies* 42 (1994 Special Issue: 'Contemporary Crisis of the Nation State?' ed. J. Dunn) 129.
15. This is the principal message conveyed by Elie Kedourie in *Nationalism*.
16. M.R. Beissinger, 'Demise of an Empire-State: Identity, Legitimacy, and the Deconstruction of Soviet Politics', in C. Young (ed.), *The Rising Tide of Cultural Pluralism: The Nation-State at Bay?* (Madison, University of Wisconsin Press, 1993) 100.
17. C. Geertz, *The Interpretation of Cultures* (London, Hutchinson, 1973) 240.

18. Young, *The Rising Tide of Cultural Pluralism* 13, 14.
19. S. Zubaida, 'Nations: Old and New', *Ethnic and Racial Studies* 12/3 (1989) 337.
20. D.L. Horowitz, *Ethnic Groups in Conflict* (Berkeley, University of California Press, 1985) 567.
21. On earlier experiences of this kind within the Habsburg Empire, see M. Teich and R. Porter (eds), *The National Question in Europe in Historical Context* (Cambridge, Cambridge University Press, 1993) 213, 259–62.
22. Geertz, *Interpretation of Cultures* 260.
23. Geertz, *Interpretation of Cultures* 308.
24. Young, *Politics of Cultural Pluralism* 459.
25. Brass, *Ethnicity and Nationalism* 303.
26. M. Ignatieff, *Blood and Belonging: Journeys into the New Nationalism* (BBC Books and Chatto and Windus, London, 1993) 16.
27 Smith, 'State-Making and Nation-Building', 257.
28. W. H. McNeill, *Polyethnicity and National Unity in World History* (Toronto, University of Toronto Press, 1986) 84.
29. *Political Studies* 42 (Special Issue: 'Contemporary Crisis of the Nation State?'); Young (ed.), *The Rising Tide of Cultural Pluralism: The Nation-State at Bay?*
30. McNeill, *Polyethnicity and National Unity in World History* 35.
31. McNeill, *Polyethnicity and National Unity in World History* 56.
32. McNeill, *Polyethnicity and National Unity in World History* 6.
33. McNeill, *Polyethnicity and National Unity in World History* 82.

10. Nationhood and political theory

I have tried to show that in spite of the understandable disdain for nationalism shown by most recent anglophone political thinkers, contemporary political theory is deeply dependent on tacitly assumed nationhood. Even those theorists who take care to avoid setting their theories within the boundaries of the nation-state betray the same assumption by their lack of concern with the constitution of political power. Liberals who theorize international justice and human rights do not in general think of themselves as utopians whose ideals have no practical relevance; nevertheless they show little interest in the possible sources of the power that would be needed to implement such ideals. Remarkable as it may seem, many contemporary political theorists rarely think about the sources, costs and limitations of political power at all, tending to assume that popular, consensual, non-coercive power will be available as required. My claim has been that the missing link in these theories is provided by nationhood, which does in some cases generate collective power of a kind that makes aspirations to democracy, social justice and human rights seem within the bounds of possibility. The account of nationhood offered above suggested that the subtle web of mediations through which nationhood constitutes powerful political communities is peculiarly elusive, hard not only to analyse but even to perceive because it makes collective power seem natural and unproblematic.

I considered the possibility that the political community tacitly assumed within political theories need not be a national one, but might instead be bound by ties of patriotism that would fit better with liberal democratic commitments. It seemed, however, that in so far as a 'patriotic' political community could actually be purged of nationhood, what remained was either too weak to supply the necessary power or else (as in the militant patriotism of the classical republican tradition) no more congenial than nationalism to contemporary sensibilities. I suggested, finally, that the dependence of apparently universalist political theories upon particular nationhood is not only embarrassing but extremely unsafe, since nationhood is not in fact something that can be taken for granted. As a phenomenon it is quite rare, and contemporary trends point at least as strongly in the direction of 'nation-destroying' as of 'nation-building'.

If my arguments are sound, they must have implications for political theory, and in this final chapter I shall consider what those implications might be. As

114

we shall see, they are not straightforward, and do not (for example) lead to any general support for nationalism or a right to national self-determination. One effect is to underline an apparent contradiction between the universalist principles of contemporary political theory and the particular solidarities that support power to act on those principles. There are affinities here with recent discussions of relativism and foundationalism, but those discussions have had little to say about the constitution of collective power. In the first part of this chapter I shall consider three possible ways of dealing with this topic, each of them currently under exploration in political theory. In summary form, the three are as follows.

One response suggests that having realized the extent to which they were taking nation-states for granted, political thinkers should explicitly stop doing so, and should instead reformulate their ideas in terms of sub-national and supra-national structures.

A second proposes that political theorists should acknowledge their reliance upon the idea of the nation-state to the point of affirming nationhood as a universal value, and that they should explore ways of reconciling it with other commitments.

Thirdly, recognizing that the nation-state in terms of which they have been thinking is an idealized version of a kind of political community that exists only in certain times and places, political theorists might adopt an openly relativistic stance, for example developing a kind of 'national liberalism' instead of the cosmopolitan kind.

BENEATH AND BEYOND THE NATION-STATE

> Although it cannot be ensured that each nation will have its own state, all nations are entitled to a public sphere in which they constitute the majority. The ideal of the nation-state should therefore be abandoned in favour of another, more practicable and just. (Yael Tamir)[1]

For many (perhaps most) political theorists, the most attractive response to the arguments put forward above would be to say that if we have indeed been unconsciously building nationhood into our theories, then we should stop doing so and start thinking in different terms. Since most states are too ethnically diverse to conform closely to the national model, and since in any case modern political problems demand cross-national solutions, it is time we adapted our thinking to take account on the one hand of sub-national communities such as minority ethnic groups, and on the other of evolving supra-national structures like the European Union. In recent years, criticism of the ideal of the homogeneous nation-state and assertion of the value of group differences has come from a variety of different perspectives,[2] but for our present purposes a recent book by Yael Tamir provides the most interesting example of this sort of approach, because Tamir is explicitly concerned with nationhood and is prepared (with qualifications) to call herself a 'nationalist'.

As we saw earlier, Tamir understands 'nations' as *cultural* communities, and sets out to defend a 'liberal nationalism' that starts from the needs and interests of individuals but argues that among those needs and interests is belonging to a cultural community and being able to perpetuate its culture. Although she rejects the nation-state as an ideal, Tamir is acute in analysing the ways in which liberal theorists have unthinkingly assumed its existence. In a chapter on 'The Hidden Agenda: National Values and Liberal Beliefs', she argues in similar terms to those used earlier in the present study that liberal political theorists have taken for granted the closed political communities of nation-states when they assumed that distributive justice is restricted in its scope, that citizenship is typically a matter of birth rather than of choice and that political obligation can be assumed to follow from membership. She concludes that 'except for some cosmopolitans and radical anarchists, nowadays most liberals are liberal nationalists.'[3]

Interestingly, however, in spite of her own sympathy for nationalist claims, Tamir does not endorse this ideal, claiming that 'the era of homogeneous and viable nation-states is over (or rather, the era of the illusion that homogeneous and viable nation-states are possible is over, since such states never existed), and the national vision must be redefined.'[4] The enticing principle that every nation should have its own state has foundered on the rocks of boundary problems and oppression of minorities. Since it is impossible to implement the idea of national self-determination in the form of making every nation sovereign over its own territory, Tamir believes that we must rethink the principle in a form that abandons the ideal of the nation-state.

The alternative she suggests requires us to distinguish in theory and practice between two realms that the nation-state purports to link into one, the intimate realm of belonging to a cultural community, and the political realm of democratic self-government. 'Nations', defined purely in cultural terms, and 'states', purely political, can (she argues) be separated in such a way that the right of a nation to preserve its culture need not be united with the democratic right of a 'people' to rule their own state. Her ideal future is one in which the pretended 'nation-states' at present in existence cede authority in both directions, downwards to their constituent 'nations' in matters of culture, and upwards to regional structures where political matters like the economy, defence and the environment are concerned. The model Tamir appeals to is an idealized version of the European Union, sheltering minority nations like the Corsicans, Basques and Catalans under a benign supra-national umbrella. She admits that the current resurgence of unregenerate claims for national autonomy in Eastern Europe and the ex-Soviet Union may seem to point in the opposite direction, but she nevertheless claims that history is moving away from the nation-state. 'It seems safe to predict that these new states will seek to join regional organizations based on economic, strategic and ecological cooperation', sharing 'one army, one currency, one passport'.[5]

Although at one point Tamir denies that she is offering a panacea,[6] her conclusions are remarkably sanguine.

> Accepting the idea that national self-determination might be attained within a larger regional framework implies that political thought has entered a new age, in which the principle of national self-determination no longer provides the sole justification for political organization. It also challenges the belief that a stable political framework requires cultural, linguistic or religious uniformity.[7]

But this confidence is misplaced. The notion that political theory and enlightened political practice might dispense with nation-states and replace them with a combination of smaller communities and larger regional structures fails even more seriously than mainstream political theory to address the problem of the nation-state. That problem, as Tamir and others observe, is that so-called 'nation-states' very often fail to live up to their ideal of a fusion of political structure with affective community. However, the problem cannot be solved by taking apart the communal and the political aspects and dreaming of a rich plurality of semi-autonomous communities presided over by a benevolent but impartial regional authority. The most likely effect of any such attempt at a divorce between the communal and the political would be to further politicize communal identity, while depriving the political structure of the affective support it needs to be able to command allegiance.

Consider, to begin with, the level of the group, community or (in Tamir's terminology) cultural 'nation'. There is no reason whatever to suppose that the problems of boundaries and identification that occur at present at the level of the 'nation-state' could be solved by devolving rights and functions to these sub-groups, since devolution would actively provoke such problems. Supporters of this kind of pluralism generally seem to suppose that although individuals should be able to choose whether or not to identify themselves with a group with which they have some connection, there are no particular difficulties about what groups exist or who might belong to them. As long as the groups remain informal this may be so, but in so far as they acquire an official status, 'group rights' and claims on public resources, there are incentives for new groups to form and for individuals to claim membership of them. Just as supposed nations have been proliferating ever since it has made political sense to frame demands in national terms, so a political environment that rewards cultural sub-groups will call such groups into existence and encourage them to use their political leverage in competition with others.

Similarly, existing groups are likely to vary in size in response to the political and economic incentives available. Even where the groups concerned appear to be defined by blood rather than by subjective identification, group boundaries are not fixed because individuals of mixed blood may or may not be counted as part of a group. In Canada, for example, there are many people with some Indian blood, and one does not have to be unduly cynical to suppose that they are more likely to find that worth acknowledging if it gives them a title to share in group rights. Eugeen Roosens, who compared ethnic identification among Indians in Canada and Bolivia, found that a 'rise of ethnic self-affirmation under the banner of "own culture", "the right to remain different", "own tradition", and "being an independent people", is related to a broader political context that rewards such self-affirmation in one way or another.'[8] Such processes are dynamic, and (following the example of classic nationalist movements within, say, the Habsburg Empire) each group that succeeded in organizing itself and securing group rights would create pressure on other sections of the population to follow suit, intensifying conflicts of interest between different groups, not to mention power-struggles inside them.

The weakest feature of the notion that problems inherent in the politics of communal identity can be solved by displacing them from the level of the nation-state is the assumption that an overarching political structure *without* the support of communal identity will be able to contain these conflicts and preside over them with benign impartiality. Most theorists who think along these lines tacitly assume the survival of existing states, and do not consider the strains to which they would be subjected by the wholesale granting of group rights.[9] Tamir's approach makes the gap in the argument particularly obvious because she explicitly envisages the end of nation-states as currently understood, and the advent of a congeries of cultural nationalities under the political wing of something along the lines of the European Union. The question being begged is, where is such a regional body to get the power to take over the state's responsibilities for defence and the economy?

Optimism on this subject can be rapidly dispelled by looking at the record and prospects of the European Union itself. There seems little immediate prospect even of a single currency for all the member states, let alone of a single foreign policy or a single army able to take effective military action.[10] Where cooperation does exist, this has been achieved through the familiar mechanisms of horse-trading between the structures that do possess political power, namely the component states. Far from rendering nation-states redundant, the European Union to date has (as Alan Milward and others have argued)[11] been developed by those nation states to serve national purposes, and while some states whose nationhood is shaky have undoubtedly found it a convenient corset, the stiffening in that corset has been provided by the collective power of those states that do represent nations.

It is of course possible that in the very long term the situation will change, and that living within the framework of common institutions will create among the population of the European Union a new European identity.[12] But if that were to happen, and the new political structure were indeed to be able to act as a single unit in critical situations, this would imply not that the European Union had superseded the nation-state but that it had itself turned into a nation-state on a grander scale: a development most likely to be brought about, if history is any guide, by confrontation with a common enemy. In other words, if a regional structure is to be able to wield the power necessary to replace nation-states, it will itself have to generate that power through popular identification of the political structure as 'ours'. If such a project can be made to work it simply moves the problems of particular loyalties and exclusiveness to a different level.[13]

I argued in an earlier chapter that the secret of nationhood lies in its ability to mediate between individuals and between different aspects of reality, and that it is that mediating role that has enabled modern nation states to mobilize their populations and to generate collective power. Nations (in so far as they exist) have been able to make artificial political structures seem natural and have made the state *our* state. These benefits are not universally available, and the power so generated has often been used for undesirable purposes. But schemes such as that offered by Tamir for replacing the nation-state underestimate its political significance in generating power, achieving peace within large territories by integrating potentially hostile groups in loyalty to a single political community, and mobilizing that loyalty to defend the territory. Looking around the world, we can see that these are not achievements that can be taken for granted.

DEFENDING THE NATION-STATE

It may be advantageous, from a universal point of view, that people have national loyalties. (David Miller)[14]

If we must dismiss the notion that we can plausibly reformulate political theories in ways that deliberately avoid their current reliance on the nation-state, should we perhaps proceed in entirely the opposite direction? Should we not only bring this suppressed element in contemporary political thinking to the light of day, but also affirm nationhood as something that is compatible with humane politics and has value in itself? A number of political thinkers have made moves in this direction,[15] but the most powerful theoretical defence of nationality and the nation-state has come from David Miller. I shall argue in this section that although Miller has raised the philosophical level of discussion of these topics, as a contribution to political theory his position is open to serious objections.

Miller sets out in a series of publications to defend both 'nationality' (which corresponds more or less to what I have termed 'nationhood') and the nation-state. His position is complex, though he himself at one point sums it up in three linked claims, firstly that belonging to a nation may be an essential part of a person's identity, secondly that nations are ethically significant in that we have special duties to fellow-nationals, and thirdly that nations have a prima facie claim to political self-determination. The emphasis of my discussion will fall upon this third claim. 'Nations' as Miller understands them are constituted by belief, but also embody historical continuity; they are communities that can take action, that are linked to a particular homeland and that have distinguishing traits that mark them off from one another. While acknowledging that there is always a large element of myth in national identity and the stories nations tell of themselves, Miller argues that this is a source of strength rather than a weakness, since its malleability makes national identity potentially inclusive and capable of benign reinterpretation.[16]

The overwhelming advantage of the nation-state, in Miller's view, is that it can draw support from strong attachments and loyalties that actually exist. His approach here (directed against the Kantian rationalism common among political philosophers) explicitly follows the philosophical style of David Hume, offering 'a philosophy which, rather than dismissing ordinary beliefs and sentiments out of hand unless they can be shown to have a rational foundation, leaves them in place until strong arguments are produced for rejecting them.'[17] Given that national identities and allegiances exist, it makes sense to build them into political philosophy, provided that (as Miller argues) the objections usually raised against them are not insuperable. If (as is generally agreed) modern societies tend towards social atomization and stand in need of more communal solidarity, then it should be acknowledged that 'nationality is *de facto* the main source of such solidarity', the most powerful force capable of inducing individuals to share burdens and make sacrifices for the common good.[18] Even ethical universalists have grounds for favouring nationality, because 'it creates communities with the widest feasible membership, and therefore with the greatest scope for redistribution in favor of the needy'.[19] Socialists in particular should acknowledge the benefits of this kind of national solidarity.[20]

In contrast to the attempts of Tamir and others to detach nationhood from states, Miller mounts a robust defence of the nation-state, arguing that both state and nation benefit from the combination. From the point of view of statehood, 'the key element is recognition of the role played by trust in a viable political community'.[21] A state will be less dependent upon force and better able to pursue a common good where it presides over a population united by shared attachment to a national community. Conversely, a nation needs political self-determination not only to preserve its culture but to be able to act as a community.[22] Miller recognizes that there is room for dispute about the precise limits of national sovereignty, and that there may be good reasons for transferring powers in various areas to supra-national bodies, but he is prepared to defend 'a presumption...in favour of national sovereignty'.[23]

Recognizing that these views are uncongenial to most contemporary political theorists, Miller identifies and confronts the objections that are likely to be raised against them. There is, for example, what he calls the 'liberal' objection, to the effect that nation-states are inconsistent with cultural pluralism, because a single national culture will suppress all differences. In answer to this, Miller denies that national identity has to mean cultural homogeneity.[24] Nationality (which is, as he stresses, something malleable, not fixed) can be an inclusive, overarching identity that incorporates sub-groups with distinctive religious and cultural traits. Indeed, he argues (turning the argument the other way round) a plural society that has distinct cultural groups but lacks such an overarching identity is unlikely to have sufficient mutual trust to be a liberal one. 'What best meets the needs of minority groups is a clear and distinct national identity which stands over and above the specific cultural traits of all the groups in the society in question.'[25]

This may appear to be similar to Tamir's ideal of an impartial political authority looking after the common affairs of a collection of sub-nationalities, but there is a crucial difference: where Tamir assumes that this overarching polity can somehow subsist without being itself the focus of national loyalty, Miller argues that such a polity needs to be sustained by inclusive national attachments if it is to be able to cope with internal diversity. The argument is framed in general terms, but the examples Miller has in mind are evidently the US and a somewhat reformed Britain.

Miller devotes considerable attention to answering objections from philosophers accustomed to think about obligations and duties in abstract and universalist terms, and worried by the idea that those whom we recognize as our fellow-nationals have greater moral claims on us than the rest of humanity. In the end, his defence relies on Humean realism. 'Philosophers may find it restricting that they have to conduct their arguments about justice with reference to national identities at all. My claim is that unless they do they will lose contact entirely with the beliefs of the people they seek to address'.[26] He could have added that, as we saw earlier, most political philosophers in any case smuggle in tacit assumptions about the significance of national boundaries under the cloak of universalist language.

The most obvious practical objection, which Miller seeks to address and deflect, is what he calls 'the Balkan objection'. 'This claims that the principle of nationality cannot in practice be realised, but meanwhile the belief that it can leads to endless political instability and bloodshed',[27] because of the impossibility of making state boundaries correspond to the conflicting claims of different groups. Since a good deal of what was said in the last chapter could be summed up under the heading of this 'Balkan objection', Miller's answer is of particular interest here, and it is at this point, I believe, that the flaws in his argument can be detected.

Not that this is immediately apparent, for his treatment of this topic seems eminently reasonable. In the first place, he denies that the principle of national self-determination is a licence for secession by any group that feels dissatisfied, since what is at stake is national identity, not just individual will. 'When we encounter a group or community dissatisfied with current political arrangements the question to ask is not "Does this group now want to secede from the existing state?" but "Does the group have a collective identity which is or has become incompatible with the national identity of the majority in the state?"'[28] In many cases, dissatisfaction among an ethnic group or subnationality could be rectified within existing borders, since there is some degree of overarching nationality in common. Arguments for secession only come into play where existing borders contain different nations 'with radically incompatible identities'.[29] Even here, however, a prima facie case for secession must be limited by numerous qualifications, to do with feasible borders, the viability of the successor states and whether new minorities would be created.

> ...the principle of nationality does not generate an unlimited right to secession. What it says is that national self-determination is a good thing, and that states and their constitutions should be arranged so that each nation is as far as possible able to secure its common future. Since homogeneous nation-states are not everywhere feasible, often this will require second-best solutions...[30]

Miller's argument does more justice than most to the complexities of nationhood as a phenomenon, to the way in which overarching versions of it can defuse potential ethnic conflicts, and to its vital role in mobilizing allegiance to a humane political order. Nevertheless I shall argue that his conclusions are unacceptable because the terms in which he frames his argument (following the conventions of contemporary political philosophy) are simply too abstract. In spite of his professed commitment to Humean realism, his theory does not take enough account of the realities of political power, and leads as a result to over-optimistic conclusions.

Consider, for example, his defence of nationality against the objection that it is a conservative or reactionary idea. Drawing attention to the mythical elements in national identity, he argues that they allow such identity to be 'reshaped to meet new challenges and new needs'.[31] Now, if nationality is malleable in this way, it certainly follows that there is no necessary connection with conservatism, but it is not clear why liberals should necessarily find this reassuring: Hitler reshaped German nationality in a way that was far from conservative. Evidently, what Miller has in mind is the reshaping of British national identity in a liberal and anti-racist direction that has taken place since the end of the British Empire.[32] This is certainly a highly significant example, but one from which it is unsafe to generalize, partly because numerous national identities all round the world are at present being reshaped in what appears to be a fascist direction 'to meet new challenges', and partly because there can be no guarantee that the transformation of British identity will continue to move in a liberal direction. Implicit in Miller's optimism are expectations about the future distribution of power within Britain, as well as about the sort of challenges the nation is likely to face.

Implicit assumptions about power are much more apparent in his treatment of the issue of secession. As we have seen, he lays down a number of conditions that must be met if a claim to secede is to be regarded as valid, conditions that read like rules intended to guide an omnipotent international tribunal adjudicating on where borders should be fixed. Indeed, the discussion is framed in terms which suggest that we should approach the question as if we were the members of some such tribunal, with the authority to decide borders and the power to enforce our decisions.[33] The catch is, however, that no such tribunal exists, and to talk as if it did exist evades the crucial problem, which is that the normal way for borders to be established and for questions of secession to be settled is not by legal process but by the exertion of power, often by war. Like most contemporary political philosophers, Miller pays no attention to the role of war in politics, and writes as if there were in existence an impartial, effective, world-wide legal order within which disputes could be settled on rational grounds and judgements enforced upon the parties. But for that to exist there would have to be something approaching a world-wide state, presumably sustained by a global version of the overarching national loyalty which (by Miller's own account) is needed to make existing states effective legal orders. In other words, he is in essence making the mistake for which he has himself criticized the universalists, that is, the mistake of neglecting the uneven realities of power and solidarity, and tacitly assuming that the human race forms a single political community within which collective power is on tap on a global scale.

Paul Hirst has observed (in the course of a notable meditation on the political thought of Carl Schmitt) that 'all legal orders and laws have an

"outside"…they rest on a politics which is prior to and not bound by law.'[34]
What is missing from Miller's argument is a sense of this 'outside', of the
power that must underpin law and of the messily Machiavellian reality of
national claims and border-changes. The point has been underlined in practice in the territory that was formerly Yugoslavia, where in spite of pretensions to international legality and proclamations by 'the international community' that forcible seizures of territory would not be recognized, it gradually became obvious that claims to national self-determination would be
settled as they have so often been settled, by force and at the cost of civil war
and 'ethnic cleansing'. This was easily predictable on the basis of historical
experience, so that it is not unreasonable to expect a political philosopher
who defends claims to national self-determination (particularly one who
takes his stand on Humean realism) to take account of their likely consequences.

How would Miller's theory be affected if he did take these factors into
account? He would, I think, have to scale down his theoretical ambition to
suit the messiness of politics. His aim of establishing general principles to
guide our practical responses to national disputes would seem less realistic.
He could still argue persuasively for the value of nationality and the nation-
state in so far as these blessings are actually established (perhaps parting the
veil of national myth for a moment to acknowledge some of their historic
costs); he could point out that political thinkers who hold up their hands in
horror at any concessions to nationalism are themselves taking for granted
the existence of political communities that are in fact nation-states; but he
would be much more hesitant about espousing national self-determination as
a principle to be adopted for general use in contemporary politics. Where the
likely costs are so great and the benefits so uncertain, a follower of Hume
would surely be inclined to try to dampen nationalist aspirations rather than
to encourage them. Above all, he would have to come to terms with the
contradiction inherent in the link between the impulse to reorder the world
according to principles of justice (by deciding, for instance, which claims for
national self-determination are allowable) and the patchy and highly contingent solidarities that in some places generate enough power to give such
schemes the deceptive appearance of feasibility.

NATIONAL LIBERALISM?

If the existence of the nation-state is a tacit premise of contemporary political
theory, it seems that we cannot deal with this embarrassment either by drop-
ping the premise of nationhood (as Tamir would have us do) or by defending
it in general terms, as Miller does. The political principles which philoso-

phers are accustomed to advance as if they were indeed legislating for all humanity appear to be linked to an idealised version of a particular form of political community that does not exist everywhere, and that cannot be promoted everywhere without undermining those very same principles. Might it be the case, though, that one way of coming to terms with the inconsistency of this position could be the adoption of an explicitly relativist stance, arguing that although the principles enunciated by contemporary political philosophers are universal in form, they are in reality not for export?

This suggestion, though subversive, is not by now particularly novel, since doubts about universality and even explicit defences of relativism have become increasingly common among political philosophers in recent years. The thinkers in question may not have acknowledged the tacit place in their theories of a national political community, but they have become much more inclined to refer to 'our' traditions, leaving readers to guess just who 'we' may be. There are degrees of explicitness in this retreat from universalism, and Rawls's position is particularly ambiguous. For all its apparent universality, the *Theory of Justice* was (as we saw earlier) implicitly limited by the boundaries of nation-states, and Rawls's later writings not only specify that he is talking about 'closed societies' recruited by birth[35] but seem to link his theory specifically with America by talking about articulating principles inherent in 'our public political culture'.[36] However, Rawls is evidently unwilling to accept that the reach of his principles could actually be limited to any particular nation state, and he specifically denies imputations of historicism and relativism.[37]

Other political philosophers, those who identify themselves as 'post-modern', have been more willing to embrace relativism and to think of liberalism as 'our' contingent heritage, though the 'us' in question remains vague and the link with nationhood is tacit or actually denied. There is an intriguing difference of tone and style here (surely linked to national differences) between the most prominent representatives of post-modern liberalism in the US and Britain, Richard Rorty and John Gray. Rorty's position, while apparently a retreat into relativism, seems in fact to have some kinship with the kind of universalist American patriotism that we encountered earlier in the case of John Schaar, while John Gray's follows a long tradition of taking English-British nationhood for granted while avoiding talking of it as such.

Rorty's overt position, while not explicitly linked to nationhood, is an uninhibited assertion not only of relativism but of 'ethnocentrism'. Rejecting 'the rationalist rhetoric of the Enlightenment', he ridicules 'the Enlightenment notion that there is something called a common human nature, a metaphysical substrate in which things called 'rights' are embedded, and that this substrate takes moral precedence over all merely "cultural" superstructures.'[38] What we must recognize is that universal principles like human equality and human rights are simply what 'we Western liberals' happen to believe. Nevertheless, Rorty seems to manage to have things both ways, asserting that liberal 'ideals may be local and culture-bound, and nevertheless be the best hope of the species.'[39] Although Rorty does not explicitly link his principles with American nationhood, Michael Billig may be right to detect in his writings that characteristically American form of nationalism that (in John Schaar's words) gives America 'a teaching mission' to the rest of the world. As Billig says,

> This nationalism, unlike some older forms, does not speak with narrow ferocity for the nation. Instead, it draws its moral force to lead the nations from its own proclaimed reasonableness. The global ambitions are to be presented as the voice of tolerance ('our' tolerance), even doubt ('our' doubt, 'our' modesty).[40]

Billig's critique seems to imply that it is Rorty's ethnocentrism that is at fault rather than his universalism, or at any rate that the latter is fatally tainted by the former. It might be argued, however, that the reverse is the case. Thus (for example) the British post-modern philosopher John Gray appears more willing to accept the practical consequences of withdrawing from universalist positions. According to him, once the philosophical task of clearing away hubristic universalist illusions has been fulfilled, 'the theorist returns to his own inheritance and tradition – in our case, to the practice of liberty'.[41] Who are 'we' here? As we saw earlier, Gray refuses to talk in terms of nationhood, which he associates with images of ethnic and religious homogeneity. But when he criticizes the market liberalism of the New Right for neglecting 'the historical basis of political allegiance in a shared history and a common culture',[42] he seems to be getting close to acknowledging the links between liberal civil society and certain specific nation-states.

Evidently there is already a strong tendency in current political philosophy for universalist political principles to be regarded as a particular and limited historic inheritance belonging to a not very clearly identified 'us', the 'we' in question often referring to 'the West' but with hints of the nation (American or British) in the background. There is of course much to be said on the other side of the question, but my concern here is not with the philosophical controversy about the foundations of universalist liberalism, but with a different and more political kind of foundation, the collective power that is the essential foundation if universal principles are to be more than utopian ideals. For if the argument of this book is accepted, it seems that universalist principles are politically as well as (*ex hypothesi*) culturally relative in that they presuppose a kind of political community that exists nowhere in perfect form, approximations to which are rather rare and quite fragile.

Nation-states of any kind, let alone of the relatively stable and relaxed kind conducive to liberal practices, are themselves a particular and limited inheritance. As we saw, Liah Greenfeld argued persuasively that liberalism was from the start bound up with nationhood as developed in England and transmitted to the US, whereas German and Russian nationalism were conceived in specifically anti-liberal forms.[43] Since those early days, the contingencies of history have given rise (perhaps temporarily) to a number of liberal nations, but also to a larger number whose embattled nationhood is not hospitable to liberalism, and an indeterminate number of states that are not nation-states at all and have little prospect of becoming so. Once again, the implication seems to be relativistic: our sort of principles and practices, linked to our sort of nationhood, are good for us; it may even be (if we are reluctant to give up universalist aspirations) that in an ideal world they would be good for everyone; but since their export requires not just the adoption of ideas but the emergence of a particular kind of political community that cannot be constructed to order, to advocate them universally seems to make little sense. In other words, even if we are prepared to brave the post-modernists and be 'ethnocentric' in asserting the values of liberalism, we seem to be limited to a kind of 'national liberalism'.

Should we mind? After all, in the nineteenth century a position approximating to this 'national liberalism' was quite common, with liberals assuming that it would be some time before the blessings of freedom and representative government as enjoyed in Britain could be extended to the rest of the world, and seeing the growth of national consciousness as part of the process that qualified benighted populations to enjoy them. The difference between then and now lies not only in the nineteenth century's unashamed sense of the effortless superiority of more 'advanced' nations, but above all in the weakening (particularly in Europe: much less in the US) of the faith in progress that justified such patronage. No doubt 'we Western liberals' are in many ways much better off without the belief that we are simply a few steps ahead on a road that all mankind will tread after us. But the alarming implication of losing faith in progress is that the survival and perpetuation of liberal principles and practices can no longer be taken for granted. If they are a specific inheritance, linked to the existence of a rather rare kind of political community which may be increasingly challenged by demographic shifts, then awkward questions arise about reconciling the principles themselves with the arrangements that might be necessary if such communities are to be defended and passed on to future generations.

The most thorny of such questions concern the boundaries of nationhood, that is to say, matters of immigration and citizenship. These are matters that many political philosophers choose either to ignore or to discuss in universalist terms – in terms of human rights, for example. But if we are to take seriously the idea that universal ideals such as human rights are not a self-evident delivery of general human reason but are in fact a specific heritage tied to a particular kind of national political community, is there not a contradiction between the demands of the universal ideal on the one hand and of its specific substrate on the other? Political philosophers seem to be committed simultaneously to universalist principles, and to the defence of political communities that reproduce themselves partly by restricting access to membership. For the point about citizenship is that it is limited, and citizenship of liberal nations is particularly highly prized and jealously guarded. As Rogers Brubaker says, 'in global perspective, citizenship is a powerful instrument of social closure, shielding prosperous states from the migrant poor.'[44] In sharp contrast alike to the trend of modernization and to the tone of liberal theory, citizenship also remains an ascribed status, and hardly anyone, however liberal and universalist their principles, argues that borders should be opened to the point of making it a matter simply of individual choice.[45]

But does the connection between nationhood and liberal democratic principles imply that immigration and/or admission to citizenship should be not only restricted but highly selective? In a wide-ranging study of national integration, Anthony Birch points to the cases where such integration has failed in the face of ethnic or religious plurality. Faced with the 'many examples of bloodshed and suffering caused by communal conflict', Birch questions the desirability of policies that tend to increase such plurality. 'A government that diversifies its society by authorising immigration that will have that effect is necessarily creating a potential social problem'.[46] Along that line of thought, however, lie policies deeply discordant with liberal principles, like the White Australia policy which up to 1972 sharply restricted Asian immigration. At the time, an Australian minister of immigration offered this defence: 'We seek to create a homogeneous nation. Can anyone reasonably object to that?'[47]

The universalist terms in which liberal political philosophies have often been framed imply obligations to humanity in general that are hard to reconcile with borders of any kind, let alone with ethnic selection of potential citizens. A persuasive attempt to justify closure in liberal terms has been made by Frederick Whelan, though the fact that it is not explicitly framed in terms of nationhood helps Whelan to avoid some of the most painful dilemmas. In the first place, there is, he observes, a 'protectionist' case (put forward, with variations, from Thomas Jefferson to Bruce Ackerman) for limiting immigration into liberal societies. Being rare, such societies could be threatened by uncontrolled immigration, particularly of migrants from non-liberal political cultures. Even universalists can therefore accept the need to protect liberal niches from which the blessings of liberalism may spread to the rest of the world.[48]

Whelan has a number of other arguments, none of which directly appeals to nationhood, though all come close to it. For example, if liberals accept (as they must) that states are unavoidable, and that a plurality of states is prefer-able to a single and possible despotic world state, then they must also accept borders, the distinction between citizens and aliens, and some degree of closure. Again, if human beings are to enjoy the blessings of democracy, people in general must be divided into self-governing 'peoples' with rela-tively stable membership; the more mutual trust is required for democracy, and the closer to a community that 'people' is to be, then the more imperative the need for a distinction between members and aliens.[49]

Though impressive, Whelan's argument avoids confronting two sources of difficulty. Crucially, his attempt to justify particular privileges in universal terms fails to take account of the uneven distribution around the world of political benefits and the nationhood to which they are linked. He says, for example,

> To act out of loyalty to one's own state, fellow citizens, or community, is indeed in a sense to exhibit a kind of preference for the interests of one's own group over those of outsiders. But statism, democracy, and community are themselves univer-sal principles: no one should be stateless; everyone can and should enjoy demo-cratic citizenship and community membership, somewhere.[50]

This assumes that there is no reason why the kind of benefits from which we are excluding aliens should not be equally available everywhere. But as we have seen, nationhood and the kind of politics it makes possible exist only patchily at present and in the foreseeable future.

The other nettle he fails to grasp is that of ethnic and cultural plurality, and the question whether (in the interests of preserving liberal nations where they do exist) consideration should be given to the ease or difficulty of integrating potential citizens. No doubt one of the reasons why he does not consider this question is that (like the vast majority of political theorists writing in English) he is based in the US and has its experience particularly in mind. Now, there is no doubt that the defence of US borders against the vast numbers of those who would like to enter poses serious practical problems and causes considerable heartache to liberals, but the US is spared some dilemmas to do with the preservation of nationhood because of the kind of nation it is. As we saw earlier, nationhood is a complex phenomenon that mediates between ethnic and political factors, and the balance between the two varies in different national traditions. As a pluralistic nation of immigrants in which (by now) ethnicity plays a comparatively small role in nationhood compared with allegiance to the Constitution and participation in the American way of life, the US faces little serious threat to its identity. In spite of current anxieties about the challenge posed to American English by Spanish-speaking immigrants, Americans can afford to be fairly relaxed about their nation's ability to assimilate newcomers, for the cultural power of the American way of life is felt across the globe.

The other nations that currently shelter liberal democratic politics find themselves faced with more difficult problems in trying to balance the extension of citizenship against the preservation of nationhood. Interestingly, this is the case regardless of the balance between political and ethnic elements in their national traditions. A comparison of French and German conduct of policy toward immigration and citizenship (undertaken by Rogers Brubaker) shows that if the more ethnic German understanding of nationhood gives rise to one sort of problem, the more political French tradition creates others.

Brubaker emphasizes that both countries have complex traditions, within which nationhood has been conceived in different ways for different purposes. Nevertheless, whereas the dominant French tradition has a political, republican understanding of Frenchness, the dominant tradition in Germany has understood Germanness in ethnic terms, essentially as something inherited from one's parents. Although Germany has played host to vast numbers of 'guestworkers' since the Second World War, and in spite of the fact that the country had until recently extraordinarily liberal provisions giving a right of asylum to refugees from persecution, German citizenship law continues to reflect this ethnic understanding of Germanness, with the result that (for example) 'ethnic Germans' from the former Soviet Union can claim citizenship, whereas the descendants of guest-workers long settled in Germany cannot. Naturalization is possible, but difficult.[51] Defending this situation, Kay Hailbronner observes that Germany (unlike the US) is not a nation of immigration, and that decisions about whom to admit to citizenship must be determined by the interests of the nation. Ethnic and religious plurality is liable to cause tensions, and 'political communities...will entrust power only to those persons from whom they can expect a feeling of solidarity and loyalty, only to those who can be expected to share common interests.'[52]

The German law of citizenship and the ethnic understanding of nationhood on which it is based have been much criticized, usually in the name of a more political and less ethnic conception. As we saw earlier, Jürgen Habermas maintains that 'The identity of a political community...depends primarily upon the constitutional principles rooted in a political culture'.[53] It is interesting, therefore, to turn to France, which has a dominant tradition of nationhood that is indeed political and explicitly republican, and to find that this generates dilemmas of its own. Like other countries, France does of course have ethnic nationalists, who have in recent years had some political prominence. Its dominant tradition, however, is that connected with the emancipatory and universalist political ideal of the Great Revolution: a secular nation of republican citizens with a civilizing mission to the rest of mankind. Unlike Germany, it has a tradition of welcoming immigrants and expecting to assimilate them, and has citizenship laws under which (in sharp contrast to the situation in Germany) those born in France of immigrant stock either gain citizenship automatically or can easily acquire it.[54]

This situation may seem analogous to that in the US. The crucial difference, however, is that the French can no longer assume that others will gratefully recognize their '*mission civilisatrice*'. France is not only beset from outside by the spread of Franglais and Americanism, but challenged from within by Muslims of North African origin who do not necessarily want to be assimilated. Some of those automatically granted citizenship (and therefore called up for military service) have tried to obtain release from this onerous privilege. For others, the secular tradition of the French republic conflicts with the religion that is an essential part of their own identity. The resulting backlash against immigrants is fuelled not only by racism but also by a more political outrage at affronts to the sacred traditions of the republic, and an anxious debate continues about how Frenchness and the republican principles that are part of it can best be preserved.[55] Evidently the existence of Habermas's 'constitutional patriotism' may not be enough by itself to bind newcomers with strong identities of their own into the nation.

The point underlined by this discussion of immigration and citizenship laws is that a post-modern retreat into relativism does not ease the tension within liberal political theory between universal principles and particular loyalties. Even if it is the case that universalist liberal principles are only 'our' principles, it is still true that 'our' principles (or at any rate the principles of most Western political theorists and publics) are universalist principles. Although, as I have argued, the political plausibility of those principles rests upon the power generated within national political communities, there is nevertheless an acute, flagrant and inescapable contradiction between the demands of our principles on the one hand and the requirements of our national political communities on the other. We can see this dilemma at its sharpest if we consider a case in which universalist Western values are linked with a form of nationhood that is exclusive, ethnic and embattled – the case of Israel.

In an interesting essay concerned particularly with the second-class status accorded to Arab citizens within Israel, Yoav Peled observes that 'the problem of maintaining viable democratic regimes in ethnically divided societies promises to be one of the more salient political issues of the new world order', but suggests that Israel is a 'successful example of a democratic yet deeply divided society', and that the partial citizenship rights enjoyed by Arab citizens are among the secrets of that success.[56] Peled suggests that in Israeli political culture, three different kinds of principles have been influential: republicanism, liberalism and ethnicity. The model of citizenship for Jews is provided by 'ethnorepublicanism', a combination of historic Jewish ethnicity with the republican ideals of Zionism, including 'a powerful connection between military and civic virtue'.[57] Full republican citizenship, including the ever-present obligation of military service, is granted only to Jews (including the millions of recent immigrants) and denied to the indigenous Arab population. Nevertheless Israel is not simply an ethnic state, for the Arabs within Israel proper (as opposed to the occupied territories) possess what Peled calls 'liberal citizenship', not sharing in 'the common good' but 'secure in their possession of what we consider essential human and civil rights',[58] including the right to vote. These rights are not negligible, particularly in a part of the world where the normal form of government is dictatorship. As Peled agrees, this arrangement is far from ideal. Israel's Arab citizens are not content with their inferior status, and the clash between equality and discrimination, between liberal universalism and ethnic and religious particularism, is a constant source of dispute in Israel. Nevertheless, he maintains that in practice this two-tier citizenship has worked, not least in leading Israel's Arab citizens (unlike those in the occupied territories) 'to conduct their struggle within the constitutional framework of the state, rather than against it', and thereby helping Israeli democracy to survive.[59]

The Israeli case sharpens and dramatizes the issues considered here. However imperfectly, Israel has given some expression to liberal democratic values in a part of the world where these cannot be taken for granted, and the rights enjoyed by Arab citizens bear witness to that. On the other hand, that oasis of comparative liberalism and democracy exists because there is a national political community with the mutual trust to be able to defend itself without and to cope with division and debate within. Given the military situation there is nothing hypothetical about questions of allegiance and loyalty, so that to protect the political community, citizenship must be limited in ways that run counter to many of the values of the community itself.

This is a case that illustrates Whelan's 'protectionist' argument for limitations on citizenship but makes it look less palatable, for its criteria are seen to be ethnic, and there seems no reason to suppose that the oasis of comparative liberalism it protects will eventually irrigate the surrounding desert. As has been stressed earlier, of course, nations vary, and nationhood does not always have as strong an ethnic component as in the Israeli case (certainly not in Britain, let alone in the US). Nevertheless, as nation-states acquire more and more diverse populations, William McNeill's prediction that the future is more likely to see a return to 'polyethnic hierarchy' than an advance to multicultural equality seems empirically plausible, and throws into even stronger relief the dilemmas of nationhood with which political theorists must somehow come to grips. In the concluding section I will consider how this might be done.

REALISM, UTOPIANISM AND MUDDLING THROUGH

> We are too fluent in the language of universal principles and exclusion, and can
> only stammer the speech of deep diversity. (Charles Taylor)[60]

Questions of citizenship, immigration, and how liberal democratic states
should respond to religious and ethnic pluralism dramatically illustrate the
central problem which nationhood poses for contemporary political theory as
well as for political practice. This problem is a tension between universalism
and particularism: not only the philosophical tension between universal validity and particular cultural traditions, but rather the political dilemmas that
arise because general humanitarian principles and projects presuppose a power
base sustained by particular solidarity, while the maintenance of that power
base contradicts the very principles it renders plausible.

It is true that this is not a new problem. In essentials it is the same as the
problem Rousseau wrestled with in the mid-eighteenth century when he was
formulating the theory of the *Social Contract*. Ideally, it might seem, universal justice would flow from the general will of all mankind. However, a
general will can exist only where there is solidarity, which weakens as it is
extended. Only in a small, exclusive political community can a general will
to justice have any force, at the cost of obligations to all humanity. The
conflict between man and citizen is inescapable.[61] I have argued that in the
two centuries since Rousseau worried about it, this dilemma of the universality of ideals versus the particularity of collective power has been in some
ways softened and concealed by the advent of nationhood, which made
possible collective power on a much larger scale than the tight little cities of
republican tradition, and at the same time made 'peoples' seem natural and
power easy to come by.

However, the dilemma remains, and it has in some ways been heightened
by the very success of some nations in generating collective power, since this
has encouraged optimism on the part of philosophers, publics and politicians
about what is politically feasible. There is an ever-increasing demand for the
implementation of humanitarian principles, and therefore for the collective
power and political will born of popular solidarity, but this is happening at
the very moment when it is becoming apparent that modernization does not
automatically create nations, and may indeed tend to weaken those that
actually exist. The collective power of national solidarity seems ever more
necessary, not only to back ambitious political agendas of global justice,
democratization and human rights, but also to withstand the fissiparous tendencies of rival religious and ethnic solidarities.

How can political theorists cope with the links and tensions between universal ideals, collective power and national solidarity? I shall consider three

possible ways of trying to arrive at a consistent solution, two of them self-consciously 'realistic' and one openly 'utopian', though my conclusion will be that none is satisfactory and that in the end we will have to live with these dilemmas rather than hoping to escape from them into consistency.

NATIONALIST REALISM

One apparently realistic solution to the problem that cosmopolitan principles and projects call on the power provided by national solidarity would resolve this dilemma by opting decisively for the nation, affirming the priority of power and solidarity and relegating universal principles to a subordinate place. This is more or less the position defended by Roger Scruton in his powerful essay, 'In Defence of the Nation'. Attacking the non-national account of the liberal state given by Bhikhu Parekh (which I discussed earlier) Scruton argues that liberal states depend upon national loyalty as a source of unity and territorial defence. He points out that liberalism on its own provides no account of social membership or social unity, and accuses liberals of a 'refusal to perceive men and nations as they are.'[62] We saw earlier that his own account of nationhood (though complex and subtle) stresses the aspects of exclusiveness and real or imagined kinship that liberals find particularly uncongenial.

Scruton makes a strong case for the dependence of liberal institutions upon the nation-state. However, his tone is explicitly anti-liberal, giving the impression that in any clash between the two, the demands of national loyalty will trump those of liberal principles. Part of his intention is indeed to challenge the liberal orthodoxy within political theory, and he speaks of censorship by the 'thought police'.[63] Now, it is true that the deep taboos associated with such subjects in the British and American academic worlds have led to the neglect of important questions to do with the membership and perpetuation of political communities as well as to over-simplified caricatures of nationhood. Brian Barry has rather more charitably attributed the dearth of serious discussion of questions to do with nationhood in post-war political theory to the understandable fears of a generation of intellectuals who had vivid experiences of Nazism.[64] For that generation (as perhaps for a new generation looking with horror at the atrocities currently being carried out across the world in the name of national liberation) nations and nationalism have been strongly associated with fear of the power of dark myths and popular irrationality, and of the danger that liberal reason would be overwhelmed by such atavistic urges.

In a piece written a few years ago I argued that liberals had good reason to be alarmed by open discussion of such themes, not so much because of the weakness of reason faced with myth but because liberalism itself has always relied upon a structure of myths about nature and humanity, myths which can easily be attacked from the Right in the name of sociological realism.[65] At the time I conceded too much down to earth realism to those who invoke ties of blood against myths about humanity because (like most political theorists) I underestimated the complexity of nationhood as a phenomenon. One of the main theses of this book, by contrast, is that nations baffle analysis precisely because of the way in which they hold together so many different areas of experience; in particular, they mediate between the natural and the artificial. Nations are certainly not 'natural' in the sense of being primordial realities, but nevertheless one of their most important features is that they *seem* profoundly natural to their members, and often to others as well. Their naturalness is a matter of myth, and none the less powerful for that.

Now, from the point of view of those with liberal commitments, this mythical quality of nationhood can in some respects have advantages, as David Miller argues.[66] Far from being stuck fast in the blood and soil of primordial ethnicity, the classic nations are quasi-natural communities that have in the course of time greatly expanded the loyalties and sympathies of their members, producing overarching communities like Britain, France or the US that transcend narrow ethnic identities but still pull off the feat of seeming part of the natural order. Powerful emotional attachments are thereby channelled in a comparatively humane direction, and (at any rate where the well-established liberal nations are concerned) supporters of nationhood can often see themselves as being on the same side as anti-racist campaigners in endeavouring (as Richard Rorty says) 'to expand our sense of "us" as far as we can'.[67]

That said, the fact remains that there are serious objections to the idea of trying to articulate a political philosophy of nationalism, besides the stumbling-block of non-universalizability that we have already considered in relation to Miller's theory. These problems arise precisely from the element of myth in nationhood. The delicate structure of mediation involved does not lend itself to philosophical dissection. Attempts to turn anything so ambiguous and elusive into clear and distinct ideas usually lead to scepticism; but a more sympathetic nationalist philosophy that affirmed myths and gave clear articulation to the vague and shifting sentiments of nationhood could easily encourage populist simplifications and turn into a fascist ideology. It is not the case (though liberals often seem to think this) that any defence of nations and nationalism amounts to low-level fascism. Nevertheless, since nationhood does involve a larger or smaller element of mythical kinship, open stress on nationhood can hardly do other than highlight potentially explosive questions of ethnicity and race. In other words, the affirmation that because nationhood grounds liberal institutions and projects, it must therefore take precedence over them, is an unstable position with a tendency to slide in a direction that would make nationhood *less* able to sustain liberalism. There may be good reasons for feeling that the sleeping dogs of nationalism are best left to lie. There is no straightforward route, then, from recognizing the immense political significance of nationhood to theorizing it as a political philosophy.

Parts of these deep waters have been explored by Scruton himself, who recognizes the importance of myths in sustaining the conservative society he wishes to defend as well as acknowledging the incongruity of a philosophical defence of myth.[68] He even plays with the idea of Plato's 'Noble Lie', remarking that a conservative 'might in all conscience seek to propagate the ideology which sustains the social order, whether or not there is a reality that corresponds to it.'[69] While this is a deeply disconcerting idea, with echoes of de Maistre and Maurras (not to mention Mussolini),[70] it would be a great mistake to suppose that it is only those who stray from the path of universalist liberalism who find themselves in that kind of mire. As Scruton remarks (and as I have argued at length elsewhere) liberalism also has its myths, which 'can be defended to the elite which recognizes them, but only in terms which must be concealed from the common man.'[71] Judgements have to be made about which myths are likely to do more damage in a particular time and place. Under most modern conditions, to resolve the contradiction between universal principles and particular solidarities unambiguously in favour of the latter would be to purchase consistency at the cost of a far more extreme retreat from liberalism than most of us would be prepared to countenance.

If this is so, should we perhaps turn our back on nationalist 'realism' with all its dangers, and opt firmly for universalist utopianism? If it is indeed the power generated in some states by national solidarity that makes ideals like universal human rights appear politically realizable, could we not resolve this dilemma by taking the opposite route to Scruton's? Instead of looking for political realism, and allowing universal principles to become diluted and constrained by considerations of power and its sources, why should not we (as political theorists) stick explicitly to the articulation of what is in principle right, leaving to politicians the messy business of trying to give those principles some practical realization?

UNIVERSALIST UTOPIANISM

This is an option that may at first sight seem attractive to many political theorists, but not (I suspect) one that is feasible in the modern climate of political activism. Just as the previous option is unstable, tending to tilt the balance too far against liberalism, so the explicitly utopian approach to politics that was for centuries an established genre has become increasingly difficult to sustain. Perhaps it was possible once upon a time to depict a just society with no notion of trying to dictate practical policy, engaging in the enterprise either as an intellectual exercise or to encourage one's contemporaries to repent of their sins. But contemporary accounts of justice, democracy and rights can hardly avoid being intended and read as programmes for action. As Rawls famously observed at the start of the *Theory of Justice*, using a revealing analogy,

> A theory however elegant and economical must be rejected or revised if it is untrue; likewise laws and institutions no matter how efficient and well-arranged must be reformed or abolished if they are unjust.[72]

Theorists inclined in this direction may nevertheless deny that it is any of their business to worry about power and its sources in particular solidarity, since the principles they offer are intended simply as criteria for what is right, and as guiding ideals for those individual voters or politicians who have a conscience. However, it is not possible to dodge questions of power by thinking in these terms or (like the Christians mentioned in Weber's essay on 'Politics as a Vocation') doing what is right and leaving the results to Providence.[73] Consider (for example) the justice of a world-wide redistribution of goods, or of a total lack of discrimination between citizens and other human beings in the award of social security benefits. Principles such as these may in Hobbes' terms be binding '*in foro interno*; that is to say,...to a desire they should take place: but *in foro externo*; that is, to the putting them in act, not always.'[74] This is not a matter of sincerity versus hypocrisy, but rather that to ignore the conditions of power is self-defeating. Any politician, government or state that made a serious attempt to implement these principles of justice would rapidly lose power, and with it the chance to take any further action on the same principles.

It seems that neither the liberal utopian nor the conservative nationalist position can resolve our dilemma. But is there perhaps another, more plausible version of realism that might do so? If (as I have argued) modern liberal democratic ideals depend for their plausibility on the collective power generated by national loyalties that are inconsistent with the ideals themselves, why not get rid of the contradiction by retreating from every one of its conflicting elements: the ambitious universalist ideals, the overweening collective power and the dangerously quasi-fascist national solidarity? This kind of solution appeals to those Oakeshottian conservatives for whom virtually all modern political theory and political programmes consist of gigantic exercises in hubris. From this point of view, universalist principles and particular solidarities are equally dangerous to the real business of politics, which is practical improvisation to keep the peace in a world where Hobbesian threats are ever-present.

NEO-HOBBESIAN REALISM

This position is stated by John Gray in an eloquent diatribe against contemporary (and particularly American) liberalism. As we saw earlier, he is extremely wary of Scrutonian affirmations of nationhood in the face of increasing ethnic and cultural pluralism. However, the preferred liberal way of coping with pluralism, a vision of a neutral state protecting the right of its citizens to choose their identity from a menu of different cultures, seems to him shallow, since it trivializes deep, inherited and potentially explosive communal differences into 'chosen lifestyles'.[75] What he recommends instead is a '*modus vivendi* pluralism', that is to say, a practice of looking for political accomodations between opposed communities. This would entail the abandonment of universalist notions of justice and rights in favour of negotiations designed to achieve as stable a settlement as possible between the communities concerned. No such settlement can be permanent, and none can be dictated by abstract considerations of justice or rights. 'Stability in political life is an artifice, necessarily fragile and easily destroyed, of the political arts – of statecraft',[76] and the 'animating value'[77] of the political arts is peace.

As a means of avoiding the tensions between universal principles and particular solidarity that we have been considering, this neo-Hobbesian version of 'realism' may seem quite attractive, particularly to those of a sceptical turn of mind. It may be argued that for a number of reasons (including the constraints of the global economy) the ideals of liberalism are unrealizable, and that the mobilization of popular power behind national banners is an evil not only because of the difficulties it causes in increasingly plural societies, but also because it encourages damaging illusions about what politics can be expected to achieve. The fact is, however, that neo-Hobbesianism is not nearly as realistic in its account of power as it purports to be. No doubt there are a great many situations around the world in which peace can only be procured through the kind of pragmatic negotiation described by Gray, which is indeed made more difficult by popular mobilization on the one hand and considerations of abstract justice on the other. But no-one whose highest priority was really peace would choose that model. The most stable of modern states, those in which internal peace seems most assured, are precisely those that do belong to a 'people'. The Hobbesian power to maintain the peace goes along with the mobilization of nationhood, and in the case of nations such as Britain, France and the US, that nationhood is itself linked to a greater or lesser extent with the affirmation of universal liberal principles. No doubt this is a messily contradictory situation, but there is no virtue in pretending that it does not exist, or in ignoring the constraints on political activity set by the existence of liberal democratic mass publics.

MUDDLING THROUGH

The achievement of clarity and consistency is a goal to which political theorists are professionally committed. This is a natural and laudable commitment, but if there is any truth in the case I have been arguing in the course of this book, it may be something of a handicap in coming to terms with nationhood. Not only is nationhood itself a sticky cobweb of myths and mediations, guaranteed to repel the clear-minded: worse, it seems also to be the source of a fundamental contradiction in political theory. By generating collective power, and thereby establishing islands of firm ground among the treacherous swamps of political affairs, nationhood has allowed Western liberal theorists and publics to develop ideals and principles that are global in scope and to perceive them as projects rather than utopias. But the problem is not only how to build Jerusalem among the swamps. More seriously, we cannot easily reconcile the commitment to build Jerusalem for all mankind with the defence of our own patch of firm ground (which may itself be subject to erosion).

I doubt whether there is any consistent and coherent answer to this dilemma. Before we give up in despair, however, we should remember an analogous dilemma, the problem of reconciling with modern Western political principles the inescapable place of war in politics. Within contemporary thought, the dominant impulse is to condemn violence and coercion out of hand. Political thinkers, secure behind the borders of stable and well-guarded states, find war morally unacceptable. In a sense this attitude may be shallow, since it is undoubtedly true that without their command of military force liberal states would have been overwhelmed long since by those who did not share such scruples. It is well that liberals should be aware of this, but it does not follow that the only intellectually honest position they can adopt is one of gung-ho militarism. True 'realism' in this area means recognizing the demands of conflicting considerations, and something similar is true in the case of nationhood.

I began this study by looking at the reasons why post-war political theorists have been unsympathetic to nationalist ideals and unwilling to concede a general right to national self-determination. The course of the argument will not actually lead us to reverse those judgements, but it should, I believe, help us to acknowledge the significance of nationhood for political theory and make us more willing to think seriously about its implications. In so far as this book contains a recommendation, it is that we should pay more regard than is usual to the tangled complexity of these issues. We need to recognize the complexity of nationhood itself, and its patchiness as a phenomenon that does not exist everywhere and is never uniform. We need to pay more attention to political power, and particularly to the sources and limits of its more consensual collective versions. Above all, we need to be aware of the inescapably conflicting demands made upon us, on the one hand by the humane ideals of universal rights, justice and democracy, and on the other by the stability and preservation of those nation-states that have in some imperfect degree given civilized politics an earthly home.

NOTES

1. Y. Tamir, *Liberal Nationalism* (Princeton, Princeton University Press, 1993) 150.
2. e.g. Will Kymlicka, *Liberalism, Community and Culture* (Cambridge, Cambridge University Press, 1989); Iris Marion Young, 'Polity and Group Difference: A Critique of the Ideal of Universal Citizenship', *Ethics* 99 (January 1989) 250–74.
3. Tamir, *Liberal Nationalism* 139.
4. Tamir, *Liberal Nationalism* 3.
5. Tamir, *Liberal Nationalism* 165.
6. Tamir, *Liberal Nationalism* 157.
7. Tamir, *Liberal Nationalism* 166.
8. E.E. Roosens, *Creating Ethnicity: The Process of Ethnogenesis* (London, Sage, 1989) 104.
9. e.g. Young, 'Polity and Group Difference' 261; Kymlicka, *Liberalism, Community, and Culture* 215. For some acid comments (based on comparisons with the havoc wrought by communal bonds in seventeenth century Europe) on the current fashion for pluralist communitarianism among political theorists, see J. Dunn, 'Political Obligation', in D. Held (ed.), *Political Theory Today* (Cambridge, Polity, 1991) 29.
10. M. Mann, 'Nation-States in Europe and Other Continents: Diversifying, Developing, Not Dying', in *Daedalus* 122/3 (Summer 1993) (issue on 'Reconstructing Nations and States') 120–33.
11. A.S. Milward, *The European Rescue of the Nation-State* (London, Routledge, 1992).
12. There may be an analogy with the emergence of British nationhood in the eighteenth century, but note that although British identity incorporated the Scots and Welsh, it was dominated by an expanded Englishness. Might there one day be a European nation incorporating smaller sub-nations, dominated by an expanded Germanness, with the French playing the Scottish role and an unassimilable England on the outside, playing the role that unassimilable Ireland played in Britain?
13. Cf. V. Harle, 'Nationalism – No! Metanationalism – Yes!', *History of European Ideas* 15/1–3 (1992) 39–45.
14. D. Miller, 'In Defence of Nationality', *Journal of Applied Philosophy* 10/1 (1993) 4. Miller's views are more extensively developed in his book *On Nationality* (Oxford, Oxford University Press, 1995).
15. N. MacCormick, 'Is Nationalism Philosophically Credible?', in W. Twining (ed.), *Issues of Self-Determination* (Aberdeen, Aberdeen University Press, 1991); J. Schwarzmantel, *Socialism and the Idea of the Nation* (London, Harvester Wheatsheaf, 1991).
16. Miller, 'Defence of Nationality', 3–10.
17. Miller, 'Defence of Nationality', 4.

18. Miller, 'Defence of Nationality', 9.
19. D. Miller, 'The Ethical Significance of Nationality', Ethics 98/4 (July 1988) 661.
20. D. Miller, *Market, State and Community: Theoretical Foundations of Market Socialism* (Oxford, Oxford University Press, 1989) 237–45; D, Miller, 'In What Sense must Socialism be Communitarian?', *Social Philosophy and Policy* 6/2 (1988–9) 68–70. This argument is challenged in B. Parekh, 'The Politics of Nationhood', in *Cultural Identity and Development in Europe*, ed. K. von Benda-Beckman and M. Verkuyten (London, University College of London Press, forthcoming).
21. D. Miller, 'The Nation-State: a Modest Defence', in C. Brown (ed), *Political Restructuring in Europe: Ethical Perspectives* (London and New York, Routledge, 1993) 141.
22. Miller, 'The Nation-State: a Modest Defence' 144.
23. Miller, 'The Nation-State: a Modest Defence' 146.
24. Though by emphasizing shared national traits he does seem to imply that fellow-nationals have to be similar in themselves, rather than being united by sharing a common world. See Chapter 7 above.
25. Miller, 'Defence of Nationality', 11.
26. Miller, 'Defence of Nationality', 14. Cf. Miller, 'The Ethical Significance of Nationality', *passim.*
27. Miller, 'Defence of Nationality', 12.
28. Miller, 'Defence of Nationality', 12.
29. Miller, 'Defence of Nationality', 13.
30. Miller, 'Defence of Nationality', 13; Miller, 'The Nation-State: a Modest Defence' 152–8.
31. Miller, 'Defence of Nationality', 9.
32. Miller, 'Defence of Nationality', 9.
33. e.g. '...we would need to be convinced that the territory demanded by G did not contain minorities...' (Miller, 'The Nation-State: a Modest Defence', 157).
34. P. Hirst, *Representative Democracy and its Limits* (Cambridge, Polity, 1990) 112. Cf. M. Walzer, 'The Moral Standing of States: A Response to Four Critics', in C.R. Beitz, M. Cohen, T. Scanlon and A.J. Simmons (eds), *International Ethics* (Princeton, Princeton University Press, 1985) 234–7; J. Leca, 'Welfare State, Cultural Pluralism and the Ethics of Nationality', *Political Studies* XXXIX (1991) 568–74.
35. J. Rawls, *Political Liberalism* (New York, Columbia University Press, 1993) 12.
36. J. Rawls, 'Justice as Fairness: Political not Metaphysical', in S. Avineri and A. de-Shalit (eds), *Communitarianism and Individualism* (Oxford, Oxford University Press, 1992) 192.
37. J. Rawls, 'The Domain of the Political and Overlapping Consensus', in D. Copp, J. Hampton and J.E. Roemer (eds), *The Idea of Democracy* (Cambridge, Cambridge University Press, 1993) 260.
38. R. Rorty, 'On Ethnocentrism: A Reply to Clifford Geertz', *Michigan Quarterly Review* 25 (1986) 530.
39. Rorty, 'On Ethnocentrism', 532.
40. M. Billig, 'Nationalism and Richard Rorty: The Text as a Flag for *Pax Americana*', *New Left Review* 202 (November–December 1993) 82.
41. J. Gray, *Post-Liberalism: Studies in Political Thought* (London and New York, Routledge, 1993) 321.
42. J. Gray, *Beyond the New Right: Markets, Government and the Common Environment* (London and New York, Routledge, 1993) viii.
43. L. Greenfeld, *Nationalism: Five Roads to Modernity* (Cambridge, Mass., Harvard University Press, 1992).
44. R. Brubaker, *Citizenship and Nationhood in France and Germany* (Cambridge, Mass., Harvard University Press, 1992) x; Cf. T. Hammar, *Democracy and the Nation State: Aliens, Denizens and Citizens in a World of International Migration* (Aldershot, Avebury, 1990).
45. Brubaker, *Citizenship and Nationhood* 31. For a range of views on this issue, see the essays collected in B. Barry and R.E. Goodin (eds), *Free Movement: Ethical Issues in the*

Transnational Migration of People and of Money (New York, Harvester Wheatsheaf, 1992).

46. A.H. Birch, *Nationalism and National Integration* (London, Unwin Hyman, 1989) 230–31.
47. Quoted in J.H. Carens, 'Nationalism and the Exclusion of Immigrants: Lessons from Australian Immigration Policy', in M. Gibney (ed.), *Open Borders? Closed Societies? : the Ethical and Political Issues* (Westport, Conn., Greenwood Press, 1988) 45.
48. F.G. Whelan, 'Citizenship and Freedom of Movement: An Open Admissions Policy?', in Gibney (ed.), *Open Borders? Closed Societies?* 16–23.
49. Whelan, 'Citizenship and Freedom of Movement', 23–34.
50. Whelan, 'Citizenship and Freedom of Movement', 34.
51. Brubaker, *Citizenship and Nationhood* 75–8, 82, 168.
52. K. Hailbronner, 'Citizenship and Nationhood in Germany', in W.R. Brubaker (ed.), *Immigration and the Politics of Citizenship in Europe and North America* (London and Lanham, Md., University Press of America, 1989) 75.
53. J. Habermas, 'Citizenship and National Identity: Some Reflections on the Future of Europe', *Praxis International* 12/1 (April 1992) 7, 17.
54. Brubaker, *Citizenship and Nationhood* 14, 35–46, 81, 111.
55. Brubaker, *Citizenship and Nationhood* 139–64; S. Hoffmann, 'Thoughts on the French Nation Today', *Daedalus* 122/3 (Summer 1993) 63–79; N.C. Moruzzi, 'A Problem with Headscarves: Contemporary Complexities of Political and Social Identity', *Political Theory* 22/4 (1994) 653–72.
56. Y. Peled, 'Ethnic Democracy and the Legal Construction of Citizenship: Arab Citizens of the Jewish State', *American Political Science Review* 86/2 (June 1992) 432.
57. Peled, 'Ethnic Democracy' 434.
58. Peled, 'Ethnic Democracy' 434. For some apposite reflections, see C. Taylor, *Reconciling the Solitudes: Essays on Canadian Federalism and Nationalism* (Montreal and Kingston, McGill-Queens University Press, 1993) 176–7.
59. Peled, 'Ethnic Democracy' 440.
60. C. Taylor, *Reconciling the Solitudes: Essays on Canadian Federalism and Nationalism* (Montreal and Kingston, McGill-Queens University Press, 1993) 200.
61. J.J. Rousseau, *Political Writings* ed. C.E. Vaughan, Vol. I (Oxford, Blackwell, 1962) 452–3; *Emile*, trans. B. Foxley (London, J.M. Dent, 1911) 7–8.
62. R. Scruton, 'In Defence of the Nation', in Scruton, *The Philosopher on Dover Beach* (Manchester, Carcanet, 1990) 323. Scruton's remarks are aimed at Bhikhu Parekh's essay, 'The "New Right" and the Politics of Nationhood', in N. Deakin (ed.), *The New Right: Image and Reality* (London, The Runnymede Trust, 1986).
63. Scruton, 'In Defence of the Nation' 304.
64. B. Barry, 'Self-Government Revisited', in D. Miller and L. Siedentop (eds), *The Nature of Political Theory* (Oxford, Oxford University Press, 1983) 122–3.
65. M. Canovan, 'On Being Economical with the Truth: Some Liberal Reflections', *Political Studies* XXXVIII (1990) 5–19.
66. Miller, 'Defence of Nationality' 9.
67. R. Rorty, *Contingency, Irony and Solidarity* (Cambridge, Cambridge University Press, 1989) 196. I have explored this line of thought in M. Canovan, '"Breathes There the Man, With Soul so Dead…": Reflections on Patriotic Poetry and Liberal Principles', forthcoming in J. Horton and A. Baumeister (eds), *Politics and Literature* (London, Routledge, 1996). Cf. T. Modood, *Not Easy Being British: Colour, Culture and Citizenship* (Stoke on Trent, Runnymede Trust and Trentham Books, 1992) 85–6.
68. R. Scruton, *The Meaning of Conservatism*, second edition (London, Macmillan, 1984) 190.
69. Scruton, *Meaning of Conservatism* 140.
70. For acute comments, see J. Rayner, 'Philosophy into Dogma: The Revival of Cultural Conservatism', *British Journal of Political Science* 16/4 (1986) 466–73.
71. Scruton, *Meaning of Conservatism* 191. Cf. Canovan, 'On Being Economical with the Truth' 9–19.

72. J. Rawls, *A Theory of Justice* (Oxford, Oxford University Press, 1972) 3.
73. M. Weber, 'Politics as a Vocation', in *From Max Weber: Essays in Sociology*, ed. H.H. Gerth and C. W. Mills (London, Routledge and Kegan Paul, 1948) 120.
74. T. Hobbes, *Leviathan*, ed. M. Oakeshott (Oxford, Basil Blackwell, 1960) 103.
75. J. Gray, 'After the New Liberalism', *Social Research* 61/3 (1994) 725.
76. Gray, 'After the New Liberalism' 731.
77. Gray, 'After the New Liberalism' 732.

Bibliography

Ackerman, B., *Social Justice in the Liberal State* (New Haven, Yale University Press, 1980).

Alter, P., *Nationalism* (London, Edward Arnold, 1985).

Anderson, B., *Imagined Communities: Reflections on the Origin and Spread of Nationalism* (London, Verso, 1983).

Arendt, H., *The Human Condition* (Chicago, University of Chicago Press, 1958).

Arendt, H., *The Origins of Totalitarianism* (London, Allen and Unwin, 1967).

Armstrong, J.A., *Nations Before Nationalism* (Chapel Hill, University of North Carolina Press, 1982).

Asad, T., 'Multiculturalism and British Identity in the Wake of the Rushdie Affair', *Politics and Society* 18/4 (1990) 455–80.

Avineri, S. and de-Shalit, A. (eds), *Communitarianism and Individualism* (Oxford, Oxford University Press, 1992).

Barber, B., *Strong Democracy – Participatory Politics for a New Age* (Berkeley, University of California Press, 1984).

Barry, B., 'Self-Government Revisited', in D. Miller and L. Siedentop (eds), *The Nature of Political Theory* (Oxford, Oxford University Press, 1983).

Barry, B., *Democracy, Power and Justice: Essays in Political Theory* (Oxford, Clarendon Press, 1989).

Barry, B., *Theories of Justice* (London, Harvester Wheatsheaf, 1989).

Barry, B. and Goodin, R.E. (eds), *Free movement: Ethical Issues in the Transnational Migration of People and of Money* (New York, Harvester Wheatsheaf, 1992).

Barth, F. (ed.), *Ethnic Groups and Boundaries: the Social Organization of Culture Difference* (London, George Allen and Unwin, 1969).

Beissinger, M.R., 'Demise of an Empire-State: Identity, Legitimacy, and the Deconstruction of Soviet Politics', in C. Young (ed.), *The Rising Tide of Cultural Pluralism: The Nation-State at Bay?* (Madison, University of Wisconsin Press, 1993).

Bellamy, R., *Liberalism and Modern Society: An Historical Argument* (Cambridge, Polity, 1992).

Beran, H., *The Consent Theory of Political Obligation* (London, Croom Helm, 1987).

Berry, C., *The Idea of a Democratic Community* (Hemel Hempstead, Harvester Wheatsheaf, 1989).

Billig, M., 'Nationalism and Richard Rorty: The Text as a Flag for *Pax Americana*', *New Left Review* 202 (Nov.–Dec. 1993) 69–84.

Birch, A.H., *Representation* (London, Pall Mall, 1971).

Birch, A.H., *Nationalism and National Integration* (London, Unwin Hyman, 1989).

Brass, P.R., *Ethnicity and Nationalism: Theory and Comparison* (London, Sage, 1991).

Breuilly, J., *Nationalism and the State* (Manchester, Manchester University Press, 1982).

Brubaker, R., *Citizenship and Nationhood in France and Germany* (Cambridge, Mass., Harvard University Press, 1992).

Buchanan, A., *Secession: the Morality of Political Divorce from Fort Sumter to Lithuania and Quebec* (Boulder, Westview Press, 1991).

Burke, E., 'An Appeal from the New to the Old Whigs', in *Works of the Right Honourable Edmund Burke* (London, Holdsworth and Ball, 1834) Vol. I.

Burke, E., *Reflections on the Revolution in France*, ed. C.C. O'Brien (Harmondsworth, Penguin, 1968).

Canovan, M., 'People, Politicians and Populism', *Government and Opposition* 19/3 (1984) 312–27.

Canovan, M., 'On Being Economical with the Truth: Some Liberal Reflections', *Political Studies* XXXVIII (1990) 5–19.

Canovan, M., *Hannah Arendt: A Reinterpretation of her Political Thought* (Cambridge, Cambridge University Press, 1992).

Canovan, M., '"Breathes There the Man, With Soul so Dead…": Reflections on Patriotic Poetry and Liberal Principles', forthcoming in J. Horton and A. Baumeister (eds), *Politics and Literature* (London, Routledge, 1996).

Carens, J.H., 'Nationalism and the Exclusion of Immigrants: Lessons from Australian Immigration Policy', in M. Gibney (ed.), *Open Borders? Closed Societies? : the Ethical and Political Issues* (Westport, Conn., Greenwood Press, 1988).

Chapman, J.W. and Shapiro, I., (eds), *Democratic Community, Nomos* XXXV (New York and London, New York University Press, 1993).

Cherniavsky, M., *Tsar and People: Studies in Russian Myths* (New Haven and London, Yale University Press, 1961).

Cobban, A., *The Nation State and National Self-Determination* (London, Collins, 1969).

Cole, J.W. and Wolf, E.R., *The Hidden Frontier: Ecology and Ethnicity in an Alpine Valley* (New York, Academic Press, 1974).

Colley, L., 'Whose Nation? Class and National Consciousness in Britain 1750–1830', *Past and Present* 113 (1986) 97–117.

Colley, L., *Britons: Forging the Nation 1707–1837* (New Haven, Yale University Press, 1992).

Copp, D., Hampton, J. and Roemer, J.E. (eds), *The Idea of Democracy* (Cambridge, Cambridge University Press, 1993).

Crick, B., 'The English and the British', in B. Crick, (ed.), *National Identities – the Constitution of the United Kingdom* (Oxford, Blackwell, 1991).

Cunningham, H., 'The Conservative Party and Patriotism', in R. Colls and P. Dodd (eds), *Englishness: Politics and Culture 1880–1920* (London, Croom Helm, 1986).

Curti, M., *The Roots of American Loyalty* (New York, Columbia University Press, 1946).

Dahl, R.A., *Democracy and its Critics* (New Haven, Yale University Press, 1989).

Daniels, N. (ed.), *Reading Rawls* (Oxford, Blackwell, 1975).

Dann, O. and Dinwiddy, J. (eds), *Nationalism in the Age of the French Revolution* (London, Hambledon Press, 1988).

Debray, R., 'Marxism and the National Question', *New Left Review*, 105 (Sept.–Oct. 1977) 25–41.

Dietz, M.G., 'Patriotism', in T. Ball, J. Farr and R.L. Hanson (eds), *Political Innovation and Conceptual Change* (Cambridge, Cambridge University Press, 1989).

Dresser, M., 'Britannia', in R. Samuel (ed.), *Patriotism: The Making and Unmaking of British National Identity* Vol. III (London, Routledge, 1989).

Dunn, J., *Political Obligation in its Historical Context* (Cambridge, Cambridge University Press, 1980).

Dunn, J., 'Political Obligation', in D. Held (ed.), *Political Theory Today* (Cambridge, Polity, 1991).

Dunn, J. (ed.), *Democracy: the Unfinished Journey* (Oxford, Oxford University Press, 1992).

Dworkin, R., 'Liberalism', in S. Hampshire (ed.), *Public and Private Morality* (Cambridge, Cambridge University Press, 1978).

Ergang, R.A., *Herder and the Foundations of German Nationalism* (New York, Octagon, 1976).

Fanon, F., *The Wretched of the Earth* (Harmondsworth, Penguin Books, 1967).

Fichte, J.G., *Addresses to the German Nation* (Chicago and London, Open Court, 1922).

Filmer, R. (ed. P. Laslett), *Patriarcha and Other Political Works* (Oxford, Blackwell, 1949).

Furtado, P., 'National Pride in Seventeenth Century England', in R. Samuel (ed.), *Patriotism: The Making and Unmaking of British National Identity* Vol. I (London, Routledge, 1989).

Galeotti, A.E., 'Individualism, Social Rules, Tradition: the Case of Friedrich A. Hayek', *Political Theory* 15/2 (1987) 163–81.

Geertz, C., *The Interpretation of Cultures* (London, Hutchinson, 1973).

Gellner, E., *Thought and Change* (London, Weidenfeld and Nicholson, 1964).

Gellner, E., *Nations and Nationalism* (Oxford, Blackwell, 1983).

George, D., 'The Right of National Self-determination', *History of European Ideas* 16/4–6 (1993) 507–13.

Gierke, O., *Natural Law and the Theory of Society 1500–1800* (trans. E. Barker) (Boston, Beacon Press, 1950).

Goodin, R., *Reasons for Welfare: The Political Theory of the Welfare State* (Princeton, Princeton University Press, 1988).

Goulbourne, H., *Ethnicity and Nationalism in Post-Imperial Britain* (Cambridge, Cambridge University Press, 1991).

Gould, C., *Rethinking Democracy: Freedom and Social Cooperation in Politics, Economy and Society* (Cambridge, Cambridge University Press, 1988).

Graham, G., 'A Refutation of Nationalism', in G. Graham, *Politics in its Place* (Oxford, Oxford University Press, 1986).

Graham, K., *The Battle of Democracy: Conflict, Consensus and the Individual* (Brighton, Wheatsheaf, 1986).

Gray, J., 'The Politics of Cultural Diversity', *The Salisbury Review* (September 1988) 38–45.

Gray, J., *Liberalisms: Essays in Political Philosophy* (London, Routledge, 1989).

Gray, J., 'Conservatism, Individualism and the Political Thought of the New Right', in J.C.D. Clark (ed.), *Ideas and Politics in Modern Britain* (Houndmills, Macmillan, 1990).

Gray, J., *A Conservative Disposition: Individualism, the Free Market and the Common Life* (London, Centre for Policy Studies, 1991).

Gray, J., *New York Times Book Review* (September 13, 1992) 26.

Gray, J., *Beyond the New Right: Markets, Government and the Common Environment* (London, Routledge, 1993).

Gray, J., *Post-Liberalism: Studies in Political Thought* (New York and London, Routledge, 1993).

Gray, J., 'After the New Liberalism', *Social Research* 61/3 (1994) 720–35.

Green, T.H., *Lectures on the Principles of Political Obligation* (London, Longmans, 1941).

Greenfeld, L., *Nationalism: Five Roads to Modernity* (Cambridge, Mass., Harvard University Press, 1992).

Greenleaf, W.H., *Order, Empiricism and Politics* (London, Oxford University Press, 1964).

Habermas, J., *The New Conservatism: Cultural Criticism and the Historians' Debate* (ed. and trans. S.W. Nicholson) (Cambridge, Polity, 1989).

Habermas, J., 'Citizenship and National Identity: Some Reflections on the Future of Europe', *Praxis International* 12/1 (1992) 1–18.

Habermas, J. (interviewed by M. Haller), *The Past as Future* (Lincoln, Nebraska, University of Nebraska Press, 1994).

Habermas, J. and Michnik, A., 'Overcoming the Past', *New Left Review* 203 (Jan./Feb. 1994) 3–16.

Hailbronner, K., 'Citizenship and Nationhood in Germany', in W.R. Brubaker (ed.), *Immigration and the Politics of Citizenship in Europe and North America* (London and Lanham, Md., University Press of America, 1989).

Hall, J.A., 'Nationalisms: Classified and Explained', *Daedalus* 122/3 (1993) 1–28.

Hallis, F., *Corporate Personality: A Study in Jurisprudence* (Oxford, Oxford University Press, 1930).

Hammar, T., *Democracy and the Nation State: Aliens, Denizens and Citizens in a World of International Migration* (Aldershot, Avebury, 1990).

Harle, V., 'Nationalism – No! Metanationalism – Yes!', *History of European Ideas* 15/1–3 (1992) 39–46.

Harvie, C., *The Lights of Liberalism: University Liberals and the Challenge of Democracy 1860–86* (London, Allen Lane, 1976).

Hayek, F.A., *Law, Legislation and Liberty* (London, Routledge, 1973).

Hayward, J., *The One and Indivisible French Republic* (London, Weidenfeld and Nicholson, 1973).

Helgerson, R., *Forms of Nationhood: The Elizabethan Writing of England* (Chicago, University of Chicago Press, 1992).

Herder, J.G., *Ideas towards a Philosophy of the History of Mankind*, (1785) quoted in A. Zimmern (ed.), *Modern Political Doctrines* (London, Oxford University Press, 1939).

Hertz, F., *Nationality in History and Politics: A Study in the Psychology and Sociology of National Sentiment and Character* (London, Kegan Paul, 1944).

Hill, C., 'The Norman Yoke', in C. Hill, *Puritanism and Revolution* (London, Secker and Warburg, 1965).

Hill, C., 'The English Revolution and Patriotism', in R. Samuel (ed.), *Patriotism: The Making and Unmaking of British National Identity* Vol. I (London, Routledge, 1989).

Hill, C., 'History and Patriotism' in R. Samuel (ed.), *Patriotism: The Making, and Unmaking of British National Identity* Vol. I (London, Routledge, 1989).

Hirschman, A.O., *Exit, Voice and Loyalty: Responses to Decline in Firms, Organisations and States* (Cambridge, Mass., Harvard University Press, 1970).

Hirst, P., *Representative Democracy and its Limits* (Cambridge, Polity, 1990).

Hobbes, T., *Leviathan* (ed. M. Oakeshott) (Oxford, Blackwell, 1960).

Hobsbawm, E.J., *Nations and Nationalism Since 1780* (Cambridge, Cambridge University Press, 1990).

Hoffmann, S., 'Thoughts on the French Nation Today', *Daedalus* 122/3 (1993) 63–79.

Holden, B., *Understanding Liberal Democracy*, second edition (New York, Harvester Wheatsheaf, 1993).

Hont, I., 'The Permanent Crisis of a Divided Mankind: "Contemporary Crisis of the Nation State" in Historical Perspective', *Political Studies* 42 (Special Issue 1994: 'Contemporary Crisis of the Nation State?, ed. J. Dunn) 166–231.

Horowitz, D.L., *Ethnic Groups in Conflict* (Berkeley, University of California Press, 1985).

Horton, J., *Political Obligation* (Houndmills, Macmillan, 1992).

Hutchinson, J., *Modern Nationalism* (London, Fontana, 1994).

Ignatieff, M., *Blood and Belonging: Journeys into the New Nationalism* (London, Vintage, 1994).

Jaszi, O., *The Dissolution of the Habsburg Monarchy* (Chicago, University of Chicago Press, 1929).

Kant, I., (ed. H. Reiss), *Kant's Political Writings* (Cambridge, Cambridge University Press, 1970).

Kantorowicz, E.H., *The King's Two Bodies: A Study in Medieval Political Theology* (Princeton, Princeton University Press, 1957).

Kaviraj, S., 'Crisis of the Nation-state in India', *Political Studies* 42 (1994 Special Issue: 'Contemporary Crisis of the Nation State?' ed. J. Dunn) 115–29.

Kearney, H., *The British Isles: A History of Four Nations* (Cambridge, Cambridge University Press, 1989).

Kedourie, E., *Nationalism*, 4th edition (Oxford, Blackwell, 1993).

Keohane, N.O., *Philosophy and the State in France: The Renaissance to the Enlightenment* (Princeton, Princeton University Press, 1980).

Khilnani, S., 'India's Democratic Career', in J. Dunn (ed.), *Democracy: the Unfinished Journey* (Oxford, Oxford University Press, 1992).

Rudyard Kipling's Verse, definitive edition (London, Hodder and Stoughton, 1940).

Knowlton, J. and Cates, T. (ed. and trans.), *Forever in the Shadow of Hitler?* (New Jersey, Humanities Press, 1993).

Kramer, M., 'Arab Nationalism: Mistaken Identity', *Daedalus* 122/3 (1993) 171–206.

Kukathas, C., and Pettit, P., *Rawls: A Theory of Justice and its Critics* (Oxford, Polity, 1990).

Kumar, K., 'The 1989 Revolutions and the Idea of Europe', *Political Studies* XL/3 (1992) 439–61.

Kymlicka, W., *Liberalism, Community and Culture* (Oxford, Oxford University Press, 1989).

Leca, J., 'Welfare State, Cultural Pluralism and the Ethics of Nationality', *Political Studies* XXXIX (1991) 568–74.

Lepschy, G., 'How Popular is Italian?', in Z.G. Baranski and R. Lumley (eds), *Culture and Conflict in Postwar Italy* (Basingstoke, Macmillan, 1990).

Lijphart, A., *Democracy in Plural Societies*, New Haven, Yale University Press, 1977.

Locke, J., *Two Treatises of Government*, ed. P. Laslett (Cambridge, Cambridge University Press, 1964) 318–20.

Lyotard, J.F., *The Post-Modern Condition: A Report on Knowledge* (Manchester, Manchester University Press, 1984).

MacCormick, N., 'Is Nationalism Philosophically Credible?', in W. Twining, (ed.), *Issues of Self-Determination* (Aberdeen, Aberdeen University Press, 1991).

MacIntyre, A., 'Is Patriotism a Virtue?' (The E.H. Lindley Memorial Lecture, Lawrence, University of Kansas Department of Philosophy, 1984).

MacIntyre, A., 'Poetry as Political Philosophy: Notes on Burke and Yeats', in *On Modern Poetry: Essays presented to Donald Davie*, ed. V. Bell and L. Lerner (Nashville, Vanderbilt University Press, 1988).

Mann, M., 'Nation-States in Europe and Other Continents: Diversifying, Developing, Not Dying', *Daedalus* 122/3 (1993) 115–40.

Margalit, A and Raz, J., 'National Self-Determination', *The Journal of Philosophy* LXXXVII/9 (1990) 439–61.

Marr, A., *The Battle for Scotland* (Harmondsworth, Penguin Books, 1992).

Marshall, T.H., *Citizenship and Social Class* (Cambridge, Cambridge University Press, 1950).

Mayall, J., *Nationalism and International Society* (Cambridge, Cambridge University Press, 1990).

Mazrui, A.A. and Tidy, M., *Nationalism and New States in Africa* (London, Heinemann, 1984).

Mazzini, J., 'To the Italians', in *Essays by Joseph Mazzini*, ed. B. King (London, J.M. Dent, 1894).

Mazzini, J., *The Duties of Man and Other Essays* (London, J.M. Dent, 1907).

McNeill, W.H., *Polyethnicity and National Unity in World History* (Toronto, University of Toronto Press, 1986).

Meinecke, F. (trans. R.B. Kimber), *Cosmopolitanism and the National State* (Princeton, Princeton University Press, 1970).

Mill, J.S., *Utilitarianism, Liberty, Representative Government* (London, J.M. Dent, 1910).

Miller, D., 'The Ethical Significance of Nationality', *Ethics* 98/4 (July 1988) 647–62.

Miller, D., 'In What Sense must Socialism be Communitarian?', *Social Philosophy and Policy* 6/2 (1988–9) 51–73.

Miller, D., *Market, State and Community: Theoretical Foundations of Market Socialism* (Oxford, Oxford University Press, 1989).

Miller, D., 'The Nation-State: a Modest Defence', in C. Brown (ed.), *Political Restructuring in Europe: Ethical Perspectives* (London and New York, Routledge, 1993).

Miller, D., 'In Defence of Nationality', *Journal of Applied Philosophy* 10/1 (1993) 3–16.

Miller, D., *On Nationality* (Oxford, Clarendon Press, 1995).

Miller, D. and Siedentop, L. (eds), *The Nature of Political Theory* (Oxford, Oxford University Press, 1983).

Milward, A.S., *The European Rescue of the Nation-State* (London, Routledge, 1992).

Minogue, K., *Nationalism* (London, Batsford, 1967).

Modood, T., *Not Easy Being British: Colour, Culture and Citizenship* (Stoke on Trent, Runnymede Trust and Trentham Books, 1992).

Morris, C.W., 'On Contractarian Constitutional Democracy', in D. Copp, J. Hampton and J.E. Roemer (eds), *The Idea of Democracy* (Cambridge, Cambridge University Press, 1993).

Moruzzi, N.C., 'A Problem with Headscarves: Contemporary Complexities of Political and Social Identity', *Political Theory* 22/4 (1994) 653–72.

Moynihan, D.P., *Pandaemonium: Ethnicity in International Politics* (Oxford, Oxford University Press, 1993).

Mulhall, S. and Swift, A., *Liberals and Communitarians* (Oxford, Blackwell, 1992).

Nairn, T., *The Break-Up of Britain* (London, New Left Books, 1977).

Nairn, T., *The Enchanted Glass: Britain and its Monarchy* (London, Radius, 1988).

Nathanson, S., *Patriotism, Morality, and Peace* (Lanham, Md., Rowman and Littlefield, 1993) 185–97.

Newman, G., *The Rise of English Nationalism: A Cultural History 1740–1830* (London, Weidenfeld and Nicholson, 1987).

Nozick, R., *Anarchy, State, and Utopia* (Oxford, Blackwell, 1974).

Oakeshott, M., *On Human Conduct* (Oxford, Clarendon Press, 1975).

O'Brien, C.C., *God Land: Reflections on Religion and Nationalism* (Cambridge, Mass., Harvard University Press, 1988).

O'Brien, C.C., 'Nationalism and the French Revolution', in *The Permanent Revolution: The French Revolution and its Legacy 1789–1989*, ed. G. Best (London, Fontana, 1988).

O'Brien, C.C., *The Great Melody: A Thematic Biography of Edmund Burke* (London, Sinclair-Stevenson, 1992).

Oldfield, A., *Citizenship and Community – Civic Republicanism and the Modern World* (London, Routledge, 1990).

Orwell, G., *The Lion and The Unicorn: Socialism and the English Genius* (London, Secker and Warburg, 1941).

Orwell, G., 'England Your England', in G. Orwell, *Selected Essays* (Harmondsworth, Penguin Books, 1957).

Parekh, B., 'The "New Right" and the Politics of Nationhood', in N. Deakin (ed.), *The New Right: Image and Reality* (London, The Runnymede Trust, 1986).

Parekh, B., 'A Misconceived Discourse on Political Obligation', *Political Studies* XLI/2 (1993) 236–51.

Parekh, B., 'National Identity and the Ontological Regeneration of Britain', in P. Gilbert and P. Gregory (eds), *Nations, Markets and Cultures* (Aldershot, Avebury, 1994).

Parekh, B., 'The Politics of Nationhood', in K. von Benda-Beckman and M. Verkuyten (eds), *Cultural Identity and Development in Europe* (London, University College of London Press, forthcoming).

Parekh, B., 'Ethnocentricity of the Nationalist Discourse', *Nations and Nationalism* 1/1 (1995) 25–52.

Peled, Y., 'Ethnic Democracy and the Legal Construction of Citizenship: Arab Citizens of the Jewish State', *American Political Science Review* 86/2 (1992) 432–43.

Pitkin, H., *The Concept of Representation* (Berkeley, University of California Press, 1967).

Pitkin, H., *Fortune is a Woman: Gender and Politics in the Thought of Niccolo Machiavelli* (Berkeley, University of California Press, 1984).

Pogge, T.W., *Realising Rawls* (Ithaca, Cornell University Press, 1989).

Rahe, P.A., *Republics Ancient and Modern: Classical Republicanism and the American Revolution* (Chapel Hill and London, University of North Carolina Press, 1992).

Rawls, J., *A Theory of Justice* (Oxford, Oxford University Press, 1972).

Rawls, J., 'Justice as Fairness: Political not Metaphysical', in S. Avineri and A. de-Shalit (eds), *Communitarianism and Individualism* (Oxford, Oxford University Press, 1992).

Rawls, J., 'The Domain of the Political and Overlapping Consensus', in D. Copp, J. Hampton and J.E. Roemer (eds), *The Idea of Democracy* (Cambridge, Cambridge University Press, 1993) 260.

Rawls, J., 'The Law of Peoples', in S. Shute and S. Hurley (eds), *On Human Rights: The Oxford Amnesty Lectures, 1993* (New York, Basic Books, 1993).

Rawls, J., *Political Liberalism* (New York, Columbia University Press, 1993).

Rayner, J., 'Philosophy into Dogma: The Revival of Cultural Conservatism', *British Journal of Political Science* 16/4 (1986) 455–73.

Renan, E., 'What is a Nation?', in A. Zimmern (ed.), *Modern Political Doctrines* (London, Oxford University Press, 1939).

Reynolds, S., *Kingdoms and Communities in Western Europe, 900–1300* (Oxford, Oxford University Press, 1984).

Riley, P., 'Rousseau's General Will: Freedom of a Particular Kind', *Political Studies* XXXIX/1 (1991) 55–74.

Roosens, E.E., *Creating Ethnicity: The Process of Ethnogenesis* (London, Sage, 1989).

Rorty, R., 'On Ethnocentrism: A Reply to Clifford Geertz', *Michigan Quarterly Review* 25 (1986) 525–34.

Rorty, R., *Contingency, Irony and Solidarity* (Cambridge, Cambridge University Press, 1989).

Rosenblum, N.L., 'Pluralism and Self-Defense', in N.L. Rosenblum (ed.), *Liberalism and the Moral Life* (Cambridge, Mass., Harvard University Press, 1991).

Rousseau, J.J. (trans. B. Foxley), *Emile* (London, Dent, 1911).

Rousseau, J.J. (ed. C.E. Vaughan), *Political Writings* Vol. I (Oxford, Blackwell, 1962).

Rousseau, J.J., *The Social Contract* (Harmondsworth, Penguin, 1968).

Sandel, M., 'The Procedural Republic and the Unencumbered Self', in S. Avineri and A. de-Shalit (eds), *Communitarianism and Individualism* (Oxford, Oxford University Press, 1992).

Sartori, G., *The Theory of Democracy Revisited* (Chatham, N.J., Chatham House, 1987).

Schaar, J.H., 'The Case for Patriotism', in J.H. Schaar, *Legitimacy in the Modern State* (New Brunswick, Transaction Books, 1981).

Schwarzmantel, J., *Socialism and the Idea of the Nation* (London, Harvester Wheatsheaf, 1991).

Scruton, R., *The Meaning of Conservatism*, second edition (London, Macmillan, 1984).

Scruton, R., 'In Defence of the Nation', in R. Scruton, *The Philosopher on Dover Beach* (Manchester, Carcanet, 1990).

Seligman, A.B., *The Idea of Civil Society* (New York, Free Press, 1992).

Seton-Watson, H., *Nations and States* (London, Methuen, 1977).

Shute, S. and Hurley, S. (eds), *On Human Rights: The Oxford Amnesty Lectures* (New York, Basic Books, 1993).

Smith, A.D., *The Ethnic Origins of Nations* (Oxford, Blackwell, 1986).

Smith, A.D., 'State-Making and Nation-Building', in J. Hall (ed.), *States in History* (Oxford, Blackwell, 1986).

Smith, A.D., *National Identity* (Harmondsworth, Penguin, 1991).

Smith, R.M., 'The "American Creed' and American Identity: the Limits of Liberal Citizenship in the United States', *Western Political Quarterly* 41/2 (1988) 225–51.

Steiner, H., 'Libertarianism and the Transnational Migration of People', in B. Barry and R. Goodin (eds), *Free Movement – Ethical Issues in the Transnational Migration of People and of Money* (New York, Harvester Wheatsheaf, 1992).

Steiner, H., *An Essay on Rights* (Oxford, Blackwell, 1994).

Szporluk, R., *Communism and Nationalism: Karl Marx versus Friedrich List* (Oxford, Oxford University Press, 1988).

Tamir, Y., *Liberal Nationalism* (Princeton, Princeton University Press, 1993).

Taylor, C., 'Alternative Futures: Legitimacy, Identity and Alienation in Late Twentieth Century Canada', in A. Cairns and C. Williams (eds), *Constitutionalism, Citizenship and Society in Canada* (Toronto, University of Toronto Press, 1985).

Taylor, C., 'Cross-Purposes: The Liberal-Communitarian Debate', in N.L. Rosenblum (ed.), *Liberalism and the Moral Life* (Cambridge, Mass., Harvard University Press, 1989).

Taylor, C. (ed. G. Laforest), *Reconciling the Solitudes – Essays on Canadian Federalism and Nationalism* (Montreal and Kingston, McGill-Queen's University Press, 1993).

Teich, M. and Porter, R. (eds), *The National Question in Europe in Historical Context* (Cambridge, Cambridge University Press, 1993).

Poems of Thomas Tickell, The British Poets Vol. XXVII (College House, C. Whittingham, 1822).

Tilly, C. (ed.), *The Formation of Nation States in Western Europe* (Princeton, Princeton University Press, 1975).

Van den Berghe, P.L., *The Ethnic Phenomenon* (New York, Praeger, 1981).

Voegelin, E., *The New Science of Politics* (Chicago, University of Chicago Press, 1952).

Vogler, C.M., *The Nation-State: The Neglected Dimension of Class* (London, Gower, 1985).

Waley, D., *The Italian City-Republics*, second edition (London, Longman, 1978).

Walicki, A., *Philosophy and Romantic Nationalism: The Case of Poland* (Oxford, Oxford University Press, 1982).

Wallace, W., 'Rescue or Retreat? The Nation State in Western Europe, 1945–93', *Political Studies* 42 (1994), (Special Issue, 'Contemporary Crisis of the Nation State?', ed. J. Dunn) 52–76.

Walzer, M., *Spheres of Justice – A Defence of Pluralism and Equality* (New York, Basic Books, 1983).

Walzer, M., 'The Moral Standing of States: A Response to Four Critics', in C.R. Beitz, M. Cohen, T. Scanlon and A.J. Simmons (eds) *International Ethics* (Princeton, Princeton University Press, 1985).

Walzer, M., *Nation & Universe* (The Tanner Lectures on Human Values, Brasenose College, Oxford, 1989).

Walzer, M., 'Notes on the New Tribalism', in C. Brown (ed.), *Political Restructuring in Europe – Ethical Perspectives* (London, Routledge, 1994).

Ware, A., 'Liberal Democracy: One Form or Many?', *Political Studies* XL (1992) (Special Issue, 'Prospects for Democracy', ed. D. Held) 130–45.

Weber, M., 'Politics as a Vocation', in *From Max Weber: Essays in Sociology*, ed. H.H. Gerth and C. W. Mills (London, Routledge and Kegan Paul, 1948).

Weber, M. (ed. G. Roth and C. Wittich), *Economy and Society* (New York, Bedminster Press, 1968).

Weil, S., *The Need for Roots – Prelude to a Declaration of Duties Towards Mankind* (London, Ark, 1952).

Whelan, F.G., 'Democratic Theory and the Boundary Problem', in *Liberal Democracy*, ed. J.R. Pennock and J.W. Chapman, *Nomos* XXV (New York, New York University Press, 1983).

Whelan, F.G., 'Citizenship and Freedom of Movement: An Open Admission Policy?', in M. Gibney (ed.), *Open Borders? Closed Societies? The Ethical and Political Issues* (Westport, Conn., Greenwood Press, 1988).

Whitehead, L., 'The Alternative to "Liberal Democracy": a Latin-American Perspective', *Political Studies* XL (1992) (Special Issue, 'Prospects for Democracy', ed. D. Held) 146–59.

Young, C., *The Politics of Cultural Pluralism* (Madison, University of Wisconsin Press, 1976).

Young, C. (ed.), *The Rising Tide of Cultural Pluralism: The Nation-State at Bay?* (Madison, University of Wisconsin Press, 1993).

Young, I.M., 'Polity and Group Difference: A Critique of the Ideal of Universal Citizenship', *Ethics* 99 (January 1989) 250–74.

Zubaida, S., 'Nations: Old and New', *Ethnic and Racial Studies* 12/3 (1989).

Index